PAST, PRESENT AND FUTURE OF KASHMIR

PAST, PRESENT AND FUTURE OF KASHMIR

Dr. Rajkumar Singh

Gyan Publishing House
5, Ansari Road, New Delhi.
Pin - 110002

Past, Present and Future of Kashmir

Rs. 720

ISBN: 81-212-0967-6

Published in 2008 in India by
Gyan Publishing House,
5, Ansari Road Darya Ganj
New Delhi-110002
Phones : 23282060, 23261060
Fax : 23285964
E-mail: books@gyanbooks.com

Lasser Type Setting by: Quick Media, Delhi
Printed at : Singhal Print Media, Delhi

Dedicated

To

Shri Ramanand Singh

Father-in-law

Contents

Preface

The book *Past, Present and Future of Kashmir* has been written keeping in view the problem of the State of Jammu and Kashmir at the centrestage of Indo-Pak relations. Following division India and Pakistan were badly engaged in their post-partition problems, the issue had got prominance since its accession to the Union of India in October 1947 which Pakistan considers based on fraud and violence because at the time will of the people was not ascertained. Apart from the four wars that were fought between the two countries, the issue had been discussed in detail at the bilateral talks and at the United Nations. Especially after the Indo-Pak war of 1965 Pakistan was convinced that it can not change status quo in Jammu and Kashmir by force and hence it began to think in terms of insurgency around India-Pakistan border in addition to the disputed territory.

Initially, the people and the political parties of the State were kept aloof from the deliberations of the two countries on the issue. Later on several groups emerged who began to emphasise the independent status of the State of Jammu and Kashmir. For the sake of 'Kashmiriyat' they, without hesitation, used violence and took part in anti-India activities. Indian misrule in Jammu and Kashmir together with Pakistan's efforts to create disturbances and insurgency made the problem a hot spot in international politics. The year 1989 witnessed an increase in violence due to Soviet withdrawal from Afghanistan which resulted in the influx of Mujahideen with agents of ISI in Jammu and Kashmir. Pakistan's evil motives and designs were further frustrated at Kargil in 1999 which the two had fought.In post-Kargil phase need for amicable steps were felt by India and Pakistan and a beginning in the right direction has been made recently. Amity must be preceded while resolving the problem of Jammu and Kashmir with Pakistan in the interests of the parties concerned.

Encouragement, co-operation and goodwishes of the institutions and individuals that I received are acknowledged with gratitude. Several central libraries as well as the book-stocks of different Departments have been consulted in the completion of the book. Librarians and staff of the institutions deserve cordial thanks.

Among teachers Dr. D.N. Mallik and Dr. Kirtyanand Singh, retired Professor and Head of the University Department of Political Science, BRA Bihar University, Muzaffarpur, have been a constant source of guide and encouragement at every stage. Colleagues Dr. Chandra Prakash Singh, University Department of History, BN Mandal University, West Campus, Saharsa, Dr. Ram Naresh Kumar, Head, Department of Chemistry, Dr. Dhirendra Narayan Singh, Department of Political Science, MLT College, Saharsa and Dr. Nand Kishore Singh, Professor and Head, University Department of Political Science and Present Pro Vice-Chancellor, B.N. Mandal University, Madhepura are thankful for their co-operation and goodwishes. Eldest brother late Suryanath Singh and elder brother Shri Bhuvneshwar Prasad Singh, father-in-law Shri Ramanand Singh, retired Professor and Head, University Department of Physics, BRA Bihar University, Muzaffarpur, deserve deep sense of gratitude for their sincere goodwishes. I express my gratitude to Shri Ranjeet Kumar for his labour in composing the book. The author is also grateful to colleagues and staff of the BN Mandal University, West Campus, P.G. Centre, Saharsa.

I must extend my sincere goodwishes and gratitude to the family members including my wife Hemlata, son Aditya Priyadarshi and Apurv Adarsh in the completion of the book.

All responsibility for the defects and misjudgements, however, rests with me alone.

Rajkumar Singh

Introduction

The problem of the State of Jammu and Kashmir had plagued India's relations with Pakistan in the Post-independence era. At the time of independence it was one of the princely states of India who failed to decide whether to join the Union of India or Pakistan before 15 August 1947. Pakistan despite Standstill Agreement with the State of Jammu and Kashmir could not fulfil its promises to supply consumer goods to the State and having found the State helpless attacked on its territories with the help of tribes. The development was alarming enough and compelled Hari Singh, the then Maharaja of State, to seek military and other supports from the Indian government. Hence the State was not a part of Indian territory the latter was advised by Lord Mountbatten first to get accession of the state completed. Acting on his advice hectic arrangements were made and Indian military forces landed there to get vacate the occupied territory of State. Since then Pakistan has been claiming because most of the people in the state were the followers of Islam, Pakistan should be its natural ally, while the legal points along with international laws on the subject favour India. Apart from deadlocks on number of other developmental issues, four straight fighting between the two had taken place with no solution of the problem in sight.

The history of the people of Jammu and Kashmir is a record of constant impulses of immigration from the north-west, west, south and east directions. The alien races, ethnic groups and various religions have influenced the cultural ethos and mode of life of people of this region. In the process of peopling of the region, the Dards in the north-west, the Ladakhis in the east, the Gujjars and Rajputs in the south and Paharis in the south-east have closely influenced the existing ethnicity of the people of Jammu and Kashmir. The racial composition of the State was also influenced by the immigrants from the territories of Turkmenia, Tadzkistan, Uzbaikistan, Kazakistan, Georgia, Azerbaijan, Turkey, Iraq, Iran and Afghanistan. It too had a close bearing of the Indo-Aryans on the racial composition of the people of state.

The political history of Kashmir begins, according to Kalhana, with Asoka, the great Buddhist emperor who erected several Buddhist temples and statues and founded Srinagari, the present Srinagar, as its capital. In afterwards, the successors of Asoka introduced a complete system of administration and during the period Buddhism attained a new horizon. Among the other Hindu rulers were Lalitaditya (724-760 A.D.), Avantivarman (855-883 A.D.), Samkaravarman (883-902 A.D.), Harsa (1089-1101 A.D.) Uccala (1101-11 A.D.). The last Hindu ruler of Kashmir in ancient period was Kota Rani, who assumed power after the death of her husband, Udyanadeva. The general condition of the people under Hindu rulers remained good and irrigation canals found later on testify that the Rajas did not spend all money on temples only. Gradually Hindu kings became weak and helpless and about 1346 A.D. Muslim rulers began to reign in Kashmir.

Important among Muslim rulers were Sikandar who succeeded Shams-ud-Din, the first Salatan-I-Kashmir and earned for himself the nickname of Butshikan or the idol breaker. He was enemy of Hindu temples, books of Hindu learning. He left worshipping people with three options - death, conversion or exile. However his son Zain-ul-Abdin was quite different from him and expressed a practical zeal in state's developmental works. From 1586-87 the valley passed from the period of the Sultans of Kashmir into the hands of the Moghul Emperors. Moghul Emperors set the revenue of the state and made it a pleasant place through planting and gardening. The period following from 1756 the rule of valley was passed into the hands of Afghans who proved the cruellest masters the valley had ever seen. The people of Kashmir were so vexed with the brute rulers and turned with hope to the rising power of Ranjit Singh. He was the Sikh monarch of Punjab and acquired Kashmir in 1819. His rule was an improvement for the people of the State.

By the time the power of the British in India expanded and they began to chalk out an strategy for annexation of Kashmir as a buffer state in the region. In 1830 Lord Hastings, the then Governor-General of India, visited Kashmir and gave Raja Gulab Singh a certificate of merit for his excellent arrangements during the tour. They both came into contact and Gulab Singh had visualised that in order to achieve his aims the British could be a powerful master. Death of Maharaja Ranjit Singh in 1839 followed the collapse of the central authority thereby opening the field for the British to act.

Treachery and internal dissension led to the signing of the treaties of Lahore and Amritsar. These treaties made Raja Gulab Singh the Maharaja of Jammu and Kashmir. The British did not care to ascertain the wishes of the people of Kashmir while bringing the territory under the subjugation of Gulab Singh. With the signing of the treaties British interference in the affairs of the state started and gradually the ruler became weak and helpless. After the death of Gulab Singh in 1857, his third son Ranbir Singh assumed power who maintained the traditions of his father and remained loyal to the British. He also helped the latter in suppressing the revolt of 1857 in various regions. He was succeeded by Pratap Singh who came to the throne on September 25, 1885. From the first day he was eager to show extreme loyalty to the British and lived in the shadow of fear. During his reign the British completed the reorganisation of civil administration and reorganised all departments. Meagre developments were made in the field of communication due to Anglo-Russian rivalry but largely the territory remained backward in sphere of education, trade and everything that could bring an enhanced way of life in the valley.

The last king before the British withdrawal was Maharaja Hari Singh who took over in 1925. The people of the State were not happy in his reign and the king had no control over administration. Public resentment and resistance against the autocratic rule of Maharaja generated disappointments in the masses that led to the formation of a political organisation in 1932. The entire political organisation in the valley was reconstituted in 1938 led by Sheikh Abdullah in the name of National Conference. The new force had a mass-base and it united the state against the oppressive policies of Maharaja to form a responsible government in the state.

After the lapse of British paramountcy over Indian territory the State of Jammu and Kashmir became an independent one like the other Princely States of India. As it could not make choice regarding accession before independence, in post-independence phase it became a bone of contention between India and Pakistan following the British withdrawal. The new state made a situational accession with the Union of India on being forced by Pakistani attack. Signing of the Instrument of Accession by Hari Singh, the then Maharaja of State, made India its legal heir while the Government of Pakistan termed the Instrument based on fraud and violence. The accession of the state was made disputed by Lord Mountbatten who wrote a letter, in addition to the Instrument, expressing the wish to have a decision in reference to the people of the State of Jammu and Kashmir. On January 1, 1948, India took the matter to the UN in the hope of solving the problem to the satisfaction of the parties concerned. The first war that occurred in 1947-48 proved helpless in making a just solution.

Accession of the State was made with the signing of Instrument by the ruler and open support of the people and their lone leader, Sheikh Abdullah. The latter was the undisputed, sole leader of the National Conference while the same position was held by Mohammad Ali Jinnah in the Muslim League. Sheikh Abdullah was opposed to joining the State of Pakistan perhaps due to the fear that his arch rival Jinnah would come to power and so he attached his lot with India. Initially on the issue of Plebiscite the strongest opposition came from him. He claimed himself as the sole representative of Kashmir and whatever he would decide, would be good enough for the Kashmiris and thus there was no need of having a plebiscite to ascertain people's wish. He, on his behalf, left no one in doubt that the State of Jammu and Kashmir belongs to India only.

The real face of Sheikh Abdullah came to the fore once he was saddled firmly and accession of the State of Jammu and Kashmir was completed. He began to misuse, rather blackmail his position in the eyes of Indian government for which he was the sole hope of national integration on the one hand and test of Indian secularism on the other. Abdullah belied Nehru's hope that the former would not only remain with India but would take an active part in the political, economic and social development of the country. At the end of 1952 it became clear that he was guided by Pakistani leaders and their thinking. His authoritarian and autocratic style of functioning in the state compelled the Government of India to dispose him from the chair and put behind the bars in August 1953.

Several official and unofficial attempts were made including the efforts of Indian government and the UN to solve this contentious issue. Solution of the Kashmir problem is important not because it is a Muslim majority area but because it has the key to normalisation of relations between India and Pakistan. For Pakistan gaining Kashmir may be a matter of religion, for India it is a part of its culture. The case of Kashmir stands apart, because Kashmir is not a case of communal conflict. It may be a case of any other conflict, but it is essentially not a case of communal conflict. It is attached with India due to old bounds and sentiments. It is not close to our minds only but to hearts too.

New Delhi, on her part, has always avoided full-fledged war with Islamabad on the issue. The initial war of 1947-48 could not get it done and the matter was put before the UN. In response to India's complain and Pakistan's explanations the world body had passed two resolutions in April and August 1948, respectively. The resolution contained three parts of which first one was related to the cease fire that had come into effect from January 1, 1949. Ceasefire between the two had left with India its major and best part while Pakistanis had control over smaller and less important parts of the State of Jammu and Kashmir. Pakistan-controlled part of the territory is called 'Azad Kashmir' but India had retained its traditional nominclature. After some years the issue of Kashmir had become a part of the cold war. While the Anglo-American bloc was inclined towards Pakistan the former Soviet Union backed India. Right from the year 1962, on number of occasions the two had tried to solve the problem through direct talk or negotiation but without success.

The war of 1965 convinced Islamabad that Kashmir could be gained only through internal rebellion and not through external aggression. Following the war India signed a Tashkent agreement which was a more disappointing for Pakistan than for India. Z. A. Bhutto, the then Foreign Minister of Pakistan, defended the agreement by saying that only when the people of Jammu and Kashmir have exercised their inherent right of self-determination and that the Declaration was only the dialogue between India and Pakistan for a permanent solution of the 'tragic dispute'. In due course the idea for self-determination was converted in the dream of a Azad, Independent Kashmir. For the purpose an organisation named Jammu and Kashmir Liberation Front (JKLF) was formed. In recent past several other organisations have also been set up to look after the ideal of Kashmir's independence and demanded integration of the portion of territory occupied by Pakistan and controlled by India. The demand of the right of self-determination and independence for the state of Jammu and Kashmir had led the problem in the direction, beyond the control of New Delhi and Islamabad.

From the viewpoint of security and integrity of Pakistan its war with India in December 1971 was the worst. The 13-day direct fight had disintegrated Pakistan and a new sovereign, independent nation–Bangladesh emerged on world's map. The agreement at Simla was the result of this war in which Pakistan accepted the problem of Kashmir a bilateral affair that should be settled between the two countries. The promises made at Simla were short lived and the two had at straight fighting in Kargil in 1999. Till now four wars had been fought between India and Pakistan keeping this problem at the centre. Even after Kargil Islamabad stood almost destroyed. It also led to the change of guard in the country–from the democratic ruler Nawaz Sharif to Pervez Musharraf, a Army General.

Despite a humiliating defeat at the battle-field Pakistan handled the aftermath well in diplomatic terms. The direct results of the war and the agreement that followed were return of PoWs, withdrawal of troops and resumption of diplomatic relations. Apart from this the Simla Pact also contained a Kashmir settlement comprising four parts. The last paragraph of the pact not only grouped together a Kashmir settlement but also bound the parties to another summit to resolve them all. 'Both governments agree that their respective heads will meet again at a mutually convenient time in the future and that, in the meanwhile, the representative of the two sides will meet to discuss further the modalities and arrangements for the establishment of durable peace and normalisation of relations'. On the issue they were also afraid of the United Nations and both the leaders – Mrs. Gandhi and Bhutto expressed willingness in the Rajya Sabha and National Assembly respectively to resolve the problem bilaterally. Unfortunately, the proposed summit was never held and promises could not be translated into action.

In the post-Simla periods several rounds of unsuccessful discussions were held between India and Pakistan and for number of years it had set the course of relations between the two.In between 1972 and 1989 Pakistan never raised the issue of Jammu and Kashmir or described it as a "Core Issue" in any of the discussions. On the other hand alienation of the people of Kashmir continued as earlier. It was made considerable headway due to the sequence of events and the general mood of the public became from anti-government to anti-India. There has been a persistent policy of denying Kashmir a right to democracy : one-party rule has been imposed on the state through manipulation of elections, opposition parties have been prevented from growing and elementary civil liberties and human rights have been denied to the people. This refusal to integrate Kashmir within the framework of Indian democracy has proved to be the single greatest block to the process of Kashmir's emotional and political integration with the rest of India. The basic premises of this policy are that the Kashmiris are unfit for democracy. This is not only an insult to the people of Kashmir but to all democratic sensibility.

From 1989 onwards militancy in Kashmir had passed through various phases. It acquired a qualitatively new terrorist character. Having permitted conditions within Kashmir to deteriorate to the level that they had reached, the Indian state had little option but to fight hard to break the insurgency. The Kashmir policy of the Government of India has been marked by the carrot and stick approach. Right from the days of arrest of Sheikh Abdullah in 1953, the brute force of the Bakshi regime failed to suppress popular unrest. It was then supplemented by lavish central aid to the state along with the supply of rice at heavily subsidised rates. More generous central aid was once again promised in exchange of Farooq's agreement to share power with the Congress in 1986. From the start, force and aid had been used as instruments to win the loyalty of the people not for the nation but the Government and party in power.

Indian misrule gave birth to an uprising in Kashmir. In course of time militancy entered a new phase. It was no longer a fight-between the militants and the security forces. It gradually assumed the form of a total insurgency of the entire population. The conspicuous failure of the state had occurred earlier in allowing matters to get to that point. The needs of party politics and security could not be reconciled. As a result grievous damage was done not only to the volitional connection of the state with the rest of the country, but also to the concept of Kashmiriyat that linked the 36 per cent non-Muslims of the State. The establishment helped Muslim zealots caputre Kashmiriyat.

In this atmosphere of total confrontation between security forces and the Kashmiri Muslims, the excesses of the militants and the killing of innocent civilians by them could hardly attract much attention. By the time Pakistan decided to start a low-intensity conflict in Kashmir based on the experience gained from the deniable war in Afghanistan it had pursued in the Eighties together with the US against the Soviet Union. General Zia had transformed Pakistan under his strategy of Islamisation. The very nature of the militant movement in Kashmir implied intolerance of dissent and use of violence as the principal means of action. Its targets were not always the personnel of the security forces and so-called informers but also civilian officials and non-officials, political leaders and common citizens.

In 1998, the Kashmir dispute attained an extra dimension when India and Pakistan became overt nuclear powers. By the time Pakistan embarked on the Kargil operation in 1999, the low-intensity conflict in Kashmir was yielding mostly negative results for Pakistan in terms of international support. The operation clearly meant to highlight the Kashmir cause, failed to make Pakistan realise that it had become too isolated internationally for the policy of highlighting to work. In afterwards offers and counteroffers were made for the settlement of Kashmir by both countries but they rejected for the reason best known to all. Just after the war Pakistan urged India to take up the Kashmir issue on "priority basis" as it was root cause of tension between the two neighbours. Meeting of leaders–Vajpayee and Nawaz Sharif in July 1998 at the SAARC Summit in Colombo had paved the way for the resumption of stalled dialogue between the two countries. They agreed, despite disagreements to move towards a solution which would be in the mutual interest.

In the post-Pokharan and Kargil periods the problem of Kashmir has the potential to create not only armed confrontation but possible nuclear war. That is why the rapprochement between India and Pakistan has been supported by overseas powers. The process of confidence–building measures initiated by India and Pakistan needs to be institutionalised and an element of irreversibility needs to be embedded in these measures. A solution could grow to become a resolution, if the mindset of the peoples in the region change. Once a framework had been created, which involved intensive dialogue between India and Pakistan it would not be difficult to find a solution. Pakistan has to be dealt with a multi-pronged strategy. Most importantly, we have to strengthen communal harmony and promote respect for pluralism within India. Pakistan will see the futility of seeing parity with India only when we are at peace domestically. Trade, contacts and economic affairs would be regulated by both sides, which would also be responsible for Kashmir's external security. Domestic policy would be decided by an elected autonomous government. In contrast to the policy adopted in Punjab which led to the untold human sufferings, the 'healing touch' policy is on the card in the state of Jammu and Kashmir. The root cause of the lack of a strategic vision in India's policy is the inability of Indian Policy–makers to look at themselves through Kashmiri eyes.

The entire series of misunderstandings reveals how difficult it has become for governments to make radical departures of policy in the information age. The only way to bring lasting peace is to eschew find goals and concentrate on the process. Open road and rail links between the parts of Kashmir, open both parts of Kashmir for tourism and trade, give both parts of Kashmir the autonomy that their constitutions normally contain, allow them to form links with each other, and do all this in step with the normalisation of relations between India and Pakistan. This can only be done in stages and trust will grow as each stage is completed.

India and Pakistan have a more than half century experience of the subject which they have seen through the Kaleisdoscope of war and terrorism, verbal duels in the United Nations, bilateral negotiations and quasi-mediation. At the end of the day it is becoming clearer to both sides that neither reference to historical claims nor the US resolutions and liberation struggles will resolve the problem. The 'final settlement' the two sides are committed to can only come through a political compromise which must be fashioned with the understanding that politics is, after all, the art of the possible.

1

Kashmir : The Political History

Gift of Nature

The land is best known as 'a garden of eternal spring' and 'tourists' 'paradise'. Nature itself when creating this valley and its enclosing wall of mountains, seems to have assured to this territory not only a distinct geographical character, but also a historical existence of marked individuality. It is bounded northwest by Afghanistan northeast by Sinkiang Province of China and east by Tibet. Kashmir is divided physically into two parts, very unequal in area, climate and population by the great Himalayan mountain system, which runs from the North boundary of Chamba State to where Nanga Parbat Mountain towers 26656 ft above the Indus. The fertile valley of Kashmir and the Jammu- Kashmir plain, which is 120 miles long and 76 miles wide, the well–watered valley and forested hills surrounding them, are drained by the Jhelum, the Chenab, and Ravi, the waterly three of the five rivers of the Punjab. The smaller but more densely populated part of Jammu Province divides itself naturally into three geographical, ethnic, economic and linguistic regions: Kashmir, the western non - Kashmiri districts and East Jammu Province, the first two drained by the Jhelum, the third by the Chenab and the Ravi. There are three similar trans – Himalayan frontier regions : the Gilgit area, Baltistan and Kargil and Buddhist Ladakh. These six main parts of the state intermingle and overlap in some respects, but the broadly distinct and homogeneous. There are no particular geographical distinctions between the West and East parts of Jammu Province to Ladakh. Only the valley of Kashmir and the Gilgit regions are clearly defined by high mountain barriers.

As a health resort, Kashmir, excluding Srinagar, has no rival anywhere in the neighbourhood of India. In consequence of the varied range of temperature and the facility of moving about, the visitor is enabled with ease to select places at elevations most congenial to him. The railway to Rawalpindi and a driving road thence to Srinagar make the valley easy to access. When the temperature in Srinagar rises at the beginning of June, visitors normally go to Gulmarg, a fashionable hill station. Writing about the unique climate of land, Walter Lawrence says, 'it is impossible to speak of Kashmir as possessing any one climate. Every hundred feet of elevation brings some new phase of climate and of vegetation, and in a short ride of thirty miles one can pass from over powering heat to a climate delightfully cool or can escape from wearisome wet weather to a dry and sunny atmosphere.' Famed for its beauty, the valley of Kashmir presents a breath- taking view — a vast carpet in a thousand shades of greens and blues, tans and lavendar, with shimmering brooks and streams, a picture of incredible beauty, with its distant features half revealed half concealed by magic mist. Throughout its known history, the name Kashmira, in its original Sanskrit form, has been used as the sole designation of the country. The Sanskrit 'Kashmira' still lives as 'Kashmir'. In Persian spelling it is Kashmir.

The Present State of Jammu and Kashmir was created by the military and Political powers of the British . Events which occurred at the close of the eighteenth century in Europe , had largely shaped the policy of the British in India. The Indian ruler Tipu sultan had earlier entered into an alliance with the French with the sole aim of driving out the British from the Indian soil.[1] When the French failed in their attempt, the Russian came forward and their shadow started lengthening over the north- western frontiers of India. Conflicts of interests gave birth to the Anglo – Russian rivalry in India and the countries surrounding it. At the moment, Russia was not ignorant of India and the most famous Russian traveller A.D. Saltikova visited India in 1841, wrote a book about the country. He travelled whole of India and prepared innumerable sketches and pictures. Although England succeeded in putting a stop to Russian 'leap forward policy 'it now began to take interest in Persia and Afghanistan, with the result that by 1837, Persia became practically subservient to Russia. Now they turned their attention towards

Afghanistan, strategically situated north of India. The British Government got alarmed and seriously chalked out their policy for creating buffer states surrounding their precious empire, which was ringed with dependent and buffer states like Siam, Bhutan , Sikkim, Nepal, Tibet and Afghanistan.

In coming years the situation worsened with Russia's moving towards the Southern and eastern regions, in 1864, when she occupied Chinkent. It was followed by the occupation of Tashkent in 1865, Kohj in 1866 and Yuni Kurgan in 1867. The Russians subjugated Samarkand in 1868. As a result, the British took effective steps in the consolidation of the scientific frontier of their Indian Empire. They extended railway lines upto Quetta and the Khyber passes. A policy of reconciliation with the Amir of Afghanistan was enunciated so as to secure a safe north–western frontier . Having done this, they desired to seal two other doors from outside influence and these were Gilgit and Leh. The British had to pursue a policy favourable to their Imperial interests.[2] Hence they had to look for some other barrier against Russia and it could be no other territory than Kashmir which lies at the crossroads of India Russia and China and could be an important Jumping – off place for military operations.

Judging from Kashmir's chronicles and other available information, the population of Kashmir had already shown even in old times , the same homogeneity that it does today. The political history of Kashmir is enshrined in four Sanskrit books. Rajatarangini, commencing with traditional history of very early times, comes down to the reign of Sangrama Deva, 1006; the second work, by Jonaraja, takes up the history in continuation and, entering the Mohammedan period, gives an account of the reigns down to that of Zain–ul-ad-din, 1420. P. Srivara carried on the record to the accession of Fath Shah, 1489. The fourth work, called Rajavalipataka, by Prajnia Bhatta, completes the history to the time of the incorporation of Kashmir in the dominions of the Moghul emperor Akbar, in 1586.

Hindu- Buddhist Period

Gonand 1, as mentions kalhana, is the first king of the valley, related to Jarasandha, the ruler of Maghda, who was a contemporary of Krishna and the Pandavas. He is one of the 52 earliest kings of Kashmir who, according to Kalhana, were not recorded in the former chronicles. The 'lost' kings included Lava and Kusa, the sons of the legendry Rama. But with Asoka, the great Buddhist Emperor of India, the history of Kashmir begins. The authentic facts of history safely held the view that Ashoka's sovereign power extended to Kashmir. He was the contemporary of Hannibal and his Kingdom extended from Bengal to the Deccan, to Afghanistan and the Punjab, and the results of whose influence may be seen to this day in Kashmir, in the remains of Buddhist temples and statues, and in the ruins of cities founded by him 250 years before Christ.[3] It was Asoka who founded Srinagari, the ancient capital of Kashmir with its' ninety-six lakhs of houses resplendent with wealth. According to Hiuen Tsiang, Asoka settled 5,000 monks in Kashmir which had in earlier times played a great part in the traditions of Buddhism. He found a hundred convents in the country but Ou-Kong who visited it in 725 A. D. found more than three hundred and a considerable number of stupas and sacred images.

The successor of Asoka, Jalauka, traditionally said to be his son, was a popular hero who not only cleared the land of the Mlecchas, but made extensive conquests and introduced a complete system of administration. With the three Turkish Kings, Huska, Juska, and Kanishka, Buddhism achieved new popularity and power. Kanishka, identified with the great Kushan ruler of north- western India, held the third great Buddhist council in Kashmir and withdrew the northern canon. Hiuen Tsiang on his visit to Kashmir in the seventh century found local traditions about that king. According to Kalhana, the eminent Buddhist teacher Nagarjuna lived in Kashmir at that time. Kanishkapura, Huskapura, and Juskapura which the three kings founded are still in existence. After the death of Asoka Brahmanism revived. While Kashmir was under Kushan rule, Buddhism was to a great extent restored, though for several centuries the two religions existed together in Kashmir, Hinduism predominating. In this Hindu–Buddhist period, and chiefly between the 5th and 10th centuries of the Christian era, the Hindu temples in Kashmir were erected.

A king remembered best in Kashmir is Lalitaditya (724-760 A.D.), a powerful ruler 'asserting his power far beyond Kashmir and the adjacent territories'. With the reputation of a great builder, of towns and temples, Lalitaditya ushered in a glorious period in the history of Kashmir.Writes Stien, "But those among them which can be identified justify by their extant ruins the great fame which Lalitaditya enjoyed as a builder . The ruins of the splendid temple of Martanda , which the king had constructed near the Tirtha of the same name are still the most striking object of ancient Hindu architecture in the valley . Even in their present state of decay they command admiration both by their imposing dimensions and by the beauty of their architectural design and decoration.[4] Kalhana describes at length the series of great temples built by the king at the town of Parihasapura which he had founded as his residence. The numberous shrines and images erected during his reign throw light on the religious conditions of Kashmir at the time Buddhism was in a flourishing condition, as it is clear from Ou-Kong who visited Kashmir (759-763 A.D.), probably only a few years after Lalitaditya's death, and the number of Buddhist temples and shrines was considerable. Lalitaditya was 'the most conspicuous figure in Kashmir history, and raised his country to a pitch of glory it had never reached before or attained to since'.[5]

After Lalitaditya, the royalty fell on evil days, and the immediately adjoining hill- tracts threw off the Kashmir suzerainty in a succession of weak rulers . From this times the kings of Kashmir 'became habituated to looking at the faces of their officials' for guidance and to following the directions of their servants. More than a century passed before the downward process was reversed by another gifted king, Avantivarman (855- 883A.D.), who brought a period of consolidation for the land. Prosperity returned and the king built a large number of temples as well as the town of Avantipura on the right bank of the Jhelum seventeen miles from Srinagar on the Srinagar – Jammu highway, where he built a temple dedicated to Vishnu. 'During his regime Suyya was known for his engineering operations for the drainage of the valley and its irrigation. He built a town which bore his name Suyyapura, the modern Sopore and prohibited by his own authority the killing of fish and birds on the lake. 'Altogether Suyya stands out as a person hundreds of years in advance of his time.[6] Under Avantivarman, the arts of peace flourished and the rights of humanity were respected. He paid minute attention to everything that tended to promote the well-being of the population. [7]

The next king, Samkaravarman(883-902 A.D.), the son of Avantivarman, a great conqueror, robbed what the temples possessed and in his avarice subjected the people to relentless oppression. The manner in which the king raised the State revenues shows, according to Stien, that 'the elaborate system of taxation which was maintained in Kashmir until quite recently, had been fully developed already in Hindu times'. Then began a period of civil war, instability, depravity and licentiousness in which intrigue and murder speeded up the succession of kings and pretenders. The people found some relief in Yasakara's reign whose administration won Kalhana's esteem for its wisdom, who showed Judicial capacity, for example, in the interpretation of legal contracts. Ananta (1028-63 A.D.), showed great personal bravery on occasion, but with the passage of time the influence of his able and pious queen Suryamati began to prevail upon him. Incidentally, Ananta acted as the Kashmir agent to king Bhoja of Malwa. 'It shows that, notwithstanding the political isolation of Kashmir and the Mohammedan conquest of the region to the South, regular intercourse and trade with the Hindu kingdoms of India proper must have continued'. [8]

After a period of disorders, Harsa (1089-1101A.D.),'the most striking figure among the later rulers of Kashmir', became king. He was born from atoms of light, according to Kalhana, and at the gaṭe of his palace at which people from various nations presented themselves, the riches of all countries seemed always to be piled up. Kalhana pictures king Harsa as a youth of powerful frame and great personal beauty, courageous and fond of display. He was well – versed in various sciences and a lover of music and art. When his reign began he showed forbearance and adopted a prudent policy. It is worth mentioning that kalhana's father, Champaka, served as Minister of Harsa, being responsible for the defence of the State's frontiers. The honest Uccala (1101-11A.D), who succeeded him from kindheartedness allowed robbers to rise to high posts in rememberance, of their past services, just as the sandalwood tree allows the snakes to climb up on it,. He was a liberal king, a capable and fairly energetic ruler, showing considerable regard for the common people. [9] Uccala was murdered and the throne changed hands from time to time largely by murder, pretenders fought with one another, and political instability led to economic dislocation. For a century and a half the land had suffered from unrest and rebellion.

The Hindu rule, according to Jonaraja, continued for another two centuries 'though the princes were weak and helpless and material prosperity of the valley more and more fading. According to Lawrence the Hindu period, must from certain points of view, have been one of great magnificence. With the plunder of conquest splendid temples and fine public works were constructed, and their ruins show that Kashmir in those days was endowed with noble buildings, while the potsherds of ancient cities on the Karewas and elsewhere suggest that the valley must have been very thickly populated. About the condition of the people little is known, but as Hindus living under Hindu kings their lot must have been fairly happy, and irrigation canals testify that the Rajas did not spend all their wealth on temples, but had some thought for the cultivators. The queen Kota Rani, the last representative of Hindu dynasty, who assumed power after the death of her husband Udyanadeva, refused the proposal of Shah Mirza or Shah Mir to marry with him and committed suicide. Shah Mir, the vizier of Udyanadeva, became the first Salatan- I- Kashmir under the name of Shams-ud-Din and succeeded by Sikandar. Thus Hindu kings continued to reign till about 1346 A.D.

The Muslim Rulers

Of the Mohammedan rulers mentioned in the Sanskrit chronicles, one who reigned about the close of the 14th century, made his name prominent by his active opposition to the Hindu religion and his destruction of temples. The new king Sikandar who earned for himself the nickname of 'Butshikan' or the idol breaker was driven mainly by fanaticism. He ordered the wholesale destruction of Hindu temples. A special establishment was set up to demolish the impressive temples at Martanda. Having wreaked his vengeance on Hindu temples, says Lawrence, Sikander turned his attention to the people who had worshipped in them and he ordered them three choices: death, conversion or exile. Those who could not flee were converted and many were killed. An enemy of knowledge, Sikandar sank all books of Hindu learning on which he could lay his hands in the Dal Lake.[10]

Sikandar was succeeded by his son Zain –ul- Abdin who was a different from his father as was Aurangzeb from Akbar. His rule lasted forty- two years and the valley not only enjoyed peace but a great development in arts, crafts, and irrigation. He built bridges and canals, planted gardens, and raised a great causeway from Andarkot to Sopore. Among the industries which he introduced into the State were carpet, papier mache, silk and paper–making. His influence was of far–reaching character and he stamped the many facets of life in Kashmir with the seal of his personality. He turned Kashmir into a smiling garden of industry inculcating in the hearts of the people some conceptions of labour and life and also implanting in their minds the gems of real progress. He provided his subjects with a code of laws and had engraved them on copper plates which were exhibited in markets and halls of justice. His impartiality was proverbial. "Though the king was kind hearted", writes Jonaraja, 'yet for the sake of his people he would not forgive even his son or minister or a friend if he were guilty'. However it is an accepted fact that up to about the beginning of the fourteenth century the population of the valley was Hindu, and that about the middle and end of the century the mass of the people converted to Islam , through the efforts of Shah-i-Hamdan and his followers and the violent bigotry and persecution of king Sikandar iconoclast. Tradition affirms that the persecution of the Hindus was so keen that only eleven families of Hindus remained in the valley. Their descendents are known by the name of Malmas, as distinguished from the fugitives and the Hindus of the Deccan, who came to Kashmir later on and are known as the Banamas. [11]

In Kashmir a long continued process of conversion to Islam had resulted in 95 per cent of the population becoming Muslims, though they retained many of their old Hindu customs. In the middle nineteenth century the Hindu ruler of the State found that very large numbers of these people were anxious or willing to return en bloc to Hinduism. He sent a deputation to the pandits of Banaras inquiring if this could be done. The pandits refused to countenance any such change of faith and there the matter ended. Conversion to Islam in those days, writes Jawaharlal Nehru, whether individual or group, probably aroused no particular opposition, except when force or some kind of compulsion was used. Friends and relatives or neighbours might disapprove but the Hindu community as such apparently attached little importance to this. In contrast with this indifferent attitude, conversions to-day attract widespread attention and are resented, whether they are to Islam or Christianity. This is largely due to political factors and specially to the introduction of separate religious electorates. Each convert is supposed to be a gain to the communal group leading ultimately to greater representation and more political power.[12] This is one of the direct effects of Islam on Hinduism though in practice it brings it into conflict with Islam in India.

In the first half of the sixteenth century the power of the Chaks, who came from the north and were Shiahs, increased and their tyranny over the Sunnis and Hindus resulted in an invitation to Akbar which brought the Moghul army to Kashmir. From 1586- 87 the valley passed from the period of the Sultans of Kashmir into the hands of the Moghul Emperors. Akbar built the great fort on the Hari-Parbat hill and he is said to have done this to encourage the Kashmiris who had fled because of Chaks' atrocities, to return to the valley. His revenue minister Todar Mal settled the revenue arrangements of the valley. But it was Jehangir, the son of Akbar, who really loved Kashmiris and who when asked at his death bed at Bahramgalle whether he wanted anything, replied "only Kashmir". It was he who had chenar trees planted throughout the valley and pleasure gardens built. The Emperor Shah Jehan kept up the tradition set by Jehangir and was a great builder of pleasure places. With the decay of the Moghul Empire, the central authority weakened in Kashmir, and the Governors became independent and high–handed.

With the downfall of Moghuls a new curse fell upon valley when it passed into hands of the Pathans who proved to be the cruellest masters the valley had ever seen. A period of Afghan rule followed from 1756 and the State entered a new and terrible phase of persecution and fanaticism. Forster had described Asad khan, one of the Governors, as internal despot.[13] His victims included Brahmans, the Shiahs, and the Bombas of the Jhelum valley. Growing a beard was made compulsory for Brahmans, but the bearing of turbans and shoes forbidden. The poll tax on Hindus was reimposed and many Brahmans either fled the country, were killed, or converted to Islam. According to Lawrence to save their daughters from degradation, Brahman parents destroyed their beauty by shaving their heads and cutting their noses. It would be wearisome to recount instances of the brutal cruelty of the Pathans, but at least the oppression became so unendurable that Kashmir turned with hope to the rising power of Ranjit Singh, the 'Lion of the Punjab'.[14] In comparison to the rule of Moghuls, Pathans were the worst. The Moghul period, if the bad times of one or two cruel subahs be excluded, must have possessed many elements of happiness for the people ......, when, however, we pass from the Moghul period to the period of Pathan we pass to a time of brutal tyranny, unrelieved by good work, chivalry and honour. [15]

Sikh and the British

Misrule in Kashmir by Afghans provided an opportunity to Ranjit Singh, the Sikh monarch of the Punjab, who acquired it (Kashmir)in 1819. This Jat Sikh had built up a kingdom in Punjab which included Kashmir and the Frontier Province. He was not only intellectually curious and inquisitive, he was remarkably humane at a time when India and the world seethed with callousness and inhumanity. He held a powerful army and yet he disliked bloodshed. 'Never was so large an empire founded by one man with so little criminality'. He abolished the death sentence for every crime, however heinous it might be, when in England even petty pilferers had to face death. Except in actual warfare; writes Osborne, who visited him, 'he has never been known to take life, though his own has been attempted more than once, and his reign will be found freer from any striking acts of cruelty and oppression than those of many more civilized monarches.'[16] The condition of Kashmir under the Sikhs, states Ferguson, was undoubtedly an improvement on that under the Afghans. The Hindus to whom the Sikhs are in many ways very near, benefited most and the disabilities under which they had been unable to practice the rites of their religion were removed. 'It was now the turn of the Muslims to suffer. Mosques were closed, the call to prayer was forbidden and capital punishment was meted out for the killing of a cow'. [17] This was harsh, but there was no reconversion, murder or exile, much less drowning in the Dal Lake.

Now Kashmir was in possession of Maharaja Ranjit Singh and by the time the British were seriously chalking out an strategy for annexation of Kashmir as a buffer state in the region. The opportunity was provided by the death of Maharaja in 1839. His death proved disastrous for the Sikh State, because his personality was the main factor which had lent stability and coherence to the Kingdom. In the post–death phase the Sikh Government of the Punjab disintegrated owing to personal jealousies and rivalries among the Sikh nobles.[18] The British who were always eager to profit by internal disorders in the Indian states, came forward and set in motion their unscrupulous diplomacy which resulted in the destruction of the Sikhs and subsequently led to the annexation of their Kingdom by the British.

Earlier, in the middle of the eighteenth century, Jammu came under the rule of Rana Ranjit Dev, a Chief of Dogra Rajput. At that time the neighbouring country was split up into a number of independent hill principalities, such as Kishtwar and Badrawar on the east, Basaoli on the South, Bhimbar and Rajaori on the west and north west. The Chiefs of these principalities were engaged in constant quarrels and nurtured rivalries against one another. This enabled Maharaja Ranjit Singh to annex Jammu and the neighbouring hill tracts in the beginning of the nineteenth century. By the time, the three brothers Gulab Singh, Dhayan Singh and Suchet Singh, the great-grand-nephews of Rana Ranjit Dev, joined the court of Maharaja Ranjit Singh. The three brothers steadily increased their influence over the Maharaja who became so much enamoured of the family that he showered wealth on them. They all were utilized by the Maharaja to extend the frontiers of his kingdom. Gulab Singh remained in the hills and was used by Maharaja to subjugate the chieftains of Jammu, Riasi, Rajaori and kishtwar. In fact, the Maharaja tried to subjugate Jammu in 1808, but the Sikhs were defeated by the Dogras. It was only after the death of Raja Ranjit Singh that the Jammu was annexed to the Sikh state. The three brothers rendered distinguished service to the Maharaja and soon rose in his estimation. Soon Riasi Rajaori and Kishtwar became a part of the Sikh Government of Lahore, through the efforts of Gulab Singh, who also extended the sway of the Sikh ruler over Ladakh and even to some parts of Tibet.[19] The trio became the most influential in the Sikh Kingdom and exercised tremendous influence over the aged Lion of the Punjab till his death.

According to the Sanad dated 4th Har 1879 Bikrami, which corresponds to June 1822, the three brothers were favoured by the Maharaja with jagirs. The Maharaja granted to Raja Gulab Singh the Government of the 'Chakla' of Jammu which had been in possession of his forefathers, in lieu of his faithful services and out of love for him. The Government of Bindaral territory (Ramnagar) was given to Raja Suchet Singh, so that he and his descendants may use its revenue themselves. Later, Dhayan singh was made Raja of Poonch under the order of the Maharaja. In the next fifteen years, they had brought under their control all the neighbouring hill principalities. After the murder of Dhayan Singh in 1843, the death of Suchet Singh in 1844 and murder of his son Hira Singh in the same year, all their estates fell to the survivor — Gulab Singh. By 1844, Gulab Singh had acquired full authority over all the territories which are included in the present province of Jammu.

Despite his high position, Raja Gulab Singh was a feudatory of the Sikh State and he could only cling to this position at the pleasure and will of the Maharaja of Punjab. Hence, he wished to achieve the position of a *de facto* ruler of his master's possessions. He came into contact with Lord Hastings, the then Governor–General of India, who visited Kashmir in 1830 and Gulab Singh was entrusted, on behalf of the Maharaja, to make necessary arrangements of transport and reception. He was granted certificates of merit by the Governor–General for his excellent arrangements. This was his first chance and he must have visualised that in order to achieve his aims, there could be no better powerful masters than the British.

Treaties of Lahore and Amritsar

Death of Maharaja Ranjit Singh in 1839 and the internal conflict that followed, led to the virtual collapse of the central authority at Lahore. The whole of the Sikh kingdom was thrown in turmoil and there occurred many insurrections in various parts, including Kashmir. In this atmosphere of chaos various claimants to the throne had offered alluring terms to the British and sought their help and support, even at cession of their territories. Ultimately, the pro- British Party led by Raja Gulab Singh proposed to barter the independence of the Sikh state for the sake of their Jagirs and principalities. They were devoid of all patriotic impulses, and always thought of personal gains at the expense of the State. The pro-British faction proposed : (i) Extermination of the Sikh; (ii) Payment of tribute by the Lahore Court; (iii) Cession of Kashmir and other territories to the British, and (iv) Stationing of the British forces at Lahore. In above terms, the intentions of the pro – British faction reveal that wanted nothing less than the complete dismemberment of the Sikh State. It also reveals that Raja Gulab Singh had already his eyes on Kashmir and he was craving to invite the British. When Jind Kour, the Maharani of the Kingdom, did not yield to conspirators, the pro – British faction changed their strategy and instigated the unruly Sikh forces to cross the river Sutlej, telling them that the East India Company wanted annexation of the Punjab. The British had decided to cross the Sutlej after November 1845, and they wanted the Sikh army to come on its own accord into the jaws of death. The pro-British faction made Maharani agreed that the Sikh troops should make necessary preparations for war with the British

The Sikh troops crossed the Sutlej on December 11, 1845. The British were ready and prepared to destroy the Sikhs. Henceforth it was a story of continuous treachery in which the commanders betrayed their own soldiers on the field. On account of treacherous conduct of their leaders, the Sikh soldiers fought desperately and in the process destroyed themselves in fighting the British in the battlefield. The battle of Sobroan was fought under such shameful treason. The British attained a great and important victory on February 15, 1846. Gulab Singh reached Kasur to hear the terms of peace, which were embodied in the Treaty of Lahore. It is undoubtedly true that Gulab Singh had been, for years, trying to cultivate the British, because he foresaw attainment of his cherished aim in their rising power. He was also in secret correspondence with them and the British Agent at Ferozepore.

The famous Treaty of Lahore was signed on March 9, 1846, which sealed the fate of the queen Mother, the infant king and the Sikh state. Lord Hardinge, with the help of Gulab Singh and others, succeeded in carrying out British policy in full and the kingdom of Punjab was reduced to the insignificant states of a small principality. By this treaty, the Sikh Government of the Punjab was made to cede in perpetual sovereignty to the British Government; by Article 3, all the country, hill and plain, between the Sutlej and the Beas; and in addition, by Article 4, in lieu of cash indemnity for the expenses of the war, the hill countries situated between the Beas and the Indus, including the provinces of Kashmir and Hazara. By the same treaty, the British agreed, by Article 12, as a reward to Gulab Singh for his services, to transfer to him territories in the hills; to recognise his independence in such territories; and to admit him to a separate treaty.[20] The new State was to be rendered weak in financial and economic resources, so that it could have no military organization. The real intention of the British was to criple the Sikhs by means of fair or foul. They decided to reduce the Kingdom of the Punjab to the State of Lahore, so that it might not become a source of danger to the British. The new State was weakened to such an extent that its absorption in the British India was only a matter of time.

Clause 12 of the treaty by which the infant Maharaja agreed to recognise Raja Gulab Singh a sovereign of such territories as may be made over to him in consideration of his services, clearly revealed the designs of the British Government in India and amply proved the existence of an early understanding between Raja Gulab Singh and the British. All under–hand dealings were exposed when only seven days after the signing of the Treaty of Lahore (March 16, 1846), the Treaty of Amritsar was concluded which made Raja Gulab Singh, the Maharaja of Jammu and Kashmir. According to Article 1 of the treaty, the East India Company made over to him, in independent possession all the hilly and mountainous country with its dependencies situated to the eastward of the river Indus and westward of the river Ravi, including Chamba. In consideration of the price the Maharaja was to pay the British Government the sum of seventy- five lakhs of rupees. Out of this, fifty lakhs was stipulated to be paid on ratification of the treaty and twenty five lakhs on or before October 1, 1846. It was not merely a commercial transaction but something more than that because the British had decided to reward the forbearance of Gulab Singh, because this was in accordance with an intended policy. [21]

On the otherhand, the whole transaction about the sale of Kashmir appears to have been completed under suspicious circumstances. It is a controversial point as to whether any amount was actually paid and adjusted in the books of the East India Company, or whether it was simply an eyewash for the world. Some analysts say that it was simply a political gift and for political reasons. The British desired to curb the revolting spirit of the hilly Chiefs as well as check any aggression from the Chinese, Gurkhas and Afghans' and this could easily be done by keeping their tested and trusted ally in the north of India. Secondly, it was necessary to weaken the Sikhs by depriving them of Kashmir; and thirdly, Gulab Singh's loyalty to the British having been severely tested, foreign aggression would be retarded, by his proximity to them than precipitated and it is in accordance with intended policy that instead of ours being in war with them, the Raja should be direct in contact with them. However, legally, as the Maharaja Dalip Singh was a minor any agreement forced upon or executed by an infant is null and void in law. Lastly, the British were not in active possession of Kashmir and as such they had no right to transfer or sale anything which did not belong to them.

At the time of signing the Treaty of Amritsar Raja Gulab Singh had assured the British that he would be able to occupy Kashmir without difficulty. But in Kashmir a bitter opposition awaited him. Kashmir was at that time held by Shaikh Ghulam Mohi -ud-Din, the Governor of the Sikh Government. The Shaikh died in April 1846 and his son Shaikh Imam–ud–Din, declared the independence of Kashmir and raised the banner of revolt. Raja Gulab Singh got initial defeat and disappointments at the hands of Shaikh but ultimately, with the help of British army, became victorious. He entered Srinagar on November 9, 1846. The capital city surrendered and normalcy was restored in the valley. The first important act, which the British did was the demarcation of boundaries between Kashmir and the Punjab. By the middle of the nineteenth century other regions such as Ladakh, Gilgit, Baltistan and Poonch were also acquired by the Maharaja and were included in the State of Jammu and Kashmir. All the distinct regions came to comprise the historical territory of the princely state of Jammu and Kashmir.

The British Government while bringing Kashmir under the subjugation of Gulab Singh, did not even care to ascertain the wishes of the Kashmiris. The whole business was transacted behind their back.[22] That is why the Kashmiris have continued to hate this transaction.[23] Although with the Treaty of Amritsar the Maharaja had secured a large measure of independence, both in internal and external affairs of the State. It was evident from the various instances which followed that the varying degrees of internal as well as external sovereignty of the Maharaja in fact became subject to the due exercise of the authority by the British Government. The British rulers violated the provisions of the Treaty by interfering under one pretext or another not only in the external affairs of the state but in the internal affairs as well. The interference of the British Government started as soon as the Treaty had concluded. At that time the magnitude of interference was not of any serious nature, but by the end of nineteenth century it assumed alarming proportions.[24]

Dogra Kings and the British

Gulab Singh died in 1857 and succeeded by his third son, Ranbir Singh, who was a model Hindu Prince devoted to his religion and to Sanskrit learning. Ranbir Singh maintained the tradition of his father and remained faithful and loyal to the British. He even refused acceptance of Khilat amounting to Rs- One lac and a Jagir in Oudh, in recognition of his services to the British in suppressing the revolt of 1857 in various regions, particularly in Delhi. He declared that he had done his duty out of loyalty and goodwill. He felt proud that he had played a useful part in suppressing the rebels and was glad that the insurgents had been crushed. Actually, with the submissive attitude to the British he wanted to prepare ground for his leap forward policy' towards the north. He wanted to regain what his father had lost in Gilgit and Dardistan and something more beyond Pamirs. At a later stage it became cleat that the Britishers were suspicious of the activities of Ranbir Singh and he was told in a diplomatic way to be careful in future. The British did not want any war with Russia and latter's extension to the outposts of Afghanistan compelled the former to have a special attention to the question of frontier defence. Incidentally Kashmir came in for their special attention and they took steps to establish a British Residency in Kashmir and Sir Oliver St. John became the first Resident in Kashmir.

After the death of Ranbir Singh, Pratap Singh, the new Maharaja camc to the throne on September 25, 1885 under the shadow of fear. As he was submissive by nature, he wanted to show extreme loyalty to the British from the first day of his accession. From the beginning of his rule, Pratap Singh felt suspicious that some intrigue was going on against him. As such, he looked towards the British for support. The British Resident in Kashmir and Raja Amar Singh hatched a conspiracy and Maharaja was told that he had a difficult task before him. As such he should consult the Agent of the Viceory; at all times and be guided by his advice; to carry out the views of the Viceroy. Subsequently in 1888, the largest army of Kashmir that any other Indian Chief ever had, was reduced. Further a British Military Adviser was appointed to carryout the re- organisation of the Maharaja's forces. The basic policy of the British was to bring the forces in every native state under its control and utilise them for furtherance of the Imperial interest. The Kashmir forces were utilised in Chitral, North West Frontier Province and the Afghan expeditions. Similarly the soldiers of the State were utilised in various expeditions in the tribal territories of the frontier. Maharaja Pratap Singh continued to remain as a non–entity in Kashmir.

The British started the reorganisation of civil administration in 1895 and reorganised all departments by 1903. Complete reorganisation was effected by the British in 1907. As Kashmir had acquired an importance in the context of Anglo–Russian rivalry, the question of developing road communications attracted the foremost attention of the British. It was necessary to have roads to fortify the military position on the frontiers as well as to resist, if necessary, an attack from Russia.[25] It was also considered advisable to connect Gilgit with Srinagar and Rawalpindi. Earlier in 1890, a railway line between Jammu and Sialkot was completed by the British and it was placed under the charge of the North Western Railway. The Banihal cart road between Jammu and Srinagar was built in 1915. With the outbreak of world war 1, the whole of the Kashmir army was mobilised for active service in the Great War and they fought against the Germans in East Africa. The total number of recruits supplied from the State for the war came to nearly sixteen thousand.

With the connivance of the British Governments and the Maharaja, despite meagre developments in transportation, the state of Jammu and Kashmir remained backward largely in education, trade and in everything that could enhance the life of the valley. Figures and data undertaken from time to time showed that though the Hindus form less than seven per cent of the population, they benefited more from the education bestowed by the state. 'Not only the rulers of Jammu and Kashmir ruined their poor subjects with the burden of heavy taxes and efficient officers,' they did not care a fig for their education. The wealth which was accumulated by sucking their blood was spent on furnishing the royal palaces, in pursuit of song and luxury and for the serving of the English; and nothing was spent out of it, for education of the subjects. In fact, this heaven had become a hell for its residents. Devoid of education and freedom, they cannot take advantage of natural blessings. The land which appears to be a heaven for outsiders was nothing less than a hell for its residents.

The Muslims of the State, viewing their educational and overall social position became both conscious and agitative. Sensing the frustration and general mood of the Muslims, the Maharaja invited a representative gathering at Srinagar in 1910 and advised them to maintain communal harmony. A delegation led by Sahibzada Aftab Ahmed met Pratap Singh in 1913 and pleaded the cause of Kashmiri Muslims. Their demands became irresistible and the Maharaja was moved to do something in this direction. An All India Mohammedan Educational Conference presented a memorandum to Maharaja Pratap Singh regarding provision of Educational facilities to the Muslims in the State. However some cosmetic reforms implemented after the Russian Revolution of 1917. Many progressive reforms were carried out and the masses were freed from heavy taxes extortion, and forced labour. Means of communication were improved; agriculture and industry were developed and educational facilities provided for. The administration was overhauled and a beginning was made towards democratic rule. It was an era of reforms in every sphere of the life of the people. For strategic point of view, his rule was remarkable for the reassertion of the Kashmir sovereignty over Gilgit that could serve as one of their observation posts on the north of India.[26]

Maharaja Hari Singh replaced Pratap Singh in 1925. He assumed the reign of administration in a troubled period. The change marked the end of an era and Kashmir left behind an autocratic phase to enter onto a modern era. Steps taken by the British Government and Maharaja failed to contain the wave of political unrest in which press media had played an important role. It wrote in India about Kashmir and its administration and complained; there is want of grip in the administration, absence of touch with the people and the negation of love and attachment on their part to the Government. The plight of the people having gone from bad to worse, prayers were made that 'His Majesty,' by his royal grace, may be pleased to extend the people of Kashmir, the new light of equality and self-determination.[27] The British Government, itself, caught in a dilemma. After the establishment of a Socialistic regime in Russia, a fear psychosis engulfed them and they feared that 'with the slightest change in the situation the imperialist pirates will again move against us.' Naturally the British alarmed by possible repercussions in British India, including Kashmir, could neither tolerate nor sympathise with the Kashmiri uprising.[28]

Public resentment and resistance against the autocratic rule of Maharaja continued despite severe repression and arrest on the part of the Government. A new generation of university-educated Kashmiri youth fresh from Aligarh, started organised resistance in 1931. It was in 1932 that a Political organisation named All Jammu and Kashmir Muslim Conference was formed. Its main purpose was to coordinate the popular movement for democratic government and social Justice. Further a split took place in the Muslim Conference in 1938 when almost its entire organisation in the Kashmir valley led by the dynamic Sheikh Mohammad Abdullah, reconstituted itself as the National Conference (NC). The new force declared its intent to end communalism by ceasing to think in terms of Muslims and non- Muslims, and invited all Hindus and Sikhs who believe in the freedom of their country from the shackles of an irresponsible rule to participate as equals in the democratic struggle.[29]

The National Conference under the charismatic leadership of Abdullah consolidated its mass following in the valley. A much more important factor was added to the Party in 1944 when it adopted a social manifesto; Naya (New) Kashmir; that promised a radical land reform that the monarchy had abolished. The All- India Muslim League, led by Mohammed Ali Jinnah continued to hold a strong foot in the Jammu region that, later became part of Azad Kashmir. But in the Kashmiri heartland, the mantle of leadership had passed to Abdullah, his Party went from strength to strength. In May 1946, the NC launched a mass agitation which it called 'Quit Kashmir,' on the model of the Indian National Congress 'Quit India' Movement of 1942, against the last Maharaja, Hari Singh. Abdullah declared that the time has come to tear up the Treaty of Amritsar...... Sovereignty is not the birthright of Maharaja Hari Singh.[30]

The Larger Imperial Design

As the British withdrawal approached, its Government on March 11, 1942 had declared to set up a Constituent Assembly in India after the end of the Second World War to determine India's Constitution.[31] It made, almost certain, the lapse of British paramountcy over India, including princely states and the State of Jammu and Kashmir. Before the State was acceded to India on October 26, 1947, a section of the people, leadership and the then Maharaja Hari Singh advocated that the state shall remain independent. This was one of the reasons which, it appears, had prevented the Maharaja of the state not to sign the Instrument of Accession as done by other Rulers of the Indian States.

The Imperial British Government while determining the legal framework for the future political status of the princely states of India had hoped that the larger princely states would remain independent, that the sub continental empire would consist of two dominions – India and Pakistan and that a number of large princely states would constitute the third geopolitical ingredient of the South Asian subcontinent. Their further expectation was that these princely states and Pakistan would sustain close linkages with the British Government. When the majority of the princely states acceded to India, the British plan went awry. The aspiration of Maharaja Hari Singh of Jammu and Kashmir to convert his state into an independent country was sort of a last opportunity which the British Government wished to utilise to strengthen its influence and to create strategic equation with Pakistan to meet this purpose.[32]

Meanwhile, Pakistan jumped the gun with the tribal and military intervention in Jammu and Kashmir resulting in Hari Singh as well as Sheikh Mohammed Abdullah deciding to accede to the Indian union. Both Lord Mountbatten, the then Governor–General of India, and British Prime Minister Clement Atlee were not happy about this development. It was on their advice, and against his own instinct, that Jawaharlal Nehru took the issue to the UN and offered a referendum Plebiscite in that state. Once the matter reached the UN the British converted it into a territorial dispute between India and Pakistan and laid the foundations of international or third-party involvement in Kashmir.[33]

The act of the tragic drama, on the eve of country's independence, was dominated as one author says, by four actors whose characters contained the seeds of tragedy. Maharaja Hari Singh was indecisive; Jinnah impatient; Nehru impulsive and apt to ignore stark realities; and Sheikh Abdullah over- ambitious and prone to fits of megalomania. Everyone of them had illusion of his own and thought that the plot of the drama would proceed in accordance with the outlines that he had drawn. But that was not to be. Miscalculations could only lead to confusion and conflict.[34] And Kashmir was soon sucked into a whirlpool of national and international controversies.

References

1. G.S. Misra, British Foreign Policy and Indian Affairs, 1783-1815, p.5.
2. F.M. Hassnain, British Policy Towards Kashmir, 1846- 1921, New Delhi, 1974, p. 29.
3. M.A. Stien, Rajatarangini, Vol. 1, P. 104.
4. *Ibid.,* p. 92.
5. Francis Younghusband, Kashmir, p. 125.
6. J.P. Ferguson, Kashmir: A Historical Introduction, London, 1961, p. 19.
7. P.N. K, Bamzai, A History of Kashmir, Delhi, 1962, p. 125.
8. M.A. Stien. *op. cit.,* p. 109.
9. B.L. Sharma, Kashmir Awakes, Delhi, 1971, p. 27.
10. Walter Lawrence, The Valley of Kashmir, London, 1895, pp. 190-91.
11. *Ibid.,* p., 302.
12. Jawaharlal Nehru, The Discovery of India, Calcutta, 1946, pp. 266- 67.
13. George Forster, A Journey from Bengal to England, London 1808.
14. Walter Lawrence, *op., cit.,* pp. 197- 98.
15. *Ibid.,* pp. 196- 97.
16. Quoted by Edward Thompson, in The Making of Indian Princes, 1943, pp. 157- 58.
17. J.P. Ferguson, *op. cit.,* p. 49.
18. Jagmohan Mahajan, Annexation of the Punjab, p. 15.

19. B.J. Cunningham, History of the Sikhs. pp. 181-218.
20. Parliamentary Papers (1846), No, 15 G.G. to the Secret Committee, February 19, 1846.
21. Life of Lord Hardinge, Oxford, 1891, p. 113.
22. P.N. Bazaz, Inside Kashmir, p. 31.
23. Statements of Sheikh Mohammed Abdullah and others in Quit Kashmir Movement, 1946. The Historic Trial of Kashmir, Weekly Khalid, Kashmir, October 1946, p. 43.
24. H.O. Agarwal, Kashmir Problem: Its Legal Aspects, Allahabad, 1979, pp. 5- 6.
25. Tyndale Biscoe, Kashmir in Sunlight and Shade, p. 30.
26. William Digby, Condemned Unheard, p. 103.
27. Kashmiri Magazine, Lahore, February 27, 1920.
28. F.M. Hassnain, *op. cit.,* p., 115.
29. Lamb, Alastair, Crisis in Kashmir, 1947 to 1966, London, 1966, p. 31.
30. M.J. Akbar, India, the Siege Within, Penguin, 1985, pp. 227- 28.
31. For the text of the declaration of the British Government, see Indian Constitutional Documents, Munshi Papers Vol. II, p, 5.
32. J. N. Dixit, "Three is a Crowd Always", The Hindustan Times, 23 December 2001.
33. *Ibid.*
34. Jagmohan, "50 Years of Kashmir's Accession to India", Ibid, 27 October 1997.

2

Kashmir : Religion and Culture

Islam : Origin and Orientation

Every religion comes into existence in a given society with its values, its ethos, customs and traditions. Often a religion comes into existence in a society when it gets corrupted or deviates widely from the acceptable path that ensures good for the whole society. A religion tries to reform a society by providing certain ideals and values. But the people adopt these ideals and values quite selectively so as not to harm their interests. Human behaviour is never determined simply by the religion one follows. It is determined by several factors — personal or group interest and inspiration, social mores and traditions and tribal or national expectations. Social changes also deeply affect what could be termed as 'religious behaviour'. Understanding religion varies according to tribal, national and ethnic considerations. There is no single or uniform understanding of religion.[1] One always finds a tension between the theological and the sociological. This tension could be creative or destructive, depending on the situation or approach of the people concerned.

The word 'Islam', which is derived from 'aslama', means surrender to the Will of God. The word has other meanings too – to be at perfect peace, to have done one's duty to the Master, to strive after righteousness, and to greet safety and salvation. It believes that in obedience of God, lies peace, prosperity, happiness, and the salvation of man. According to Islam, the other prophets who preceded Muhammad were all true prophets, and Islam is nothing but a confirmation of the true faith taught by previous religions and teachers. Religion is certainly a vital force in every society and Muhammad made Islam a permanent force of vitality by giving it a natural and rational basis.[2] He emphasised the universal concept of religion such as the unity of God and the unity of the human race. The essence of tawhid or the unity of God as a working idea is equality, solidarity, brotherhood and freedom. It is a change from heterogeneity to homogeneity, from diversity to unity and from confusion to order.

Islam's concept of the unity of man had very deep and far-reaching effects on the social, political, economic and moral way of life of the Muslims. It is eminently human because it takes man for what he is. The prophet was sent not to make life more difficult, but to facilitate it. The requirements of Islam are easy and simple. The striking feature of Islamic teaching, which is so well brought out is the equality and brotherhood of man. It attempts to level the barriers of caste, colour and class and takes its stand on the bedrock of love, liberalism and brotherhood. The Quran says, 'Oh people! be fearful of God who has created you all from the same single soul'. This unity of man was of great social value. It removed all discriminations in human society and had established the value of merit, ability and the capacity to wield the sword that mattered most, and not the race, colour or the social distinction. In the Muslim period of Indian history, slave after slave succeeded to political power and established a Slave Dynasty itself, holding power for nearly a century.

An impression has been created that Islam is intolerant of other religions. The Quran emphatically declared, 'There is no compulsion in religion', and again 'Unbelievers who worship other things than God need not be blamed lest they should abuse God in their ignorance. It is true that jehad or holy war is permitted in Islam, but Jehad is a fight against those who fight against you. It is a defensive war sanctioned by the prophet at an extraordinary period when the Kuraish were bent upon wiping out the Muslims. It does not permit the Muslims to commit aggression. Later theologians have interpreted jehad as a struggle to create something new and change the order through intellectual power, and it is not necessarily the use of physical force.

Unfortunately, this intolerance is the common heritage of all the three semitic religions –Judaism, Islam and Christianity. The misfortune of Islam is that it has no Reformation, no Renaissance. This situation, said Sri Aurobindo, needs to be corrected. "We must strive to remove the causes of misunderstanding by mutual knowledge and sympathy and spread the just views of Mohammedan history and civilisation". What is wanted is some new religious movement among the Mohammedans which would remodel their religion and change the stamp of their temperament.[3] Although Islam has had no reformers because of the belief in the immutability of the doctrine. The same conviction guides the Christian Right, mainly in the US. They oppose Darwin's theory since it negates the Word of God in the Bible. Lots of people all over the world have the feeling that Islam is intolerant and violent. And this is true enough. The concept of Kafir and Jehad are wholly unacceptable, especially in its present form and interpretation.

Apart from this Islam had a bad press. The belief that Islam harboured more subversives than any other religion had been widespread. But as the understanding of the Quran is greatly influenced by the social norms and ethos of the prevailent society, the verses, such as, 'Then fight and slay the pagans wherever ye find them. And seize them, beleaguer them. And lie in wait them. In every war, simply reflect the merciless times when they were written. In his *Study of History*, Arnold Toynbee wrote that 'in matters of race, the promptings of this old fashioned Syriac oracle (*the old Testament*) are very clear and savage'. Toynbee had regarded *the old Testament* as 'representative of the Syriac religious genius in its young and callow phrase ; and even in this phase, towards its latter end, there was an outburst of spiritual experience and spiritual creation recorded in the Books of prophets – which points towards the *New Testament.*[4]

In fact any religion, particularly those that have existed over long periods of time and continue to be practised – speak to us in many voices. Their multivocality, which expresses the diversity of historical experience, allows for a degree of internal and external critique. For example, the concept of a global Islamic umma is at best a theological one and not reflected in the realities of life or politics. The per capita Gross Domestic Product (GDP) of United

Arab Emirates (UAE) is $ 17,400, while that of Yemen is $ 260. And both are not just Muslim countries, but are part of the even more supposedly close knit Arab family. There are deep societal fissures within Islamic nations; the Sunni-Shia divide is only the most prominent.

Islam started as a great revolutionary movement based on equality, human dignity and justice. These ideals were partly acceptable to the tribal society of Mecca. Equality and human dignity was acceptable in a limited way within tribal social boundaries. Members of a tribe could be accepted as equals, but not those of other tribes. Members of other tribes could be accepted only as a client, not as an equal. Hence, the concept of universal brotherhood and inter-tribal equality created social tension throughout the Islamic history. Within Arab society, these became explosive after the death of the prophet. By the time the prophet died, different tribes of Arabia had embraced Islam. Sociologically speaking, 'hostile' tribes also entered the fold of Islam leading to tension between them. The lofty ideals received a setback when the tribe of Quraysh claimed the Caliphate quoting a 'hadith' and superiority over other tribes. These concepts were never accepted sociologically. Islamic society soon transformed into a feudal society. The reasons for embracing a religion could be quite varied. Some embrace it collectively along with other members of the caste or tribe or nation; some embrace it for political or economic advantages ; and some after studying the religion. Normally the social structure does not change, but religious practices do. Arab society has remained tribal in structure till this day. Had Islamic ideals and values prevailed, Arab society would have undergone radical changes and tribal norms and values would have been replaced by Islamic ones. Thus, it would be very difficult to talk of a 'pure' Islamic culture. Each Muslim society has its own distinct tribal or national or ethnic culture even though ritual practices may be the same.

The continued presence of religion in the public sphere is justified on two grounds. First it is argued that religion per se is not responsible for the kind of hostility and hatred that we witness among members of different communities today. Second, and more importantly, it is argued that 'communal violence' is a contemporary phenomenon embodying a system of rationality that is characteristic of modernity. Industrial development displaces large sections of the population from their original surroundings, resulting in a deep sense of dislocation and alienation. At the same time it fails to provide an alternative set of values and along with it, a sense of belonging to these people. To offset this deficiency they try to reclaim and assert their traditional identities more stridently. The alienation generated in the process of modernisation provides the material for the growth of orthodox religious forms.[5]

In more positive term, the principles of modernity claim that the theme of tolerance, which defines a liberal democratic framework, is an attribute of all lived and practised religion. Continuous interaction with members of other communities in the course of everyday life, generates a degree of tolerance and diversity in which religious boundaries become fuzzy as members of one community participate in the religious and cultural practices of the other. In contemporary India, despite the increasing incidents of communal violence, we find Hindus visiting 'gurudwaras' and rubbing shoulders with the Muslim pilgrims at the Chishti Dargah in Ajmer.

Early in the eighth century, in 712, the Arabs had reached Sind and occupied it. For nearly 300 years there was no further invasion of or incursion into India. About 1000 A. C. Sultan Mahmud of Ghazni (Afghanistan), began his raids into India and annexed the Punjab and Sind to his dominions. He was unable to conquer Kashmir. This mountain country succeeded in checking and repulsing him. He was far more a warrior than a man of faith and like many other conquerors, used and exploited the name of religion for his conquests. His raids are a big event in Indian history, though politically India as a whole was not greatly affected by them and the heart of India remained untouched. Mahmud repeated incursions from the north west that brought many new elements into India's closed thought and economy. Above all they brought Islam, for the first time, to the accompaniment of ruthless military conquest. So far, for over 300 years, Islam had come peacefully as a religion and taken its place among the many religions of India without trouble or conflict. The new approach produced powerful psychological reactions among the people and filled them with bitterness. There was no objection to a new religion but there was a strong objection to anything which forcibly interfered with and upset their way of life.

India is a land of many religions, despite the dominance of the Hindu faith in its various shapes and forms. Before Islam, Jainism and Buddhism had been absorbed by Hinduism. Also, there were Christianity and the Hebrew religion which had reached India probably during the first century after Christ, had found a place in the country. Historically, Hindu society had shown a peculiar ability to absorb and culturally assimilate groups which entered its fold from outside, even with military power. Islam was the first exception. Islamic groups had much greater cultural self-confidence, and clearer self-recognition in terms of doctrines and observances. This prevented an absorption into Hindu society in the treacherously insidious way that had been the common fate of earlier intruders. However, the Indian Islam eventually developed many peculiarities which must be put down to its constant transactions with indigeneous religious forms.

Islam and Kashmir

After the Delhi Sultanate, a small Muslim state grew up in Jaunpur. Right through the fifteenth this was a centre of art and culture and toleration in religion. An attempt was even made to bring about a synthesis between the religious faiths of Hindu and Muslim. About this time in Kashmir, an independent Muslim King, Zainul-abdin, became famous for religious toleration, encouragement of Sanskrit learning and old culture. The new ideas of Islam were troubling people's minds all over India. As of old India was trying to absorb the foreign element and herself changing somewhat in the process. A new type of reformer who deliberately preached this synthesis arose. In the fifteenth century there were a number of Hindu reformers, like Ramanand in the South, Kabir, his more famous disciple, Guru Nanak in the north. The influence of these reformers went far beyond the limits of the particular sect that grew up after them. Hinduism as a whole felt the impact of the new ideas, and Islam in India also became somewhat different from what it was elsewhere. The fierce monotheism of Islam influenced Hinduism and the vague Pantheistic attitude of the Hindu had its effects on the Indian Muslim.[6] A large number of Indian Muslims were converts bred up in and surrounded by the old traditions; only a comparatively small number of them had come from outside.

However, the synthesis of the above two cultures continued to remain a distant dream even today. The fact that political authority lay with Islamic groups made it impossible for Brahminical society to ignore it entirely, the insidious aggrandisement of Hindu religious practice did not succeed against the Islamic culture. Gradually, indigeneous society allowed the two types of Islamic groups—the military entrants and the large masses of indigeneous converts—to settle down into existence groups or circles of their own obeying in an indirect sense the exclusivistic logic of the Hindu social order. Muslim ruling dynasties came to control the upper layers of political authority while Hindu groups controlled commercial, craft and other productive practices and an effective protocol emerged for the prosecution of everyday business. But it would be a misjudgement to believe that such transactions in mundane matters would form the base of a culture which became wholly mixed in every respect. Because the mundane is less important than the sacred for pre-modern mentalities, the significance of such transactions was comparatively meagre.[7] The sacred, for both communities, remained largely exclusive and unmerged, and intolerant of excessive contact, despite the efforts of Bhakti saints and Sufi mystics to produce syncretic forms. The Muslims were profoundly influenced by the environment, by Hinduism, its social organisation and culture as a result of which, Hindu-Muslim masses became least indistinguishable. Many converted Hindus were not Muslimised. Instead of materially changing their outlook, they continues to breathe in their traditional environment, retain their old world socio-religious ideas and even sought to import these into their fold.[8]

The new direction and their activities, which was confined to a few, failed to resolve the doubt and confusion of their minds. Hindus had looked back and sought consolidation in ancient times. Old philosophy and literature, art and history, had brought some relief. Ram Mohan Roy Dayananda, Vivekananda, and others had started new movements of thought. They kept the rich streams of English literature in their minds and were also full of ancient sages and heroes of India. The proselytising zeal of Islam strengthened conservatism in the orthodox circles of the Hindus. Just as the Protestant Reformation in Europe was followed by the Counter-Reformation and efforts of the Roman Catholic Church to set its own house in order, so to protect their position against spread of Islam, the Hindus wanted to make themselves as orthodox as possible and increased the stringency of caste rules and formulated rules of conduct in Smriti works with a rigidity unknown before.[9]

For the Muslim masses this idea was not new and they were acquainted with these tradition. But the Muslim upper classes, despite the Indianisation of conquerors and immigrants–Arab and Afghan, Turk and Turkoman, Mongol Mongoloid in several respects, began to realise that it was not proper for them to associate themselves with these semi-religious traditions, and any encouragement to them would be contrary to the spirit of Islam. They searched for their national roots elsewhere. They concentrated on Islamic history and to the periods when Islam was a conquering and creative force in Baghdad, Spain, Constantinople, Central Asia. But these all were limited and did not really affect the general outlook of Indian Muslims. At best, the Indian Muslims derived some psychological satisfaction from a contemplation of Islam's past greatness.

The case of Islam in the present state of Jammu and Kashmir is an exception. The history of Kashmir, reveals Stien, has always borne a local character. It cannot be doubted that this fact has been a decided advantage for the preservation of historical traditions.[10] It is, like the rest of India, a cauldron in which religions, races, and languages meet, melt and mingle. Here is a confluence of Indian, Tibetan, Central Asian, Greek and Iranian cultures. Hinduism principally prevails in the province of Jammu, Islam in the valley and northern areas and Buddhism in Ladakh. There are also a few Sikhs and Christians. Kashmir's chronicles and other available information, the population of Kashmir had shown already in old times the same homogeneity that it does today.

Considering the history of the people, it is not surprising that Hindus and Muslims have much in common and they share many customs and practices on occasions of birth, marriage and death. If comparison be made between the customs of the Hindus and the Muslims, it would be seen that there are many points of resemblance, and the curious prominence of the walnut and the salt and the use of the mendhi dye in both religions; there is the fixing of the marriage day ; the visit paid by bridegroom to the bride's house after marriage; the giving of money and Jewels ; the dress and the title of the bridegroom as maharaja and of the bride as maharani ; the giving of presents on the fourth day after death, and the celebration, respectively of the birthday and the day of death. According to Lawrence, the Rishis, the order of Muslim holy men, the Babas and the Makhdum Sahib Pirzadas are always looked upon as pure Kashmiri and are called Wami, as distinguished from the Saiyads and Saiyad Pirzadas, who found their way to the valley from foreign countries.[11] After the end of the Hindu rule Sanskrit remained for a considerable period the medium of official communication and record in history. The continued popular use of Sanskrit among Muslims was proved by the Sanskrit inscriptions on tombstones at Srinagar near Martand and elsewhere.

It is clear from the brief account that nothing did greater harm to the development of secular ideals and religious tolerance in Kashmir than Sikandar, the Chaks, and the Pathans. Their blind obsession with the craze to add to the number of the faithful and to destroy the religious movements of their forefathers closed their hearts to the call of humanity as it shut their eyes to their ancestors' dreams in store. However, the persecutions and destruction were launched by the rulers who were mostly outsiders, alien to the culture of the people, not by the people themselves. The Hindus and Muslims in the valley did not split apart, and irrespective of the suffering and indignities heaped upon the Hindus by the fanatics who were incapable of seeing a view other than their own, the relations between the two communities continued to be friendly and cordial. This fact was of tremendous importance.

But cordial relation between the two communities was too good to last. It was the foreign zealots who came into the valley and instigated Muslim rulers to give no quarter to Hindus. People's attitude was sound and since most of the Muslims were Hindu converts and the two communities had so much in common in language, culture, thought and customs, they had nothing to quarrel about. What is at stake in Kashmir is the long preserved tradition of religious tolerance. Over the centuries and after many trials and tribulations has emerged there a way of life, based on tolerance, an attitude to fellowmen preserved from the curse of suffocating creeds, a faith in the coexistence of many religions and cultures.[12]

Western View of Islam

The continuous enjoyment of political power for over 1,000 years had given the Muslims a self-confidence which was based on a faith in Islam, which they believed would never let them down. But as a result of the renaissance in Europe, with the age of reason, the invention of gun powder, the geographical explorations, the industrial revolution and the colonial expansion of the European powers, Islamic glory became a thing of the past. The mainstream of the intellectual and creative section of the society fell into the grip of traditionalists who valued piety more than progress. Islamic decline became more apparent from the eighteenth century, when the French Revolution gave new concepts of democracy and nationalism to Europe, and the Muslims were left far behind in every sector of human life. With them declined a civilization which had consistently flourished in the major areas of three continents, Asia, Europe and Africa. Even their political authority was seriously challenged by the British in India, the Dutch in Indonesia, the French in Western Africa and the Russian in Central Asia. Islam's darkest hour was when the Allied fleet anchored in the Golden Horn after the First World War. The question before Islam was not how to find new channels for its expansion, not even to retain the superiority they had enjoyed, but to survive and escape total annihilation and humiliation.[13]

It is true that the Islamic faith in the past had elevated human dignity and had promoted human happiness on earth, but possession of knowledge without acting on it is useless. The Muslims are unable to meet the challenge posed by Western countries. This created fundamental doubts among the educated Muslims in Islamic values and ideas, and they were inclined more and more towards an appreciation of western culture and outlook. This tended to cut the Muslims off from the Muslim way of life. Muhammand Ali of Egypt, Sir Syed Ahmed Khan of India and Mustapha Kemal of Turkey are examples of this change towards Westernization and modernization. But this does not mean that the Muslims did not resist the European onslaught. They fought every battle in India including the one in 1857. Apart from this several movements were started to revise the tenets of Islam, each in their own way.

The West regarded Islam as an archaic, conservative, rigid, dogmatic and primitive order which they wanted to change through the secular traditions of Voltaire and Tom Paine and through the impact of Graeco-Roman culture. Their aim was to project emphatically, the western secularism, based ultimately on the Greek ideals of justice, order, reason and humanity, which were not tagged on to any religious label. It was not a clash between Islam and Christianity as religions, but a clash between two cultures; the highly industrialised and politicised European culture with vastly superior military power. Islam could not meet this challenge as it was not prepared, for it.[14] The educational system they practised, the political institutions they had built up, the economic structure they evolved, the military discipline they followed, and the type of cultural life they led might have been very progressive from the medieval viewpoint of feudal society, but not from the western standard which was not far wrong in thinking that the Islamic world was still in the primitive stage. The matter became much worse when not only the westerners but also the western-educated Muslims began to think the same way. Hence Islam came under fire both from within and without.

There is a section of the people in the west and in India who consider Islam as an autonomous factor in the global power matrix.

The vulnerability of Middle East oil to ideological Islam has sharpened this perception among strategic thinkers in the West. In the case of the general public, particularly in the US, the situation faced by Israel has also contributed to the process. The West has given the world science and technology. It has also introduced the concept of democracy and human rights. But it has also rubbished India, China-and Muslim world. They have imposed on these civilizations. Missionaries have been sent with foreign funds to subvert the religion and culture of those people. Muslims resent it more because they have recent memories of their power. Many Muslim countries were occupied. Even after 'independence', their governments were either toppled or turned into puppets. Their oil wealth still goes to enrich the West. Their oil revenues are diverted to arms purchases. Neighbouring countries are encouraged and armed to fight each other. According to Paul Kennedy, there is an annual flow of over $ 40 billion from the poor countries to the rich countries.[15] In Pakistan, they have installed a series of generals. Even the Western media devote the greatest attention to the Third World in times of disaster, crisis and confrontation while they conceal facts about themselves. During the Cuban missile crisis in 1961, the Western media said Khrushchev had yielded to Kennedy and agreed to withdraw those missiles. They almost suppressed the fact that, in return, the US had agreed to withdraw its missiles from Turkey which were aimed at Russia.[16]

The recent militant image of Islam has come basically from the use of religion to generate political consciousness in the Middle East where external involvement, on account of oil and Israel, has not permitted democracy to take root. The fear of confrontationist Islam as typified by Professor Huntington's vision of clashing civilisations began with the rise to power of militant Islam in once West-friendly Iran and the resilience it has displayed in several countries including Egypt, Algeria, Sudan, Pakistan, Libya, Lebanon and Afghanistan. His characterisation of Islam locates a particularly menacing, primordial 'civilization' in the crescent-shaped Islamic bloc of nations, from the bulge of Africa to Central Asia. 'Islam' he proclaims, 'has bloody borders'. And he speaks of the historic clash between Muslims and Hindu in the subcontinent.[17]

This, however, represents American conservatism perhaps, shaped by a sour mix of 'anti-democratic authoritarianism, genuine paranoia and intellectual bankruptcy. Commenting on Huntington's concept Edward Said has summarised its essential character, 'A penchant for dividing the world into pro–and anti–American ...an unwillingness to report political processes, an imposition of patterns and values ethnocentric or irrelevant or both, pure misinformation, repetition, an avoidance of detail, an absence of genuine perspective.[18] This form of thinking, which presents 'Islam' as a 'resurgent atavism', is threatening 'the destruction of democratic order in the Western world.[19] The Western academia and media, particularly after the Iranian Revolution of 1979, had developed the segments to demonise Islam as a faith, and to depict Muslim societies, with varying degree of candour and crudity. In realpolitik terms the West has always been selective in its dealings with Islam. It has opposed Islamism in Egypt, Algeria and Saudi Arabia but has been supportive of it in Chechnya, Bosnia and Kashmir. Singling out Islam as a fundamentalist religion is clearly not a practical, long term proposition when it is the second largest religion in the world, and there are 39 countries spanning three continents where Muslims make up a majority. One fifth of humanity is Muslim by religion.[20]

The State as Today

Similar to the West, despite the evidence of powerful grass-roots efforts at unity, harmony and cooperation, much of the political, military, diplomatic, media and intellectual establishment in India viewed the Kashmir question explicitly or implicitly, through the Jaundiced and distinctly 'communal lens of Hindu Muslim conflict. In this view there is sufficient scope for deadly consequences for human lives, especially when it permeates entire institutional apparatuses of power and control.[21] This attitude of the administration is heavily responsible for today's state of affairs in Kashmir. It has changed the face of the Kashmiri into a blurred, featureless mask. And all these have nothing to do with democracy and secularism in Kashmir. Even much alike in Bosnia-Herzegovina, many Kashmiris do feel 'they are being killed and destroyed because they are Muslims. But they have, on the whole, have shown significant restraint and temperance in the face of extreme provocation.

Kashmiri Muslims are indeed devout Muslims. But it would be grave injustice to them not to recognise the fact that they are also proud Kashmiris. They are perhaps the only community of the subcontinent that has a recorded history of 5,000 years.[22] Evidently, Islamic consciousness has always been a prominent and integral component, along with other political ideals and forms of identity, of Kashmiri nationalism and its democratic struggle. The upsurge of 1931 was in many ways the revolt of the politicised elements of a subjugated Muslim population against a Hindu autocrate, bureaucracy and military. And there are deep historical reasons for the enmeshing of Islamic consciousness with Kashmir's nationalism and democratic movements in the modern period. Islam is rooted in Kashmiri tradition and that tradition is permeated with the Islamic spirit has enabled Kashmiris to reconcile cosmopolitan affiliation with territorial nationalism. The Kashmiri Muslim has remained a Kashmiri as well as Muslim .... Kashmiri Muslims ... do react like any other Muslim community when their religious interests are endangered. But they are unlikely to submerge their Kashmiri identity in the name of Islam.[23]

Kashmiri's movement for their identity has been hijacked by fundamentalist elements. The credit for this lies first of all with the repressive measures practised by the Indian state and second, with the Pakistani regime, who exploited the situation in its favour and began to sponsor such elements, mainly underemployed Afghan mujahideen and Pakistani religious radicals, but also men from the Sudan, Lebanon and Egypt, among other countries, fighting in Kashmir.[24] It provided us a convenient mechanism to justify our policy of repression and blinding 'ourselves' to what 'our' relationship with Kashmir has really been. This institutionalised ideological rhetoric as Edward Said puts it, of defending national unity against the encroachment of those bloody borders' serves the purpose of producing the 'illusion', if not the actuality, of consensus'. It also means that Indians are left with little opportunity to view Kashmir 'except reductively, coercively, oppositionally. Although the State swears by 'secularism', it has done little indeed to secularise a civil society that remains extremely backward, ridden by caste prejudices and religious intolerance, superstitious beliefs and obscurantist practices. In Hindu-Muslim relation in particular, the pre-partition legacy of communal division has been allowed to intrude into politics, lending legitimacy to both Hindu and Muslim fundamentalism.[25]

Historically speaking, the Kashmiri identity has played a far more important role in its politics than the Muslim identity. Before 1947, the political support by Indian leaders in particular by Gandhi and Nehru to the struggle of the people of Kashmir against an autocratic rule, and later at the time of partition, to their right to choose between India and Pakistan attracted them to Hindu majority India instead of what was called the homeland of Muslims. As Kashmiri Muslims felt that their Kashmiri identity was threatened by the Muslim raiders from Pakistan who tried to annex them to that country forcibly, they sought Indian help and welcomed the Indian Army. The Muslim majority state acceded to India in 1947 when communal violence had peaked in the subcontinent. When the issue arose before India's Islamic community as to how to define India, it was accepted that while India was not Darul Islam (land of Islam), it was also not Darul Harb (land of discord), since the free practice of Islam was in no way hindered. That Pakistan had to resort to cross-border infiltration and send in Pakistan and Afghan mujahideen to carry out terrorist outrages in the Muslim majority State of Jammu and Kashmir is proof that there is little support for Pan-Islamism among Indian Muslims.[26] The people in Jammu and Kashmir are aware that most of the Kashmiri casualties, almost all Muslims, were victims of terrorists from across the border, claiming to act in the name of Islam.

This Kashmiri identity is a misfit in the monolithic structure of Pakistan, which did not recognise any identity other than that based on religion. The federal democratic and secular framework of India, on the other hand, promised in 1947 a better guarantee for the defence and growth of Kashmiri identity. The accession of the Muslim-majority state of Jammu and Kashmir to India, in which Kashmiri leaders played a key role, revitalised and revalidated Indian secularism.[27] The zigzag attitude of Kashmiri Muslims to their relations with India cannot be explained in terms of Hindu-Muslim relations in the country or in the state. It was not so much a failure of secularism in India or in the state as that of federalism and democracy at both level due to which Kashmiri aspirations could not be fulfilled. There is no doubt that a large number of Kashmiri Muslims are alienated from India today but no pro-Pakistan sentiment is yet visible. Their alienation is more as Kashmiri than as Muslims.[28] However, it is partly true that due to over a decade of militancy, religious identities have become more pronounced. The Kashmiri Muslim has remained a Kashmiri as well as a Muslim. Kashmiri Muslims do react like any other Muslim community when their religious interests are endangered. But they are unlikely to submerge their Kashmiri identity in the name of Islam. True to the tradition of Kashmir is the fact that 'the cult of Buddha, the teaching of Vedanta, and the mysticism of Islam have one after another found a congenial home in Kashmir', and its society has 'imbibed the best of Buddha, the best of Hinduism and the best of Islam.

Hinduism : Origin and Orientation

The first use of the word 'Hindu' is found in a Tantrik work of the eight century which means a people and not the followers of a particular religion. But it is clear that the word is a very old one, as it occurs in the Advesta and in old Persian. It was used then and for a thousand years or more later by the peoples of western and central Asia for India, or rather for the people living on the other side of the Indus river. Although Arya dharma, Vedic dharma, Buddhism and Jainism all arose in India and were integral parts of Indian life, culture and philosophy, they are not a Hindu by faith. So, it is entirely misleading to refer to Indian culture as Hindu culture. In later ages this culture was greatly influenced by the impact of Islam, and yet it remained basically and distinctively Indian.[29] Before the coming of Christianity and Islam, the old faith and philosophy of Hinduism were chiefly a way of life and an outlook on the world. But when a more rigid religion developed, with all manner of ritual and ceremonial, it became something more and at the same time something much less than that composite culture. A Christian or a Muslim could, and often did, adapt himself to the Indian way of life and culture, and yet remained in faith and orthodox Christian or Muslim. The Indian philosophical outlook, which had been the dominant feature of Indian culture had met so many incursions of foreign element successfully by a new synthesis and a process of absorption.

Hinduism, as a faith, is vague, amorphous, many-sided, all things to all men. In the past it embraced many beliefs and practices, from the highest to the lowest, often opposed to or contradicting each other. Its essential spirit seems to be to live and let live. According to Mahatma Gandhi's, search after truth through nonviolence means, 'A man may not believe in God and still call himself a Hindu'. Hinduism is a relentless pursuit after truth ...... Hinduism is the religion of truth. Truth is God. Actually Gandhi took some conceptual resources of the Indian cultural tradition for the reconstruction of modernity. But he does not claim that tradition is a monolithic tradition, wholly based on those principles. He grants that there is the play of untruth and violence in Hindu tradition as in any other civilization. He writes : 'we are all guilty of having oppressed our brothers. We make them crawl on their bellies before us and rub their noses on the ground .... Has the English government ever inflicted anything worse on us ?'[30] Gandhi maintains that the most distinctive and the largest contribution of Hinduism to India's culture is the doctrine of 'ahimsa', which he adds, is a 'living force in the lives of India's millions even today.[31] Thus there are two aspects of Hinduism. There is, on the one hand, the historical Hinduism with its untouchability, superstitions, worship of stocks and stones, animal sacrifice and so on. On the other, we have the Hinduism of the Gita, the Upanishads and Patanjali's Yoga Sutra which is the acme of ahimsa and oneness of all creation, pure immanent, formless imperishable God.[32]

Hinduism is not just only a name of conflicting creeds which it contains, but the spiritual life, devotion, and endeavour which lie behind the creeds, the unity, the indefinable self-identity, which, however, is by no means static or absolute. Throughout the history of Hindu civilization there has been a certain inspiring ideal, a certain motive power, a certain way of looking at life, which cannot be identified with any stage or cross-section of the process. The whole movement and life of the institution, its entire history, is necessary in order to disclose to us this idea, and it cannot therefore be expressed in a simple formula. This continuous element that runs through all its stages from the earliest to the latest, from the lowest to the highest and fully expressed in the highest, it is also present in the very lowest. All through the years, coherent perspective, as a common element has been its essential spirit, that any account of Hinduism would seek to express.[33] In it, there are certain governing conceptions, controlling ideas, deep and dynamic links which bind together the different stages and movements. The unity of Hinduism is not one of an unchanging creed or a fixed deposit of doctrine, but is the unity of a continuously changing life.

At its highest Hinduism is a universalist religion. It accepts the infinite possibilities of movements towards the divine, and does not seek to limit or confine us to any particular formulation. Each one of us has to seek our own path, and Hinduism welcomes and accepts the multiplicity of paths to the divine. The key to the continued dynamism of Hinduism despite so many challenges and persecution lies in its remarkable capacity for creative rearticulation by a whole succession of seers and social reformers. The entire panorama of Hinduism from Vedic times down to the present day can be looked upon as a series of challenges and creative responses.

Later on the common elements of Hinduism met the challenges posed by Christianity, Buddhism and Jainism successfully and they were absorbed by the former. Occasionally there were local troubles or conflicts between a Hindu ruler and the Buddhist Sangha, or organisation of monks. It should also be remembered that Hinduism was at no time wholly displaced by Buddhism. Even when Buddhism was at its height in India, Hinduism was widely prevalent. Buddhism died a natural death in India Hinduism, says Keith, 'has a strange genius for converting what it borrows and assimilating it'. If that is true of borrowings from abroad or from alien sources, still it is more applicable to something that come out of its own mind and thought. Buddhism was not only entirely a product of India; its philosophy was in line with previous Indian thought and the philosophy of Vedanta.

From the beginning of Hindu history in every stage there is an attempt to reach a harmony. Only the harmony is a dynamic one. When this dynamic harmony or organic rhythm of life is missing it means that the religion stands in need of reform. During the Mughal period, the Hindu society of the country was more or less untouched. Even Mughal rulers were strong so long as they put themselves in line with the genius of the nation and tried to work for a common nationality and a synthesis of the various elements in the country. In spite of widespread conversions, Hinduism, in all its varieties, continued as the dominant faith of the land, solid, exclusive, self sufficient, and sure of itself.

Religion had always exercised great influence on the people in their social ways and habits. The epochs in which religion stood for deeper philosophies in quest of the Absolute, were the epochs when society represented vitality and tolerance, vigour and elasticity. At other times, when religion meant only the outer form and rituals, the pattern of social outlook became stereotyped. In the eighteenth century, for most men, religion meant rigid rules and restrictions regarding social life. To maintain religious purity, people became intolerant of others and developed excessive sectarianism. Extreme dependence of people on the priestly class and of the priestly class on irrational practices made religion synonymous with bigotry and orthodoxy.[34]

In the nineteenth century, the impact of the West on India became visible with shock and change in ideas. The first reaction, limited to the small English educated class, was one of admiration and acceptance of almost everything Western. Repelled by some of the social customs and practices of Hinduism, many Hindus were attracted towards Christianity and some notable conversions were took place. An attempt was made by Raja Ram Mohan Roy, Keshab Chandra Sen, Dayanand Saraswati, Vivekanand, and of late by Rabindranath Tagore and Mahatma Gandhi to adapt Hinduism to this new environment and presented a rationalist and social reform basis. The Brahmo Samaj of Raja Ram Mohan Roy with Keshab Chandra Sen as his successor gave it a Christian outlook and influenced the people of Bengal. Swami Dayananda Saraswati's Arya Samaj was very popular among the Hindus of the Punjab. It was a crushading and reforming movement from within, as well as a defensive organisation for protection against external attacks. Next to him was Vivekananda, who with his brother disciples, founded the non-sectarian Ramakrishna Mission of service. Rooted in the past and full of pride in India's heritage, his approach to life's problems was a kind of bridge between the past of India and her present. It was through the writings of Tagore, that all the modern languages of India have been moulded partly and helped to bring into harmony the ideals of the East and the West and broadened the bases of Indian nationalism. Needless to say what Gandhi did for reformation and solidification of Hinduism.

Hinduism and Kashmir

'The Valley of Kashmir' says Lawrence' is the 'holyland' of the Hindus, and I have rarely been in any village which cannot show some relic of antiquity. The architecture of Kashmir was called by Cunningham the 'Arian order partly because it was the style of the Aryas, or Arians of Kashmir and partly because its interculminations are always of four diameters, an interval which the Greeks called Araiostyle.[35] According to an old Hindu legend the 'Valley of Kashmir', was originally a lake in which lived a demon called Jalodbhava (waterborn). He caused great distress to all neighbouring countries by his devastations. The great saga Kasypa, the father of all Nagas, while engaged in a pilgrimage to holy places in north India, heard the causes of this distress from his son Nila, the king of the Kashmir Nagas. To punish the evil-doer, Kasypa appealed to Brahman and other gods for help. It was the efforts of Vishnu that the lake became dry and the demon was slain with the god's war disk Kasypa then settled the valley which had thus been produced.[36] The earliest inhabitants, according to the Rajatarangini, were the people called Naga, a word which signifies 'snake'. The other races mentioned as inhabiting this country and the neighbouring hills were Gandhari, Khasa and Daradae. The Khasa people were supposed to have given the name Kashmir. In the Mahabharata the Kashmir and Daradae were named together among the Kshattriya races of northern India.[37]

Hinduism prevails principally in the province of Jammu, Islam in the Valley and northern areas, and Buddhism in Ladakh. There are also a few Sikhs and Christians. In the time of King Asoka in 245 B.C. one of the Indian Buddhist missions was sent to Kashmir and Gandhara. After his death Brahmanism revived. While Kashmir was under Kushan rule, Buddhism was to a great extent restored, though for several centuries the two religions existed together in Kashmir, Hinduism predominating. As Buddhism decayed, Hinduism took its place until the time of the Mongol invasion. In this period and chiefly between the 5th and 10th centuries of the Christian era, the Hindu temples in Kashmir were erected. In the 6th and 7th centuries Kashmir was visited by some of the Chinese Buddhist pilgrims including Hsuan Tsang who spent two years (631-633 A.D.) in Kashmir. The great temple of Shiva Pravaresvara which the King Pravarasena II had built was present in Kalhana's time. The ruins of the splendid temple of Martanda which the king Lalitaditya (724-760 A.D.), had constructed near the Tirtha, are still the most striking object of ancient Hindu architecture in the valley.

The Hindu period in Kashmir witnessed several Hindu kings including Avantivarman (855-883 A.D.), who brought the consolidation of the land and Harsa (1089-1101 A.D.) who, as Kalhana called 'was born from atoms of light.' The Hindu period according to Lawrence had been one of importance; with the plunder of conquest splendid temples and fine public works were constructed, and their ruins show that Kashmir in those days was endowed with noble buildings, while the potsherds of ancient cities on the Karewas and elsewhere suggest that the valley must have been thickly populated. About the condition of the people little is known, but as Hindus living under Hindu kings their lot must have been fairly happy, and irrigation canals testify that the Rajas did not spend all their wealth on temples, but had some thought for the cultivators. Hindu kings continued to reign till about 1346 A.D. When Udiana Deva was put to death by his Mohammedan vizier, Amir Shab, who ascended the throne under the name of Shams-ud-din. Of the Mohammedan rulers, as mentioned in Sanskrit chronicles, one, who reigned about the close of the 14th century was Sikandar.

He made his name famous for his active opposition to the Hindu religion and his destruction of temples. He was best known as Butshikan, or the 'idol-breaker'. It is a generally accepted fact that up to about the beginning of the fourteenth century the population of the valley was Hindu, and that about the middle and end of the century the mass of the people converted to Islam. 'Tradition affirms that the persecution of the Hindus was so keen that only eleven families of Hindus remained in the valley. Their descendents are known by the name of Malmas, as distinguished from the fugitives and the Hindus of the Deccan, who came to Kashmir later on and are known as the Banamas.[38] About that time the position of Hindu and Hinduism started going down and witnessed some improvements during the reign of the great Mughal King Akbar. Hinduism received its due place when the rule of Dogras took birth. The condition of Kashmir under the Sikhs, states Ferguson, was undoubtedly an improvement. The Hindus to whom the Sikhs were in many ways very near, benefited most and the disabilities under which they had been unable to practice the rites of their religion were removed.

However, Zain-ul-Abdin, son of Sikandar did not follow in his footsteps and the chief glory of his reign was religious tolerance. The toll tax on Hindus was remitted and the Hindus were given grants of land and assistance in many other ways. Repair of the Hindu temples was taken in hand and Hindu learning revived. All measures of appeasement and assistance encouraged the Brahmans who had fled from the valley in Sikandar's time to return. More Brahmans came from the South. He enacted laws which guaranteed them a just administration and trial of their cases according to their own customs. The king built two temples near Ishabar and abstained from meat-eating during the holy festivals of the Hindus. He forbade killing of birds and fish in several waters sacred to the Hindus. He was much impressed with the teachings of the Hindu scriptures and had many including the Mahabharata, translated into Persian. Many Hindus were appointed to high posts of trust and honour. Except some rare the religious tolerance had existed between the followers of the two religions chiefly to the fact that the Kashmiri Musalmans never really gave up the old Hindu religion of the country. Lawrence mentions two reasons for this tolerance – the strict prohibition of cow-killing and strong rule under which the people had lived for generations and which would not brook any quarreling between Hindus and Muslims.

Hindutva : Origin and Orientation

Hinduism is a tolerant, accommodative, eclectic and inclusive way of life.' Hindutva is an intolerant and chauvinistic caricature of the great tradition it seeks to upsurge. Originally portrayed by Savarkar the old Hindutva project of creating a 'Hindu Sangathan took recent shape in seeking to create a hot-house unity around a single book and church. It provides further impetus to 'Hindu consolidation' on the one hand and defines the Muslim once more not just as another Indian but as 'the other' on the other.[39A] It appeals directly to one's emotions. Its ideology is full of fire and brimstone. Its slogans hit us in the solar plexus. It dredges tribal memories and clothes them in the garb of patriotism. While all the time railing against jehadis, it wages a ceaseless jehad of its own. It has created a heady cocktail of history, myth and religion, and flaunts it as 'cultural nationalism'. The notion has emerged from the dilemmas of the interpretation of India's civilization as a multi-national or perhaps a multi-national 'country'. When analysed further the notion of 'country' is distinct from 'nation'. Practically in political terms' country, turns out to be no different from 'nation. For the Indian state, India's cultural or civilizational unity is the same thing as its national unity and national existence.

To equate Hindutva with Bharatiyata is to create an avoidable semantic and conceptual confusion. Hinduism is one of the great religions of the world, and to seek to confine it to India or to give it an exclusivist and majoritarian interpretation is to do it a disservice. It is certainly true that Hinduism has provided the broad cultural and religious framework that has held India together despite its astonishing linguistic, ethnic and political diversity and divisions. Hinduism is an essential for an understanding of Indian culture and civilization as Islam is for the Arab World and Roman Catholism for Latin America. Hence, all Indians are not Hindus and all Hindus are not Indians. There are millions of Hindus living around the world who, while certainly having special regard for India as their spiritual motherland, are yet loyal and patriotic citizens of their respective countries. Three other world religions – Jainism, Buddhism and Sikhism – were born here, while four religions – Zoroastrianism, Judaism, Christianity and Islam – came to us from West Asia and also flourished here. Along with the Baha'i faith as well as some new Buddhist sects, they represent a rich, pluralistic religious mosaic that needs to be carefully nurtured.[40]

In terms of India, Nehru defines 'unity in diversity', the essence of Indian history, is the ideological basis of this position. This 'unity of diversity' is not the same as the Hindutva (Hinduness) as a Hindu state, but is only a liberal assimilationist view of the same Indian nation as the product of an Indian culture that was identified as Hindu culture. This liberal interpretation of Nehru extends to 'secular' and can identify Shivaji as the symbol of 'a resurgent Hindu nationalism'. Nationalism as pointed by Benedict Anderson, has to be related to 'the large cultural systems that preceded it, out of which – as well as against which – it came into being'. Out of fragmentation of the old sacred community arose the nations of Europe. But in India's case the unity of India or unity in diversity is a civilizational unity as Rabinder Kumar puts it, 'the political identity of the Republic of India should be in terms of a 'civilization-state' rather than a nation state. To cite Rajni Kothari,' We need to remember that the essential identity of India is cultural, not political or economic. It is one civilization that has withstood various vicissitudes and still endured, largely because of its basic identity being cultural. It never had a political centre except very recently.[41] The basis of this Indian culture has been defined as the upper caste Hindu culture of the Hindi belt. Although it may be called Ram Rajya, but it is not a revivalism that seeks to bring back some values of the past. Rather, this is a use of the past to define something new–a uniform, homogeneous national culture centered on the cultural tradition of Bharatvarsha and Aryavarta. This attempt to fashion a homogeneous national culture out of a civilization has led to a clash of cultures and languages.

The base of Indian culture, and cultural continuity, as noted by Nehru, had been rooted in three major social forces. Caste, the autonomous village and the joint family. But in new India, urbanisation, modernisation and democratisation gradually erode them all. Here lies Nehru's dilemma and in an effort to find the 'binding ingredient' of the India he spoke of India as a 'sentiment' which went far back into the remote periods of Indian history. He also spoke of it as a conflict between two approaches to the problem of social organisation, which are diametrically opposed to each other; the old Hindu conception of the group being the basic unit of organisation and the excessive individualism of the west, emphasising the individual above the group. As a possible solution, Nehru suggested, must be a melding of these two with religion, philosophy and science interrelated. 'We can never forget the ideals that have moved our race, the dreams of the Indian people through the ages, the wisdom of the ancient, the buoyant energy and love of life and nature of our forefathers .... We will never forget them or cease to take pride in that noble heritage of ours.[42] However, this melding of ideas was partly success because all- India institutions–the Government of India, the army, the universities, large corporations and the like over time engender an accommodation of values which help to shape a new national consciousness. In the early years of independence this experience of national consciousness was limited to the leadership class. The public life of this new middle class tends towards modern values of individualism and scientific thought because these pan-Indian institutions are modern. In their private lines and familial relations, these same people tend to maintain many of their old religious and philosophical instincts, values and persuasions.

The prevalent dualism in new middle class and as its urban section became more modern, further removed from the rural life of the masses of Indian villagers. At the same time arose their personal and spiritual problems which left them alienated from themselves. They are not at home. Having two sets of values and living in two different world's is at best discomfiting. Granted, life under the British Raj made many a middle class Indian adept at living in two worlds. As put Nirad Chaudhuri,' one cannot be at home in the new India without finally being at home with oneself. One possible solution to this dilemma on the part of Hindu majority in

India is to follow the theocratic lead, which need to restore inner spiritual integrity, not only among the middle class, but also for the urban poor. This appeal was noted prominently in Farhang's analysis of Khomeini's victory in the Iranian revolution.[43] The power of such fundamentalist, which aims to restore or revive inner spiritual integrity, would result in political balkanisation and the dreams of both Nehru and Gandhi would have died. In Nehru's fine phrase, India will no longer be India.

As a Tool in Politics

Nehru while discussing India's cultural heritage, was at pains to visualise the decline in it in the nineteenth century and simply called for a revival of ideas and values which were indigeneously India. But he paid little attention to that modern religious movement known sometimes as the Indian renaissance or the rise of neo-Hinduism, beginning with the reform work of Rammohan Roy and reaching to the present day influence of Gandhi and himself. The political use of Hindu religion begins under the impulse of colonial modernity in which proposals were advanced for a 'semiticised' unitary Hinduism. Originally it was first proposed by nationalists who thought that Hinduism suffered in comparison with Christianity because of its lack of effective ecclesiastical organisation. The idea of Hinduism itself is quasi-political in origin, in the sense that people did not wish to be Hindus in this abstract sense until they felt political need to do so. It is therefore easy to exploit it for overtly political purposes.[44]

Use of religion for political purposes or for gaining victory in elections was almost unknown for Indian Political parties at the time of independence. It is curious to note that communal politics gained strength after about forty years of national government. If this was entirely due to the forces of traditionalism it should have appeared at that period when forces of modernity had gained enormously in Indian society and economy. Evidently, these political forces have much more to do with modernity than is usually conceded by the secularists in India. The functioning of democracy and democratisation of society – the decline of the cultural deference in which the lower classes held the more privileged, educated ones, a new style of functioning came to be represented in the political arena. Since the sixties, Indian politics has been a massive alteration in style, language, modes of behaviour, reflecting far more the actual cultural understanding of rural Indian society rather than the Westernist cultivation of the elite which inherited power in the Nehru years. It was more compounded by the forgetfulness and negligence of Nehruvian state who not merely failed to create conditions for a common sense in Indian politics, through which liberal, secular political ideas could be communicated dialogically to them, rather, its neglect of cultural institutions like primary education which contributed to a further division in society. As a result the benefits of development were so unequally and unjustly distributed that it prepared ground for two types of political dissent – an economic critique of class and an indigenist critique of modernist cultural privilege. The second kind of resentment, naturally, has predominantly found cultural expression through regionalist and communal politics, through the politics of Hindu and Hinduism.

Apart from this, a sea change of tremendous significance occurred both in Hindu religious community and in its relations to others. As pointed by Ravinder Kumar, prior to the nineteenth century, 'Hinduism was innocent of any notion like the 'umma' in Islam; or the 'community' in Christianity; which could form the basis of a cohesive social formation. In the changed circumstances the Hindu community was now called into action, not as one of the various Indian communities, but as the Indian community. It was not only the religious revivalists, but the modernising reformists as well who identified the Hindu community with Indianism and patriotism. Most important, the cultural artefacts of Hinduism – whether in dress or language or any other aspect of social life – were defined as the expressions of 'Indianness'. Steps were taken deliberately to create a Sanskrit-based, Hindu language, Hindi, as against the earlier composite language. Further, there are two variants of this expression of Indianness. One is the overt religious concept of Hindutva; and the other is the 'secular' expression of Indianness as based on ancient Indian culture. The first is a religious, the second a cultural concept; but both together relate Indianness to the tradition of what is now identified as Hindu civilisation. The cultural traditions of religious communities, to the extent they insist on being recognised as different from this 'core', are deemed 'foreign'.[45] It is partly in reaction to a Hindu-based Indianness, and more importantly, reflecting the limitations of their own elites bourgeois ambitions, the Muslim and Sikh religious communities have raised and supported moves for their own brands of capitalist homogenization. Hindu-based Indianness, as well as Islamic and Sikh fundamentalism, are all attempts of forging bourgeois nations and homogeneous national cultures out of the different existing religions' cultural systems.

On the lines drawn above the political parties of India may be grouped as religion-leaned and secularism-leaned. Hindu Mahasabha and the present day Bharatiya Janata Party represent the first while Congress and others reflect the later. The communal politics, in recent years, had suffered from an acute indetermination of the ends and the means. For the political Party, the utility of the issue is in keeping it alive, so that the more the building of Rama temple is delayed the more election can be won through rhetoric against those who are obstructing its construction. Once the temple is built, this great electoral issue is lost or has to be rediscovered at some other site. Politicians who would have to run administrations of course immediately appreciate the problems of running a permanent movement. But the more religious inclined wing of the communal groups obviously see the formation of a government as a means towards the construction of the temple.

Earlier in the seventies several proposals were made for a judicious deradicalisation of the BJP's slogans from groups inside the party itself. The decade also witnessed communal propaganda seemed to bring in few dividends and the destiny of the Jana Sangh irreversibly on the decline. At the juncture it was felt inside the party that it should subtly shift its appeal to the middle class. Instead of the traditional appeal to Hindu Chauvinism, it should try to project itself as a substitute for the Congress, asking for support not because of its ideological differences with the Congress, but its similarity - offering a cleaner, more efficient, less corrupt government. After the dramatic success of the rathayatras, its own agenda was rewritten in a retrograde direction, but it is remarkable how clearly the party has not rejected its other, more secular constituency. From the early 1980s, Hindu communal organisations increased the scale, range, aggressiveness and violence of their operations under the general direction of the militant Hindu ring-wing party Rashtriya Swayam Sevak Sangh (RSS) and its mass fronts : the Vishwa Hindu Parishad (VHP), which coordinates religious bodies, and the Bharatiya Janata Party (BJP), its electoral wing.

Hindutva and Kashmir

The State of Jammu and Kashmir has a number of distinct areas which differ from each other from the point of view of language, culture, administration and religion. These are Jammu, the Kashmir Valley, Ladakh, Baltistan and Gilgit, each having a separate administration and language. From the religious point of view, the western part of Ladakh and the whole of the Valley, Baltistan and Gilgit are predominantly Muslim. Eastern Ladakh is a Buddhist region. In eastern Jammu Hindus and Sikhs are in good numbers although not in majority.[46] At present three out of six districts have a Muslim majority – Doda (63.59 per cent), Poonch (88.87 per cent), and Rajouri (60.97 per cent). The other three are Udhampur, Jammu and Kathua. Udhampur has a substantial Hindu majority of 65 percent but a tehsil Gool Gula Garh in it, has muslim majority. The other two Jammu and Kathua, have massive Hindu majorities of between 80 and 90 per cent. Between a quarter and a third of Jammu's Hindu population is low-caste, and Hindus also tend to be somewhat concentrated in urban areas, like Jammu and Udhampur towns. However, insurgency in the valley has spread with a vengeance to Doda district, whose Muslim majority is almost entirely Kashmiri. A large number of Kashmiri youth from Doda have joined various guerilla organizations. Doda's highly mountainous terrain, and its relatively easy accessibility from the Valley makes it an ideal guerilla haven, and Kashmiri insurgents with bases there have been posing a major challenge to the Indian security forces. At best it is more accurate to characterise Jammu as a patchwork or mosaic of religions (Hindu, Muslim, Sikh), ethnic (Kashmiri, Rajput, Gujjar, Dogra, Punjabi, etc.) and linguistic (Kashmiri, Dogri, Hindi, Pahadi and Punjabi among others) groups.[47]

The Jammu region of the State as going by certain social and economic indications has suffered greater inequity and retardation than the Valley. Even Hindus were disproportionately represented in provincial – level government employment, most of these are reportedly Pandits, leaving only 10 per cent according to one estimate, for Jammu residents. Most professional and technical institutions and industrial plants established since 1947 are located in the valley and most state-owned corporations and banks are based there as well with Jammuites poorly represented among their employees. Indeed, Jammu lags behind the valley even in road construction and rural electrification.[48]

Despite social and economic backwardness of the Jammu region, Jammu's Hindutva communalist politicians, from the late 1940s, have been rabidly hostile even to the thought of a negotiated agreement with Kashmir's leaders which would address Jammu's regional problems, and foster harmonious co-existence and cooperation between Jammu and Kashmir's religious and ethnic groups. It was Maharaja Hari Singh who limited accession to Defence, Foreign Affairs and Communications – an arrangement endorsed by Abdullah. Abdullah's long association with Gandhi and Nehru persuaded him to join India, but he needed a constitutional buffer to convince his people that they would not be dominated by Hindu-majority India. These fear were kept alive by the Praja Parishad and the Jana Sangh, who did not disguise the communal character of their campaign against state's autonomy.[49] In April 1950 after resigning from the Union Cabinet, Shyama Prasad Mookerjee, who later on October 12, 1951, set up a new Political Party, named Jana Sangh, was determined about building a platform with issues that could fetch votes in the 1952 elections. He under a pact with RSS supremo M.S. Golwalkar agreed to provide cadre and *Sotto Voce* retain a grip. The Jana Sangh guided the Praja Parishad's separatist movement in Jammu.

Praja Parishad was founded in Jammu in 1947 by Balraj Madhok, an RSS activist who later became the all-India President of the Bharatiya Jana Sangh. Since the early 1950s, the Praja Parishad activists, a motley collection of disgruntled monarchists and dispossessed landlords worked under their banner and slogan—One Flag, One Constitution, One Premier for all of Mother India. The Jammu people were also genuinely alarmed at the Sheikh's opposition to the complete integration of the State with India. The unsettled condition of the Hindu and Sikh refugees from Occupied Kashmir served as an irritant to them. They agitated vociferously for the complete abolition of the state's autonomy, and its total 'integration' with the rest of the country. Unfortunately, Sheikh Abdullah became extremely bitter and categorised this as Hindu revivalism which was trying to swamp the Muslims of Kashmir and the Muslim-majority areas of Jammu. The Sheikh took this opportunity to give vent to his hostile feelings against Dogra community of Jammu, which he naturally linked with the Hindu community of Punjab and the rest of North India. He treated the Jana Sangh agitation as a symptomatic of the general Hindu mentality and this he expressed in bitter language which added further grist to the mill of Jana Sangh propaganda.

In the very first annual session of the Jana Sangh which was held in Kanpur in December 1952, Shyama Prasad Mookerjee demanded the deletion of Article 370 and Jammu be made a separate state. He, in a letter to Prime Minister Nehru wrote on January 9, 1953, 'None knows better than you the peculiar characteristics of the different parts of the State of Jammu and Kashmir. Kashmir Valley, Jammu and Ladakh represent different types of people, their language, their outlook, their environment, their habit and modes of life, their occupations differ from one another in many vital respects. Historically and politically they came to be united into one homogeneous unit which we naturally should not like to disrupt or destroy.[50] Nehru, on the otherhand greatly distressed by these harmful developments. He was anxious on the disastrous effects which the Jana Sangh-Praja Parishad agitation was likely to produce on the Muslim mind in Kashmir. Although he was agreed with the Jana Sangh's views that Jammu and Kashmir should be fully integrated with India and he was taking steps in that direction. But there are other forces like Pakistan and the Security Council which could not be ignored and it was not in India's power to do whatever she likes in respect of this state. Referring to Jana Sangh's demand that at least Jammu should be integrated as was also demanded by Shyama Prasad Mookerjee Nehru said that this would amount to subscribing to the two-nation theory and would destroy the *raison-d'-etre* of India's existence in the valley. Nehru, in his reply to Mookerjee on January 10, 1953, warned', the Jammu agitation, if it succeeded, would ruin our entire case relating to the state .... what effect do you think has the Praja Parishad agitation on such persons in the valley or elsewhere.[51]

Sheikh Mohammad Abdullah, the then Premier of the State, told bluntly in a letter to Mookerjee on February 4, 1953, that Jammu was but part of the Jana Sangh's wider national agenda', Many of the parties who are at present supporting the Praja Parishad are not satisfied with the present pattern of the Indian constitution. Some of them have demanded openly that it should conform to Hindu ideals.' The situation due to Jana Sangh supported agitation of Praja Parishad went bad to worse and at last Nehru sent B. N. Mullik, the Deputy Director incharge of Internal Affairs, Intelligence Bureau, to try to persuade the agitationists to call off the agitation by explaining that Kashmir was already an integral part of India and no further agitation was necessary — the Constituent Assembly of Jammu and Kashmir, was also going to recognise this position. The special privileges provided under Article 370, would gradually disappear and Kashmir would be like any other State of India. Therefore, it would be wise on the part of the Hindus of Jammu to hold their patience a little longer and assist in this natural process of integration.[52] He was of the view that if such agitations that were based purely on emotionalism and not reason were allowed to grow, no democracy could function. He said that the Jana Sangh's agitation had given him a shock and for the first time he had started feeling doubtful about the future of Kashmir.[53]

One possible solution to the regional disparities of socio - economic resources and revenues between the Jammu and Kashmir is the comprehensive, organic decentralisation and devolution within Indian-administered state. Keeping in view the grievances of the people of Jammu two official Commissions were set up in 1968 and 1979 respectively. On both occasions the commission recommended the idea of a multi-tiered, decentralised institutional framework for the whole of Indian-administered Jammu and Kashmir. The absence of requisite political will to implement this formula has been an obstacle in its implement. However, the underlying reason for this failure was that both Congress and Hindutva Communalists, at all India and provincial levels, have consistently and vehemently opposed any suggestion of decentralised internal government in Jammu and Kashmir, and of equitable power–sharing between the regions (Jammu, Kashmir, Ladakh) that comprise it. It was perhaps due to the fact that the people of Kashmir have practically disenfranchised for extended periods lasting decades, and this subversion of democratic process and institutions led to the total destruction of federal autonomy. Only a democratically-constituted, substantively autonomous Jammu and Kashmir government can possibly delegate authority to lower levels, including the constituent units.

The current Hindutva programme on Kashmir, which occupies a central position in BJP's India-wide strategy to capture state power, demands 'abrogation of Article 370, and, occasionally, 'trifurcation' of Jammu and Kashmir, leading ultimately to union territory status for 'Buddhist majority' Ladakh and reconstitution of Hindu-majority' Jammu as either a separate state or as part of the neighbouring Indian state of Himachal Pradesh, where BJP is strong and well organised. A demand to this content was made to Governor G.C. Saxena, which, he categorically rejected on May 13, 1992. It again gained momentum in recent past when none other than L. K. Advani, the Deputy Prime Minister lent support to it when he went to Leh on June 7, 2000, and assured the Ladakh Buddhist Association that they can discuss it 'within the four corners of the constitution.

Advani gave this assurance when he knew that he was on a charged territory which is communally polarised. As noted a correspondent that trifurcation has been given new respectability' by him. The Home Minister overlooked the fact that Article 3 of the Constitution, which empowers Parliament to diminish the area of any state, makes its application to Kashmir contingent on the consent of the legislature of that state. The centre has no power at all whether to set up a Jammu state or to endow Ladakh with UT status. Similar ignorance governed plans of considering a regional council for Jammu which Minister of State for Home I.D. Swami told an RSS delegation on July 18, 2002. Earlier the matter was also discussed at VHP's central advisory board at Hardwar on June 23, and adopted a resolution branding the Farooq Abdullah regime as a Muslim Sultanate. It demanded that the five Hindu-dominated districts of Jammu should be made a separate state. A Union Territory be carved out of areas north east of the Jhelum river in the Kashmir Valley for settling Hindus there and Ladakh be given the status of a 'Union Territory'. Among the confusions, Advani, during his visit to RSS headquarter, made a significant statement in which he said,' we are not in favour of trifurcation because, besides other drawbacks, it may convey to the world that we are not particularly interested in the valley, we are only interested in Jammu and Ladakh. But we don't want a partition on the basis of religion after the partition of our country on the basis of it.

However, in case of Jammu and Kashmir, both Congress and the BJP have attempted to exaggerate and inflame inter-regional differences, manipulate them to stoke communal antagonism between Hindus and Muslims as well as Buddhists and Muslims, and exploited regional grievances, particularly in Jammu and Ladakh. For example in 1983, Indira Gandhi capitalised on widespread discontent in Jammu to launch a blatantly communal campaign that sought to win Jammu for Congress by polarising the state along regional and communal lines, although it won 38 percent of the Jammu vote and several seates. The BJP has openly supported an agitation which was launched by the people of Ladakh in 1989 demanding the area be detached from Jammu and Kashmir and made a Union Territory. There is no doubt that the region needs better representation of its interest at the state level, as well as local autonomy and a more equitable share development funds, the interest of both parties played a leading role, turned explicitly sectarian and communal instead of organising itself as a broad-based movement for regional rights. Although with the help of these tactics the party has been able to widen its electoral support in the Jammu region to some extent, yet its mischievous opportunism is revealed by the fact that the Party has adopted a self-contradictory posture of demanding autonomous government for the Jammu region but opposing autonomy for Jammu and Kashmir as a whole. The reality is that any autonomous status would be conferred not on any particular religions, regional or cultural group but on the state as whole, and would potentially - if regional diversities are taken into account in the process of institutionalisation of the autonomous regime - benefit all the constituent regions and all sectors of the population.

Buddhism : Origin and Orientation

Buddhism had started at a time of social and spiritual revival and reform in India. It enfused the breath of new life in the people, it tapped new sources of popular strength and released new talent and capacity for leadership. It influenced Indian life in a hundred ways, as it was bound to be remembered that it was a living, dynamic, and widespread religion in India for over a thousand years. Even in the long years of its decline in India, and when later it practically ceased to count as a separate religion here, much of it remained as a part of the Hindu faith and in national ways of life and thought. Its permanent effect had little to do with dogma or philosophic theory or religious belief. The ethical, social and practical idealism of Buddha and his religion that influenced our people had left their imperishable marks upon them. It was like the ethical ideals of Christianity and Islam to which we may not pay much attention, but their human, social and practical approach influenced many people who were not attracted by its religious forms and beliefs.

The teachings of Buddha went deep down into the hearts of the people. 'Go unto all lands', had said the Buddha to his disciples, 'and preach this gospel. Tell them that the poor and the lowly, the rich and the high, are all one, and that all castes unite in this religion as do the river in the sea'. His message was one of universal benevolence, of love for all. For 'Never in this world does hatred cease by hatred; hatred ceases by love.' And 'Let a man overcome anger by kindness, evil by good. According to him 'one may overcome a thousand men in battle, but he who conquers himself is the greatest victor'. Not by birth by his conduct alone, does a man become a low caste or a Brahmin. A man's position in society is determined not by birth (Jati) but by worth, by conduct and by character rather than by descent. From social point of view he also concentrated on the means of livelihood that are of two kinds, right (Samyak) and wrong (mithya). Buddha refused to concede that a man's life could be compartmentalized, with his professional conduct governed by one set of standards and his private life by another, or that the former constituted a neutral field to which ethical considerations need not apply. He even went on prohibiting essentially unethical occupations such as those of the butcher, the dealer in poisons and the weapon-maker.

Buddha preached without any religious sanction or any reference to God or another world. He relies on reason, logic, experience and asks the people to seek truth in their minds. He himself said about the teachings,' One must not accept my law from reverence, but first try it as gold is tried by fire.' Ignorance of truth was the causes of all misery. Whether there is a God or an Absolute or not, he does not say. He neither affirms nor denies. He had repeatedly warned his people against learned controversy over metaphysical problems. He is reported to have said, 'Truth was to be found in life itself and not in argument about matters outside the scope of life and therefore beyond the ken of human intellect. He had sown the seeds of revolt against the conventional practice of the religion of his day. It was not his theory or philosophy that was objected to. The old system was free and flexible in thought, allowing for every variety of opinion, but in practice it was rigid.

The Indian Buddhism passed through three great phases of development, traditionally known as the Hinayana, the Mahayana and the Vajrayana, each with its own characteristics and its own spiritual ideals. The Hinayana, 'Little Vehicle or 'Lower Way', was so called by Mahayanists because it teaches the attainment of salvation for one self alone. It insists upon the necessity of the monestic life, with which indeed, it tends to identify the spiritual life altogether. The laity simply observe the more elementary precepts, worship the relics of the Buddha, and support the monks, by which means merit (Punya) is accumulated and rebirth in heaven assured. While mindfulness, self control, equanimity, detachment, and the rest of the ascetic virtues are regarded as indispensable, in the final analysis emancipation is attained through insight into the transitory and painful nature of conditioned things a well as into the non-selfhood of all the elements of existence, whether conditioned or unconditioned. The Hinayana adhered, in some measure, to the ancient purity of doctrine and circumscribed it in a Pali Canon. At present, Ceylon, Burma and Siam are the Hinayani countries and even now looked down upon the Buddhism that prevails in China and Japan.

The Mahayana, literally 'Great Vehicle' or 'Great Way', is so called because it teaches the salvation of all. With the decline of early Buddhism, this Mahayana form developed. In it Buddha was made into a god and devotion to him as a personal god developed. Predominantly devotional and metaphysical in character, its ideals is the Bodhisattva, the heroic being who, practising the six or ten perfections throughout thousands of lives, aspires to the attainment of Buddhahood for the sake of all sentient beings. Its perspective was infinitely vaster than those of the Hinayana. The earlier vehicle is regarded by the Mahayanists not as wrong but only as inadequate, the provisional rather than the final teaching, given out by the Buddha to disciples. On the mundane level, all followers of the Buddha are united through their common devotion to the Bodhisattva ideal. Faith as a means of attaining Enlightenment, ranks co-ordinate with Wisdom. The Buddha is regarded not only as an enlightened being but also as the embodiment of the Truth and Reality behind the universe.

Contrary to the earlier, Mahayana spread out in every direction, tolerating almost everything and adapting itself to each country's distinctive outlook. In India it began to approach the popular religion; in each of the other countries - China, Japan and Tibet - it had a separate development. According to Radhakrishnan, 'Buddhism begins with a dualistic metaphysics looking upon knowledge as a direct awareness of objects. In the next stage ideas are made the media through which reality is apprehended, thus raising a screen between mind and things. These two stages represent the Hinayana schools. The Mahayana school went further and abolished the things behind the images and reproduced all experience to a series of ideas in their mind.[54] In the field of philosophy the Mahayana is represented by the two great schools of the Madhyamikas and the Yogacarins, the first founded and systematized by Nagarjuna (150 A.D.) and the second by Asanga (400 A.D.). Both are based primarily on the doctrine of Sunyata as taught in the Perfection of Wisdom sutras ; but there are important differences of approach which give to each of their special character. The Madhyamikas or followers Mean emphasise Wisdom, and their method is dialectical. They reduce mind and matter directly to Sunyata, the truth of which is revealed the exposing the self-contradictory nature of all statements about the Absolute.[55] Brahminism and Buddhism acted and reacted on each other, and inspite of their dialectical conflicts or because of them, approached nearer to each other, both in the realm of philosophy and that of popular belief. The Mahayana especially approached the Brahminical system and forms. It was prepared to compromise with almost anything, so long its ethical background remained. Brahminism made of Buddha an avtar, a God. So did Buddhism.

The Vajrayana, 'the Diamond Vehicle or Adamantive Way', is so called because, like the irresistible Vajra, meaning both thunderbolt and diamond, it immediately annihilates all obstacles to the attainment of Buddhahood. It is predominantly yogic and magical in character, and its ideal is the Sidha, 'a man who is so much in harmony with the cosmos that he is under no constraint whatsoever, and as a free agent is able to manipulate the cosmic forces both inside and outside himself'.[56] It aims at the realisation of Sunyata not only mentally but also physically. The Vajrayana differs from the Mahayana less in respect of doctrine than in its methods. Its goal is the transmutation of the body, speech and mind to initiate into the Body, Speech and Mind of the Tathagata. All these Buddhist systems of philosophy have their origin in the Upanishads, but they do not accept the authority of the Vedas. It is this denial of the Vedas that distinguishes them from the so-called Hindu systems of philosophy which developed about the same time.

Buddhism and Kashmir

With the coming of Buddhism in Kashmir, a new chapter began in its history. The whole credit for spread of Buddhism in the valley must go to the great kings like Asoka of Gupta dynasty and

Kanishka, the most famous king of Kushan. It was after the terrible slaughter in the war of Kalinga that Asoka decided to abandon warfare in the full tide of victory. He refrained from any further aggression, and his mind turned, under the influence of Buddha's gospel. Undoubtedly Asoka was a Buddhist and much of the ideology of Dhamma which he enunciated was inspired by Buddhism. A careful analysis of the inscriptions reveals that they were of two categories. Some were specially addressed to the Buddhist Church or Sangha and were concerned entirely with matters relating to the Sangha. But the majority of the inscriptions are however, addressed to the public at large and deal with questions of wider interest. It is in this second category of inscriptions that the king expounds his ideas on Dhamma. Asoka's Dhamma aimed at creating an attitude of mind among his subjects in which social behaviour had the highest relevance. It stressed toleration, non-violence, respect for those in positions of authority, including both the Brahmans and the Buddhist monks, consideration and kindness towards inferiors and the general acceptance of ideals conducive to human dignity.[57]

It was Asoka, wrote Stien, who founded Srinagari, the ancient capital of Kashmir with its ninety-six lakhs of housed resplendent with wealth.[58] According to Hiuen, Tsiang, Asoka settled 5,000 monks in Kashmir which had in earlier times played a great part in the traditions of Buddhism, Arhat Madhyantika having first spread the Buddhist law in the land. He found a hundred convents in the country but Ou-Kong who visited it in 725 A.D. found more than three hundred and a considerable number of stupas and sacred images. Asoka's empire was extended from Bengal to the Deccan, to Afghanistan and the Punjab. The results and influences of Buddhism may be seen to this day in Kashmir, in the remains of Buddhist temples and statues and the ruins of cities founded by him.

The new awakening in the history of India, that did not arise out of political necessity but of compassion born knowledge, found a particularly fertile soil in Kashmir, where people loved knowledge and learning. Hiuen Tsiang found in the seventh century the people of Kashmir as love learning and well instructed. Kashmir played a great part in the traditions of Buddhism. For centuries it served as a centre of spread of Buddhism to the Central Asia. The two major routes from India to Central Asia led one through the high Kashmir passes of the Gilgit into the Wakhan and the second through Gandhara. The route through Gandhara was less difficult and it was this route that the early Buddhist missionaries to Central Asia selected. The Buddhist missionaries began to go to foreign lands in the reign of Asoka who had renounced war and violence as an instrument of State policy.

Apart from life Buddhism also affected the art and architecture of Kashmir. This is seen as much in the painted scrolls presented to their Jajmans to this day. About the people of Gilgit and their past history Toynbee wrote, 'Gilgit's past is almost a blank. Although wrapped in obscurity Gilgit appears to have had a similar experience. Her people must once have been Buddhists before they became Muslims. Her eastern neighbour Ladakh is still Buddhist today, and her Western neighbour Afghanistan was Buddhist till the ninth century of the Christian era'.[59]

Buddhism achieved new popularity and power with the three Turkish kings, Huska, Juska and Kanishka. It spreaded further under Kanishka whose capital was at Peshawar and empire extended to the Kabul in west and Kashgar in north. Kanishka, identified with the great Kushan ruler of north-western India, held the third great Buddhist Council in Kashmir which drew up the northern Canon or "Greater Vehicle of the Law". In the seventh century Hiuen Tsiang, on his visit to Kashmir, found local traditions about that king. It was during the period that a great schism like Buddhism divided into two sections – the Mahayana and the Hinayana. A great controversy between the two arose and the issue was put to great assemblies, to which representatives came from all over the country. Kashmir was situated near the centre of the empire and was full of this debate and of cultural activities. One name stands out in this controversy, that of Nagarjuna, who lived in the first century A.C. He was a towering personality, great in Buddhist scholarship and Indian philosophy, and it was largely because of him that Mahayana triumphed in India.

Culture

Man varies to each other in respect of physical form and social heritage or culture. This social heritage is the key concept of cultural anthropology and called culture in modern anthropology and social science. The word culture is at times used synonymously with civilization, but it is better to use the two terms distinctively. Man in order to live continually alters his surroundings and on all points of contacts with the outer world creates an artificial, secondary environment. He makes houses or constructs shelters ; he prepares his food more or less elaborately, procuring it by means of weapons and implements ; he makes roads and uses means of transport. This material outfit of man – his artifacts, his buildings, his sailing craft, his implements and weapons, the liturgical paraphernalia of his magic and religion – are one and all the most obvious and tangible aspects of culture.[60] Thus culture comprises inherited artifacts, goods, technical processes, ideas, habits and values. Social organisation cannot be really understood except as a part of culture; and all special lines of inquiry referring to human activities, human groups and human ideas and beliefs can meet and become cross fertilized in the comparative study of cultures. In its internal aspect it includes all inner expressions of the human mind, in spiritual, moral and material life – social intercommunications, art, literature, science and technology etc. Externally, it is to be equated with society in its broadest sense. It is a slow and unconscious coagulation of myriads of elements, through succcssive generations, representing what may be called miracles of mind. Cultural contacts may result from silent, peaceful social or commercial intercourse, from work of saints, preachers, evangelists and scholars, from migrations of peoples or from invasions, or militaristic or imperialistic wars of expansion.[61]

The place of religion in culture is very important. It, in its ethics, sanctifies human life and conduct and becomes perhaps the most powerful force of social control. In its dogmatics it supplies man with strong cohesive forces. It grows out of every culture, because knowledge which gives foresight fail to overcome fate; because lifelong bonds of cooperation and mutual interest create sentiments, and sentiments rebel against death and dissolution. The cultural call for religion is highly derived and indirect but is finally rooted in the way in which the primary needs of man are satisfied in culture. Among other things, culture makes man surrender some of his self-love and self seeking. For human relatives do not rest merely or even mainly on constraint coming from without. Men can only work with and for one another by the moral forces which grow out of personal attachment and loyalties. The love of parents for children and of children for their parents, that between husband and wife and between brothers and sisters, serve as prototypes and also as a nucleus for the loyalties of clanship, of neighbourly feeling and of tribal citizenship. Cooperation and mutual assistance are based, in savage and civilized societies, on permanent sentiments.[62]

Cultural Harmony and Kashmir

The cultural history of Kashmir forms part of the cultural history of India where, as it is clear from the *Upanishads*, developed a spirit of inquiry which refused to be satisfied with mere scriptural authority. This is why it developed system after system of philosophical thought and spiritual discipline remarkable for their variety and independence. This thought ranged over a wide spectrum, from nihilism, through faith in matter, mind or both or neither, or doubt, or the sole reality of the subject or the object, or of time, space and cause, to a universal spirit which is at once power, light, and joy. In the history of India, love of knowledge has shown a marked tendency to triumph over more religious or sectarian discipline.[63] Nehru, in his writings, regarded Kashmir as seat of Indian culture and observed that it has always been in history for thousands of years – not always politically but essentially – a part of India, for hundreds of years, it was politically a part of India long before the British came. Culturally, of course, it has one of the biggest seats of Indian culture and learning throughout history for about 2,000 years. Some of the first books on Indian history were written on Kashmir.

This creative phase of renaissance in Kashmir was a creative one and took over the enervated every field of intellectual activity. It had given us many classics in different branches of learning– philosophy, poetic, religion and literature. The process of patronizing the intellectuals and creative geniuses that started with king Lalitaditya (7th century) went unabated till the time of Jayasimha (1127-1149 A.D.) with a few exceptions. King Lalitaditya is the best remembered in Kashmir as a powerful ruler asserting his power for beyond Kashmir and the adjacent territories. From conquered countries he brought learned men and skilled artisans and devoted himself to great works. With the reputation of a great builder, of towns and temples, he ushered the kingdom in a glorious period in the history of Kashmir. Apart from this there was a great impetus for the composition of new and original works in Kashmir. Works on poetics practically commenced from the 8th century A.D. with Udbhata and Vamana. Works on the Trika system of philosophy began to be written about the same time and historical works also fall in the same period. The other kings like Jayapida (779-813 A.D.) and Avantivarman (855-883 A.D.) were enlightened and generous and they kept the flame of learning ever kindled during their reign. A king's popularity and success were measured in terms of his respect for learning. According to Kalhana, 'during his time king Jayapida invited scholars from all parts of India in large numbers. Of Avantivarman Kalhana says that during his reign Sidhas, such as, Bhatta Kallata were born for the benefit of the world. Encouragement from the rulers and a creatively lively academic environment made Kashmir a virtual seat of learning which bewitched scholars from every corner of the country. And consequently and rightly, too, an adage earned currency among the scholars that the real of thc scholarship lay in Kashmir.

The reasons for this intellectual revolution are not far to seek. Firstly the literary glory and creative upsurge of Kashmir was at its peak during this period and was largely responsible for creating an intellectually fertile atmosphere in which nothing mean could ever aspire for recognition. Sociologically knowledge-seeking and intellectual activity were the values supremely, cherished by the society and individuals alike. According to the social psychology deep-rooted values in the sub-conscious mind of society act as a formative principle and impart a direction, depth and meaning to the cultural and creative adventures of the ages. Knowledge seeking became the cult of the then India, not to talk of Kashmir alone. Secondly, foreign emissaries like Hiuen-Tsiang and I-Tsiang visited India so that there was ample opportunity for exchange of ideas between the great nations like China, Persia, Greece and India. Thirdly, Kashmir Saivism emerged as a critique of the different schools of Buddhism and a constructive continuator of Bhartrhari's philosophy of language which had attained a high degree of intellectual advancement. Fourthly, the kings of the period were enlightened and generous enough to keep the flame of learning ever alive during their reign.[64] The period ranging from the 9th to 12th century was most creative. The creative vitality is reflected not only by the number of authors and texts, but also the impact it made on the other system.

About the period of the Turkish conquests there were three classical languages in India, Sanskrit, Arabic and Persian. It is of particular mention here what encouragement was given to Sanskrit even by Muslim rulers such as king Zain-ul-Abidin (1420-1459 A.D.). Sultan Hasan Shah (1472-1484 A.D.) and Emperor Akbar. At the same time they also encouraged the development of vernacular or regional literatures, such as, Kashmiri and the first secular poem, Banasuravadha, was written during the reign of Zain-ul-Abidin. He himself was a linguist, knowing not only Islamic languages but also Sanskrit and Tibetan which he could speak. He enriched Sanskrit language with translations of Arabic and Persian works into it, and had Sanskrit works – *Mahabharata* and *Rajtarangini*, translated into Persian. He successively ordered Jonaraja and Srivara to complete Kalhana's *Rajtarangini.* Hasan Shah was the patron of Sitikautha – author of *the Mahanaya-Prakash*, and Srivara Pandita– author of the later edition of the *Rajtarangini.*

The great Moghul king, Akbar, also patronised Sanskrit learnig and wanted the gems of Sanskrit literature to be translated into Persian. He commissioned Bhanuchandra and his disciple Siddhichandra to write a commentary on Bana's Kadambari. Ramachandra wrote Ramavinoda for an officer of Akbar. A Persian-Sanskrit dictionary (Parsi Prakash) was compiled by Bihari Krishnadas. Many other Sanskrit works were written under orders of Akbar or of his nobles. The reign of Akbar witnessed the translation into Persian of several Sanskrit classics. Centuries later Abu-l-Fazl referring to the Moghul Emperor Akbar's rule in Kashmir, remarked that, 'at the present time under the sway of his Imperial Majesty, it is the secure and happy abode of many nationalities.[65] Kashmir, according to Stien, has always had an over-production of intellect. Bilana's classical example, among other evidence, shows that Kashmiri scholars have been as ready in old days as at present to leave their homes for distant places, wherever their learning could secure for them a livelihood.

All the three Muslim rulers patronised as well as ordered the translations of Sanskrit works into Persian and Arabic and vice-versa, so that the exchange of ideas was mutual and not unilateral. But there was a great difference between the initial and final periods of the creative phase. These Muslim rulers of the final period, however, were not the rule but exceptions who gave a fillip and stimulus to Sanskrit learning in brilliant contrast to the wicked performance of the Muslim rulers in general who took it as a religious duty to destroy the culture of Kashmir; whereas in the initial period such rulers were exception as were not generous, nor enlightened. This difference among the rulers speaks by itself of the difference between the two periods. No doubt, the Arabs were keenly interested in studying Sanskrit works and translating them. Al Biruni was an ardent student of Sanskrit learning. But this example was not followed by other Turks. About 1200 A.D. Sanskrit had ceased to be a living literature. It had become unrelated to life and aspirations of the people, spiritual and social. Sanskrit scholarship had lost the initiative and creative impulse of ancient and early medieval period and the output had deceased. Some writers attribute this to the Turkish conquest and occupation of large areas by the Muslims in Northern India, attended with plunder and destruction of temples, monasteries and centres of learning. To some extent there was change in emphasis from Sanskrit to the local languages was partly responsible for the dazzling flame of classical Sanskrit tradition. Later, the Hindu society in Kashmir began to disintegrate making the decline of Sanskrit study. Persian language began to spread its influence. The place of Sanskrit was usurped by Kashmiri language which was born afresh by a mixture of Persian and Sanskrit.

To the Kashmiri who knew the traditions of his land, but practically nothing of the world outside it, has always a vision of humanity and cultural harmony. It is full of wonderful religious compromises. The mosque of Shah-I-Hamdan in Srinagar built after the fashion of a Buddhist temple, with a flat roof, an open spire with a gilded ball has within it a spring which is sacred to the Hindus and dedicated to Kali, the goddess of nature. Beneath the mosque and right on the waterfront is a Hindu temple which is much used. Similarly on the walls of the Bota Masjid which stands below the castle hill of Srinagar the pictures of Buddhist saints are to be found which are hidden by whitewash. This mosque was formerly a Buddhist temple.[66] The tolerance of conflicting religions is clear from the conduct of many kings, ancient and medieval, in the history of Kashmir. For centuries Buddhism and the orthodox creeds existed peacefully side by side in Kashmir. Royal and private individuals who were credited with the foundation of Buddhist stupas and viharas, for instance, endowed with equal zeal shrines of Shiva or Vishnu. In Kalhana's time every contemporary royal personage or minister who is praised for his Buddhist endowments, showed the same pious liberality also in regard to Brahmanical temples and establishments.

One thing which helped religious tolerance was perhaps the absence of a caste system in the valley. While Brahmans are frequently mentioned in the chronicles, there is hardly any reference to a hierarchical division of society constituting ascending or descending social steps in order of dignity, rights and responsibilities. In consequence distinctions in dress, food, social customs and ceremonies based on caste status are rare. The sacred shrines of the two communities are situated together and frequently their fairs at these shrines are held on the same day. Much of the delightful tolerance which exists between the followers of the two religions, wrote Lawrence, was chiefly to the fact that the Kashmiri Musalmans never really gave up the old Hindu religion of the country.

The intellectual ferment in Kashmir has been in progress for the past many centuries. It has produced, within the small area of the valley, eminent philosophers, grammarians, historians, astronomers, poets, and men of letters. It is a pity that the land which was a living shrine of the goddess of learning succumbed to foreign influences and was forced to pass through a process of complete degeneration and total eclipse of its cultural identity. The process has been so thorough and its after-effects so severe that the Kashmiris today have yet to realise their real cultural identity. Any threat to the growth of compassion and mutual tolerance in Kashmir is therefore an axe aimed at the very root of its people, the root which is part of the more complex roots of India as a whole.

References

1. Asghar Ali Engineer, "An Unfinished Revolution," The Hindustan Times, 23 July, 2002.
2. B. Sheik Ali, Islam : A Cultural Orientation, Delhi, 1981, p. 14.
3. Sri Aurobindo, Karmayogin, Vol. II, p. 24.
4. Amulya Ganguli, "Image of Islam," The Hindustan Times, 1 October 2001.
5. Fundamentalists revival in Iran and other Asian countries including India, could be viewed in this context. See A. Nandy, "The Sociology of Sati," The Indian Express, 5 October, 1989.
6. Jawaharlal Nehru, The Discovery of India, Calcutta, 1946, p. 244.
7. Sudipta Kaviraj, 'Religion, Politics and Modernity,' in Upendra Baxi and Bhikhu Parekh, eds., Crisis and Change in Contemporary India, New Delhi, 1995, pp. 302-3.
8. Dr. J.N. Sarkar, Thoughts on Trends of Cultural Contacts in Medieval India, Calcutta, 1984, pp. 59-60.
9. *Ibid.,* p. 58.
10. M. A. Stien, Rajtarangni, Vol. I, London, p. 30.
11. Walter Lawrence, The Valley of Kashmir, pp. 287-88.
12. B. L. Sharma,Kashmir Awakes, Delhi, 1971, pp. 63-64.
13. B. Sheik Ali, *op. cit.,* pp. 137-38.
14. *Ibid.,* pp. 138-39.
15. Paul Kennedy, Preparing for the Twenty-first Century, p. 224.
16. K. R. Malkani, "Inside the Muslim Mind", The Hindustan Times, 13 October 2001.
17. Samuel Huntington, "The Clash of Civilization ?", Foreign Affairs (Summer), 1993, pp. 22-49.

18. Edward Said, Covering Islam : How the Media and Experts Determine How We See the Rest of the World, Newyork, 1981, pp. 35-40.
19. Ibid., p. 51.
20. Verghese Koithara, Society State and Security : The Indian Experience, New Delhi, 1999, p. 186.
21. For detail see Tavleen Singh, Kashmir : A Tragedy of Errors, Delhi, 1995.
22. Balraj Puri, "Many Faces, One Image," The Hindustan Times, 20 September 2001.
23. Ibid., Kashmiriyat : The Vitality of Kashmiri Identity,' Contemporary South Asia 4, 1 March, pp. 60-61.
24. Sumantra Bose, The Challenge in Kashmir : Democracy, Self-Determination and a Just Peace, New Delhi, 1997, p. 82.
25. Sumanta Banerjee, "The Politics of Violence in the Indian State and Society, in Kumar Rupesinghe and Khawar Mumtaz, eds., Internal Conflicts in South Asia, Oslo, Norway, 1996, p. 92.
26. The Times of India, Editorial, 31 December 2002.
27. Sumantra Bose, *op. cit.*, p. 87.
28. Balraj Puri, *op. cit.*
29. Jawaharlal Nehru, *op. cit.*, pp. 74-75.
30. The Collected Works of Mahatma Gandhi, 24, New Delhi, p. 211.
31. R. Iyer, ed., The Moral and Political Writings of Mahatma Gandhi, Vol. 1, Clarendon, 1986, p. 455.
32. *Ibid.*, Vol. 2. p. 262.
33. S. Radhakrishnan, 'Hinduism', in A. L. Basham, ed., A Cultural History of India, New Delhi, 1975, pp. 60-61.
34. P. N. Chopra, B. N. Puri and M. N. Das, A Social, Cultural and Economic History of India, Vol. III, Delhi, 1974, p. 77.
35. Walter Lawrence, *op. cit.*, p. 169.
36. As quoted in B. L. Sharma, *op. cit.*, p. 8.
37. Edwin R. A. Seligman, ed., Encyclopaedia of the Social Sciences, Newyork, 1954, p. 289.
38. Walter Lawrence, *op. cit.*, p. 302.

39. B. G. Verghese, "Mythology of Hate, "The Hindustan Times, 6 June 2002
40. Karan Singh, "Keep the Light Shining," *Ibid.,* 20 January 2003.
41. As quoted in Dev Nathan, 'India : From Civilization To Nations', in Kumar Rupesinghe and Khawar Mumtaz, eds., *op. cit.,* pp.18-21.
42. Jawaharlal Nehru, *op. cit.,* p. 522.
43. Leroy S. Rouner, "Civil Loyalty and the New India', Upendra Baxi and Bhikhu Parekh, eds., *op. cit.,* pp. 177-79.
44. Sudipta Kaviraj, *Ibid.,* pp. 312-15.
45. Dev Nathan, *op. cit.,* p. 24.
46. Dinesh Chandra Jha, Indo-Pakistan Relations, 1960-1965, Patna, 1972, p. 47.
47. Sumantra Bose, *op. cit.* pp. 92-93.
48. Tremblay, Reeta C., 'Jammu : Autonomy Within Autonomous Kashmir ?', Raju Thomas, ed., Perspectives on Kashmir, Boulder, Westview press, 1992, pp. 156-57.
49. Ajit Bhattacharjea, "Kashmir : The Actors Change, But the Show Must Go on," The Hindustan Times, 3 July 2000.
50. A. G; Noorani, "Divide and Drool," Ibid., 20 August 2002.
51. B. N. Mullik, My Years With Nehru, Kashmir, New Delhi, 1971, pp. 29-30.
52. *Ibid.,* p. 30.
53. *Ibid.*
54. Jawaharlal Nehru, *op. cit.,* p. 174.
55. Bhikshu Sangharakshita, 'Buddhism', A. L. Basham, ed., *op. cit.,* p. 94.
56. E. Conze, A. Short History of Buddhism, Bombay, 1960, p. 10.
57. Romila Thapar, 'Asokan India and the Gupta Age'. *Ibid.,* p. 42.
58. M. A. Stien, *op. cit.,* p. 104.
59. Arnold J. Toynbee, Between Oxes and Jumna, London University Press, 1961, p. 132.
60. Edwin R. A. Seligman, ed., *op. cit.,* p. 621.
61. Sherwani Haroon Khan, Cultural Trends in Medieval India, Bombay, 1968, p. 4.

62. Edwin R. A. Seligman, *op. cit.*, pp. 641-42.
63. Benjamin Walker, Hindu World, An Encyclopedic Survey of Hinduism, vol. II, London, 1968, p. 127.
64. Navjivan Rastogi, The Karma Tantricism of Kashmir, Vol. I, Delhi, 1979, pp. 95-99.
65. Ain-i-Akbari.
66. B. L. Sharma, *op. cit.*, p. 60.

3

Accession : Diplomatic, Social and Legal

Diplomatic

Before Accession

Maharaja Hari Singh of Dogra Dynasty became the king of the State of Jammu and Kashmir in 1925. His period witnessed both the partition of the subcontinent in August 1947 and accession of the State to the Union of India in October that year. It had little to do with the partition of the country in two dominions but a moment of great importance came after the lapse of British paramountcy when the State was to choose between a secular India and an Islamic Pakistan. Needless to say its importance for the newly created dominions. If for India it is a matter of having a successful secular state and national prestige, for Pakistan Kashmir is near, dear and vital : near in geography; dear in religion ; vital in strategy.

The rule of Dogra dynasty in Jammu and Kashmir was, in general, an oppressive one. It was authoritarian and had no democratic content. The settlement of the Kashmir Valley was commenced in 1887 and again it was took up in 1889. For the first time permanent hereditary occupancy rights were bestowed on those who agreed to pay the assessment fixed and entered in his or her name. As a result of this people lost proprietorship of their own land. The new system provided payment of land revenue partly in cash and partly in kind. The economic conditions of the people were far from satisfactory. As the Dogra rulers gave preference to Hindu Dogra of Jammu, particularly the Rajputs to which the ruling family belonged, the most affected community of the system was Muslim. A Kashmiri Hindu writer, G.N. Kaul, paints a Dickensian picture of Srinagar in the early 1920s- prostitution; thievery, beggary, disease, illiteracy and unemployment were apparently rife, while '90 per cent of Muslim houses were mortgaged to Hindu moneylenders'. The plight of Sikhs was equally frightful according to Kaul, while Pandits (Kashmiri Brahmins) seemed a little better-off.[1] Another Pandit writer and political activist, Premnath Bazaz wrote, 'The poverty of the Muslim masses is appalling. Dressed in rags and barefoot, a Muslim peasant presents the appearance of a starving beggar ..... most are landless labourers, working as serfs for absentee landlords ....almost the whole brunt of official corruption has been borne by the Muslim masses ...... rural indebtedness is staggering.[2]

The extension of British control to Kashmir also alienated the Kashmiris in administration. The imperial design began to reorganise civil departments to fill important posts in which administrators were brought into the State from the Punjab. The reason given was the absence of adequately educated and trained personnel in Kashmir for various branches of the administration. Thus employment which could have given a new lease of life to the sagging economy of the land was given to outsiders whose interests lay not in the State but elsewhere. The hue and cry which the measure raised led in due course to a distinction which was made between resident and non-resident subjects. The new definition helped the resident of the province of Jammu rather than those of the Valley, Ladakh or Northern areas. The distinction was based not on religion but on clan. But with the exception of the Dogras all the other communities were discontented.

Under British Imperialism, the national awakening which came to British India by the turn of the century spread in the late twenties to the State as well. The waves of modern ideas and thoughts began to make their impact on the people. The fight for independence in India also aroused consciousness amongst the people of Kashmir who from time to time, rose against the autocracy of the rulers. In this they had all the sympathies of the leaders of Indian national. However, the first popular reaction to the State Government's policy was communal. It was totally against the genius of the people who had suffered from time to time at the hands of bigoted kings and counsellors but who had not fallen out amongst themselves as religious communities. For the first time the majority community attempted to organise itself on religious lines for the attainment of political objectives. It was an ugly development because it showed that the young Muslim leaders educated at Lahore and Aligarh had been infected by the virus of communal politics which the British were busy developing in British India. In Jammu and Kashmir its proof came on 13 July 1931 when a Muslim mob looted Hindu houses and shops, killed three Hindus and wounded scores. This led to some retaliation on the part of the Hindus.

This tragic development was a much more serious threat to the people's hunger for secular democracy for which their genius and long history had fitted them and under which alone they could create conditions for helping the flowering of their innate respect for all faiths, intellectual, independence, traditional tolerance, and cooperation with fellow citizens of various races, creeds and languages. The struggle for India's freedom deeply influenced the Kashmiris who staged, in July 1931, a rebellion to liberate themselves from ancient slavery by demanding basic human and political rights and removal of innumerable grievances in social, political and economic fields.

A new generation of university - educated Kashmiri Muslim youth including Sheikh Mohammad Abdullah an M.Sc. from Aligarh University, with his colleagues and supporters, formed a political organisation in 1932 named the All Jammu and Kashmir Muslim Conference. Initially as the Party had no carefully worked out programme except perhaps for more jobs for Muslims in the administration. It therefore tried to rouse the Muslims from their slumbar and make them aware of their rights and responsibilities. In the absence of a sound political programme, this inevitably tended to inflame religious passions with their inevitable eruption into disorder, loot and harassment of non-Muslim. In public meetings, Abdullah recited verses from the Holy Quran in a sonorous and melodious voice with which he was gifted. He aroused passions of the Muslim and stirred their emotions against the atrocities perpetrated by the Hindu Monarchy. This brought him much popularity among the backward, ignorant and religion-ridden masses.

Within weeks he became a hero of the Kashmiris, cynosure of less fortunate public men and rival of the old guard. The two main elements which brought Abdullah into prominance in public life were the arousal of religious passions of the Kashmir Muslims against Dogra rule and Hindu-dominated administration and application of rowdyism against his rivals.

As a result of the popular agitation Maharaja Hari Singh was forced in 1932 to appoint the Glancy Commission which recommended a limited franchise, covering the ten per cent of the population, together with a legislative assembly consisting of nominated and elected members. As the agitation for responsible government grew, the ruler issued Regulation 1 of 1934. The regulation declared the intention of the Maharaja to provide for the association of his subjects in the matters of legislation and the administration of the State. This Regulation consisted of 46 sections which dealt with the legislative, executive, and judicial powers of the rulers. It referred to the subjects which should be reserved from the operation of the Regulation, made provisions for the constitution of the legislature of the State, conferred authority on the Council to make rules for specified purposes, but operating directly under the control of the ruler.

In a tragic development as early as 1933, Kashmiri Muslims were divided into two political sects, the Bakras (the adherents of Mirwaiz Yusuf Shah) and Shers (the followers of Sheikh Abdullah). The progressive leaders of the Muslim Conference, Sheikh Abdullah in particular, took no time to realise that in a land with a multi-religious and multi-linguistic society, a communal party would not be a success, for it could never reflect the problems and dreams of the masses who were not concerned with jobs for the few or for the few Muslims acting as top leaders. Their problems were not only political but also social and economic and they had to make up a frightening leeway before they could begin to feel that they were living in the twentieth century. Sheikh Abdullah, in his Presidential address at the first session of the Muslim Conference made it clear that 'the Kashmir movement is not communal but has come into existence to get the grievances of all classes of people redressed'.

'We assure our Hindu and Sikh brothers that we are prepared to help them in the same manner as we do the Musalmans. Our country cannot progress until we learn to live amicably with one another'.

As the rift between the two sects of the Muslim Conference widened, Abdullah began to search the possible support from All India Congress leadership and national press. The traditional attitude of the people of Kashmir to themselves, their government and their faith had reasserted itself and was seeking to undo the mischief which the earlier activities of the Reading Room Party and Muslim Conference had done. By this time the pattern of politics in India had begun to affect the political movements in the State. The struggle between the Indian National Congress with its secular, democratic programme for the masses and the Muslim League which drew its inspiration from the Muslim faith recognised no state borders, overflowing into Jammu and Kashmir as it did into other princely states. Latterly religion, in any real sense of the word, has played little part in Indian Political conflict, though the word is often enough used and exploited. In political matters, religion has been displayed by what is called communalism, a narrow group mentality basing itself on a religious community but in reality concerned with political powers and patronage for the interested groups.[3]

The leaders of the Muslim Conference failed to get rid of their differences and a split developed in 1938 when almost its entire organisation in Kashmir Valley, led by the dynamic Sheikh Abdullah, reconstituted itself as the National Conference (NC). This new force declared its intent to 'end communalism by ceasing to think in terms of Muslims and non-Muslims ; and invited' all Hindus and Sikhs who like ourselves believe in the freedom of their country from the shackles of an irresponsible rule' to participate as equals in the democratic struggle.[4] The sixth session of the Conference was held in Jammu in March 1938 and Abdullah, as its President declared, 'Like us the large majority of Hindus and Sikhs in the State have immensely suffered at the hands of irresponsible Government. They are also steeped in ignorance, have to pay large taxes and are in debt and starving. Establishment of responsible government is as much a necessary for them as for us.'[5]

As the ruler was an autocrat, unwilling to part with power, the popular demand was not satisfied and political unrest continued. The Maharaja promulgated the Jammu and Kashmir Constitution Act 14 of 1939. It consisted of 78 Sections divided into six parts and dealt with the executive, the legislature, the judicature, miscellaneous provisions, and the like. However, all that he did on one or two occasions was to throw them a crumb or two. His authority remained undiminished. The Regulations were issued without sharing the substance of constitutional power with the people. For example, Section 5 of the Act, like Section 3 of the earlier Regulation, recognised and preserved all the inherent powers of the ruler. Section 4 of the Constitution declared that all rights, authority, and jurisdiction, appertaining to the government of the State, were exercisable by the ruler except as provided under the Act or under specific direction from the Maharaja. In substance the constitutional powers of the ruler under the act were exactly the same as those under the earlier Regulation.

On the other side when Abdullah converted the Muslim Conference into National Conference throwing open its membership to non-Muslims also at least a few Hindu and Sikh members of the small urbanised intelligentsia responded enthusiastically. The new party had full backing of Abdullah's compelling personality and charismatic leadership and it swiftly consolidated its mass following in the Valley. Although the organisation essentially remained as it was before : the same communal outlook, the same approach to life and the same goal to achieve, it adopted in 1944 a social manifesto, 'Naya Kashmir', promising radical land reform once the monarchy had abolished. As a follow up of the Indian National Congress in May 1946, the NC launched a mass agitation which it called 'Quit Kashmir, clearly modelled on Quit India Movement of 1942, against the Maharaja Hari Singh. Abdullah declared that the time had come to tear up the Treaty of Amritsar .... sovereignty is not the birthright of Maharaja Hari Singh. The movement was a symbolic one as held by many that it was not a question of revolt but a matter of right as well. The manifesto was divided into two parts, the constitution of the State and the National Economic Plan. It emphasised the equality of citizens before the law in matters of fundamental rights and the right to work, and asked for an elected national assembly with a council of ministers responsible to it. In Manifesto's foreward Abdullah said, 'We shall build again the men and women of our State who have been dwarfed for centuries of servitude, and create a people worthy of our glorious motherland.'

In 1941, a section of Muslims, led by Ghulam Abbas, broke away from the National Conference and formed the Muslim Conference. The socially conservative Muslim Conference, which increasingly leaned towards Mohammed Ali Jinnah's All India Muslim League and its campaign for Pakistan. While Jinnah was not responsible for the creation of a communal atmosphere in India which had been carefully nourished by the British in pursuit of their policy of 'Divide and Rule', he converted it into a weapon which in time brought about, in the name of religion, one of the biggest bloodbaths in human history. To him there was nothing in common between Hindus and Muslims and he made it a point to exploit their real or imaginary differences for political purposes. Once the cry for Pakistan was raised at Lahore in 1940, it began to cast its shadow on some of the Muslim leaders of Jammu who had already resigned from the National Conference and revived the Muslim Conference. Narrow sectarian considerations began to infect Kashmir politics as they were already poisoning Indian political life.

The gulf between National Conference and Muslim Conference began to widen and the latter was supported by Muslim League. The difference which divided them was basic. National Conference in spite of its vascillating leadership under Abdullah was seeking its natural level in traditional, tolerant politics, while some Muslim Conference leaders under the inspiration of outside leaders, who had no sympathy for the history and achievements of the Kashmir people, were pulling it out by the roots. Muslim League which supported them was fully busy in planting seeds of violence and conflict in the State, and in a sense seeking to destroy the soul of its people. The Muslim Conference, like the Muslim League believed in equality before the law but only for Muslims. Non-Muslims were outside the pale of what they conceived to be democracy or freedom. On the otherhand, there was no chance of their compromise with the Maharaja Hari Singh, the then ruler of Jammu and Kashmir.

Abdullah, on account of his basic differences with Jinnah and being frustrated and crest fallen, returned to the Congress fold and with redoubled vigour championed the cause of Indian nationalism and communal unity. Obviously no alternative was left to him but to be on the side of India for in Muslim Pakistan under Jinnah he could easily visualise the end of his political career besides public humiliation and even something worse. Abdullah was welcomed in the Indian National Congress because he became the trumpet-bearer of anti-Pakistan tirades, the loudest opponent of two-nation theory and a staunch supporter of Indian nationalism. The few Muslims in public eye who adhered to Congress ideology were particularly patronised by Jawaharlal Nehru irrespective of the veracity of their statements or sincerity of their professions. Abdullah had an additional merit of belonging to a state where Muslims were in a preponderating majority. Therefore, he was lionised, his courage admired, his honesty and sincerity applauded. This enabled Sheikh to get more than what he wanted and deserved : international fame and stable public position.

For the period, it seemed that the ideological unity between Abdullah and the Congress leaders was not forced by events but had a much deeper base. Abdullah's regard for Mahatma Gandhi and Jawaharlal Nehru was genuine. They both had always supported the State people's struggle against the Indian princes as also Abdullah's struggle against the Maharaja of Kashmir. The Congress led by Mahatma Gandhi and Jawaharlal Nehru had always stood for the oppressed people of the States against their rulers in the same way as Sheikh Abdullah had championed the cause of the people of the Kashmir Valley against the Dogra ruler. The Indian leaders considered the rulers to be a creation of the British and propped up by them to serve their own imperialistic ends, and this was exactly the view which Sheikh Abdullah held of the Kashmir ruler. Against the background of developments in India and the machinations of Muslim Conference he challenged the validity of the Treaty of Amritsar and called upon the ruler to Quit Kashmir. He was arrested.

tried, and sentenced to three years' imprisonment. Incensed by the oppressions of the ruler, Nehru had rushed to the Valley in support of the people and had courted imprisonment by the Maharaja. He was detained by the State authorities at Uri until he was assured by Maulana Azad, then President of the Indian National Congress, that the Working Committee had decided to take the matter into its own hands,[6] when he returned from the State. Thus, strong bonds of unity had been forged between the Kashmiri people and the Indian people, who were both fighting for their liberation.

Accession

With the lapse of British Paramountcy in the subcontinent on 15 August 1947, the Dominions of India and Pakistan assumed their independent and divided existence. Partition was accepted as a disagreeable necessity by the Congress leadership : it entailed the bifurcation of Bengal, the cradle of modern Indian nationalism, the division of the rich and fertile Punjab, and the secession of strategic areas commanding the north-west approaches to India. The creation of a theocratic Islamic state juxtaposed to India was seen as a threat to India's secular democratic experiment, and partition was seen as a case of 'strategic and political secession' from India.[7] For the people of Pakistan it was not only liberation from foreign rule : it also meant freedom from the threat of a majority rule in a caste-ridden social system where they would have been destined to be a permanent and stagnant religious minority.

In 1947, there were 562 Princely states. These had hitherto preserved a degree of independence, and their rulers had direct relations with the British Crown, the paramount power. The future of these states was not adequately or fairly dealt with at any stage of the negotiation of transfer of power in 1946-47. Their future was far from clear and the subsequent near-war tension between India and Pakistan over the future of some of them was exacerbated by what Ian Stephens calls 'the impetuous and unprincipled haste with which the British, under Lord Mountbatten's lead extricated themselves in August 1947 from their governing responsibilities.[8] The Indian Independence Act which was enacted by the British Parliament on July 18, 1947, came into force from the 'appointed day', i.e., from 15 August, 1947. Sub section (b) of Para 1 of Section 17 laid down that as from the appointed day 'the suzerainty of His Majesty over the Indian States lapses, and with it, all treaties and agreements in force at the date of the passing of this Act between His Majesty and the Rulers of the Indian States .....'[9] In other words, the Crown was not to have any relationship with the Indian States.

The effect of the above provision was that those States which did not accede to either of the new Dominions by 15th August became independent and sovereign. The State of Jammu and Kashmir was one of them. It bordered on both India and Pakistan and was not originally incorporated into India at the time of partition. In the case of Kashmir, all the emotions which in the past have hampered the settlement of territorial problems in other areas of the world, are present on both sides : the nationalist sentiments of both India and Pakistan : the fundamental split between the secular and the religious state which in the first place brought about partition ; the attempt, in which both Muslims and Hindus among the Kashmiri have played a part, to transform a backward agrarian community into a welfare State ; the struggle of the great powers over the control of a strategic area which lies at the crossroads of Pakistan, India, Russia and China, and could be an important jumping-off place for military operations ; and the desire of the Kashmiris to determine their own destiny.[10] Unfortunately for Kashmir, as well as for India and Pakistan, it is one of those territories which because of their desirability, seem destined to be bones of contention between neighbouring nations.

After the enactment of the Government of India Act, 1858, the Crown became the Paramount Power in respect of the Indian States. The relationship between the Crown and the Indian States was maintained by the Political Department which was set up under the direct charge of the Governor-General. The Department had Residents and Political Agents in all important States or group of States. Lord Mountbatten, the then Governor-General of India, was an old friend of the Maharaja - they had both been ADCS on the Staff of the Prince of Wales when he toured India in 1921.

Mountbatten, in the background of partition and independence visited Kashmir on June 19, 1947 and stayed there for four days. He apparently persuaded the Maharaja to make up his mind for accession with either of the Dominions. He was also quoted as having told the Maharaja that he may accede to Pakistan if he wished in which case the State Department would not take it as an unfriendly act.[11] However, had he, as the Governor-General of India, given a simple advice to the Maharaja for acceding to the Dominion of India, it was not unlikely that the Maharaja would have done so by August 15, 1947. Pakistan by that date had not existed, and therefore there could have been no interference by it and the Kashmir problem might have settled for ever.

Maharaja Hari Singh, the ruler of the State of Jammu and Kashmir, failed to take any decision before August 15, 1947. What reasons prompted him not to accede to the State to either of the Dominions was perhaps the fact that he had three alternatives. He was free not only to accede to either of the dominions but he had also an alternative to declare the independence of the State, and thus, the State could remain as an independent and sovereign state. His momentary decision turned the course of events more than anything else. Had he acceded to Pakistan, India would have been accepted his decision, as Lord Mountbatten, then Governor-General, had already assured the ruler on behalf of the Government of India.[12] Similarly, if he had chosen to cast his lot with India, no problem would have arisen, because before 15th August Pakistan had not even come into existence.

The Ruler, in his decision to remain independent, was supported by Ram Chandra Kak, the then Prime Minister of Kashmir. He was a man without vision and equally bereft of tact and political judgement. The Maharaja was also supported on this issue by the Muslim Conference - a political party of the State which since 1944 had been competing with the National Conference, another Political Party, for the loyalty of the Kashmiri Muslims. In May 1947, before the lapse of Paramountcy, the Acting President of the Muslim Conference in a Press statement, pleaded for independence and assured to the Maharaja for the support and cooperation of the eighty per cent Muslim of the State. The Party assured the Ruler that he would be acclaimed as the first Constitutional King of a democratic and independent Kashmir.[13] Ghulam Ahmad, the Deputy leader of the Muslim Conference Party made an appeal to Maharaja on May 21, 1947, to declare Kashmir as an independent State. Sheikh Abdullah, a prominent leader of the State, had also pleaded in the past on a few occasions for the independence of the State.[14] Later on Nehru, while recalling the State's decision, stated in Parliament,' The house is aware that on the lapse of Crown Paramountcy on the 15th August, this year, Kashmir did not accede to either Dominion. We were of course, vitally interested in the decision that the State would take. Kashmir, because of her geographical position with her frontiers with three countries, namely, the Soviet Union, China and Afghanistan is intimately connected with the security and international contacts of India. Economically also Kashmir is intimately related to India. The carvan trade routes from Central Asia to India pass through the Kashmir State.'[15]

Insistence of the Prime Minister of the State and the persuasion of the Muslim Conference had led the Maharaja to cherish the dream of an independent State of Jammu and Kashmir, which at that time was looking real. But events moved fast and the ruler who had dreams of an independent Kashmir, offered a standstill agreement to both India and Pakistan. After the visit of Lord Mountbatten in June 1947, leaders of the Indian National Congress visited the State that followed the replacement of the Prime Minister of Kashmir by a militant Dogra, Janak Singh, and later by Mehar Chand. The Prime Minister of Kashmir in a telegram on August 12, 1947, announced his dicision to negotiate standstill agreements with both India and Pakistan. The 'Standstill Agreement' contained the provisions which were merely temporary arrangements to maintain status quo and to avoid administrative vacuum after the lapse of paramountcy. The subject-matters of Standstill Agreements which were offered to India and Pakistan were different.

Offers made to Pakistan in a telegram under the standstill agreement included communications, supplies, Post office and telegraphic arrangements, and 'nothing else'. The Government of Pakistan accepted the offer by an exchange of telegram on August 16, 1947. By this agreement Pakistan had assumed responsibility for carrying on communications and supply functions of Kashmir. In an effort to impress the Maharaja with the urgency of accession to Pakistan, a virtual blockade was imposed by which badly needed supplies like food grains, cloth, kerosene, salt and suger were completely stopped. This pressure was serious, because it is not easy for Pakistan to obtain these essential supplies from India on account of the difficulty of communication.[16] This was how the Pakistan Government honoured the standstill agreement. The action of Pakistan was condemned by the Maharaja of the State. On October 15, 1947, Mehar Chand, the then Prime Minister of Jammu and Kashmir complained to the British Prime Minister against Pakistan for violating the terms of Standstill Agreement. But no reply came from the British perhaps because of the fact that the suzerainty of His Majesty over the Indian States had lapsed and all treaties and agreements with the Rulers of Indian States had terminated.

The telegram which sent to the Government of India stated that the 'Jammu and Kashmir Government would welcome Standstill Agreement with the Union of India on all existing matters with the outgoing British India Government. It was suggested that the then existing arrangements should continue pending settlement of details of formal execution of fresh agreements. Thus, the offer made to India was extended to many other subjects besides those contained in the telegram sent to Pakistan, such as, external affairs, control of fears and defence etc. The language of the Standstill Agreement permitted the Indian Government even to use force should the state be attacked by any foreign power, in the same way as could be done by the British Government under the Provisions of the Treaty of Amritsar, 1846.

In response to the telegram under Standstill Agreement, the Government of India did not show any haste and refused to accept as it was sent. Its reply said, 'Government of India would be glad if some duly authorised minister could fly to Delhi for negotiating Sandstill Agreement between the Kashmir Government and Indian Dominion. It also did not like to put any sort of pressure on the

Maharaja. Nehru recalled, 'Nevertheless, we did not put the slightest pressure on the State to accede to the Indian Dominion, because we realised that Kashmir was in a very difficult position. We did not want mere accession from the top but an association in accordance with the will of her people. Indeed, we did not encourage any rapid decision. Even in regard to a standstill agreement, no speedy steps were taken by us, although Kashmir had entered into a standstill agreement with Pakistan soon after the 15th August'.[17] But it is also not unlikely that the Government did not accept the offer as it was the general policy of the States' Department not to sign Standstill Agreement until the Instrument of Accession had been signed by the Ruler of the State. Since the Maharaja had not signed the Instrument of Accession, the Government of India was not expected to accept the offer.

Virtual economic blockade of Pakistan against the State of Jammu and Kashmir despite Standstill Agreement with it and India's refusal to extend any help without the sign of Instrument of Accession had worsened the situation in the State. As a fuel to the fire, a well-organised rioting began in Poonch against the Maharaja's administration. The State troops took a harsh action aganist the Muslims inhabiting that area in which violence spread quickly and gave the disturbances a communal appearance. On October 21, 1947, a tribal invasion on the State was mounted from across the North West Frontier Province (NWFP) and West Punjab (both in Pakistan), and within a day the raiders reached Muzaffarabad. They were to march to Srinagar, in order to occupy it so that the fate of Kashmir be decided with the sword. The State forces were not only completely inadequate but were not prepared to meet the challenge. The result was that the raiders succeeded in occupying a considerable part of Jammu Province, more especially in the Poonch town, Mirpur Kotlly, Bhimbhar, Jhanger and Naushera. The areas which the raiders forcibly occupied later came to be known as 'Azad Kashmir'

As a result, Srinagar became a threatened capital and thereupon the Government of Kashmir requested the Government of India for military aid to defend the State. The situation was discussed at a Special Meeting of the Defence Committee on October 25, 1947, which was called by the Governor-General Lord Mountbatten. The Committee also considered the request of the Maharaja for arms and ammunitions and decided to send V. P. Menon to Srinagar to study the situation on the spot. On his return from Srinagar he reported to the Defence Committee regarding 'the urgency and the supreme necessity of saving Kashmir from the raiders'. Because on that very moment Kashmir was an independent country, Mountbatten considered it improper to send the troops to which the Defence Committee agreed. Menon again rushed to Jammu, where the Maharaja was staying and returned with the Prime Minister of Kashmir and Ruler's request for troops with the offer for the accession of the State to the Dominion of India. A day after on October 27, 1947, the Instrument of Accession, which was signed by the Maharaja, was accepted by the Defence Committee and the Governor-General of India. On that very date (27 October), the first contingent of Indian troops landed in Srinagar and the raiders were halted.

In pursuance of the one of the conditions that the Maharaja would introduce popular government in the state, immediately after the accession, as a stop-gap arrangement, the Maharaja invited Sheikh Mohammad Abdullah, President of the National Conference to form an interim Government and to carry on the administration of the State. Abdullah was appointed head of the emergency administration and on March 5, 1948, the ruler issued a proclamation constituting, *inter alia*, popular government with a Council of Ministers consisting of the Prime Minister with effect from March 1, 1948. Though under the proclamation a popular interim government was set up, the constitutional position still was that the popular government had theoretically to function under the constitution of 1939. As the popular government was installed in office, in practice, the autocratic authority of the ruler was broken, and power passed from his hands to popular leaders who had opposed him and suffered at his hands. Even more important was the fact that the head of the new government was a Muslim who had been principally responsible for awakening political consciousness among the Muslim masses of the State, and he was assisted in his task by Muslim as well as non-Muslim colleagues.[18]

India's insistence on the transfer of *de facto* authority from the Maharaja to the State Prime Minister and his cabinet opened a new and decisive chapter in the history of the people. Kashmiri leaders and the people were determined to strip him of all authority and to make sure that never again would he usurp popular rights or stand in the way of their own vision of what was good for the people. The Ruler also began to realise that sooner or later, in the interests of a smooth administration, he would have to go. In 1949, Maharaja Hari Singh went into voluntary exile and his place as constitutional head of the State was taken over by his son Yuvraj Karan Singh. But in the circumstances hereditary monarchy had become a misfit and the abolition of which would be consistent with the Republic of India of which the State now formed an integral part. Following the constitutional provisions and its implementation on January 26, 1950, Yuvraj issued a proclamation on May 1, 1951, convoking a constituent assembly on the basis of free elections. The Constituent Assembly appointed two committees, which among other things, considered the position of the Head of the State. The Committee, recommended that the form of the future constitution of Jammu and Kashmir should be wholly democratic, that the institution of hereditary rulership should be terminated and that the office of the Head of the State should be elective.[19] The Yuvraj was later elected by the Constituent Assembly of the State as the 'Sadar-i-Riyasat. Thus, came to an end the Princely rule in the State of Jammu and Kashmir and the head of the State was henceforth to be an elected person. The fate of the hereditary ruler came to an end.

Role of Leaders : Kashmir

At the time of independence leaders of the National Conference and All Jammu and Kashmir Muslim Conference were languishing in Jail because of their movements against the autocratic rule of Mahraja Hari Singh. Both these parties of Jammu and Kashmir had drifted apart due to individual as well as ideological factors that even led to form their attitudes as pro-Indian and Pro-Pakistan. Sheikh Mohammad Abdullah in person and National Conference as an important political Party of the State had a long suffering history for the people of Kashmir. Owing to the fact that the party had modelled its policies and programmes on the basis of Indian National Congress, the likemindedness of its leader Sheikh Abdullah with Jawaharlal Nehru and Mahatma Gandhi was not uncommon. On the otherhand, the All Jammu and Kashmir Muslim Conference was known for its pro-Pakistan allegiance and was backed by the Muslim League with its leader Mohammad Ali Jinnah. From the beginning it had fought for interests of Muslims only and had therefore, supported the accession of the State of Jammu and Kashmir with Pakistan.

Sheikh Mohammad Abdullah was the first leader of the state to be released by the Maharaja on September 29, 1947, when the critical decision of state's accession was to be taken. In 1947, the people of Kashmir hailed Sheikh Abdullah as messiah when he claimed, with justifiable pride, that he had achieved azadi for them after four centuries of slavery under Moghuls, Afghan, Sikh and Dogra kings respectively. It was their greatest hour in history to be ruled by a Kashmiri rather than a foreigner.[20] After release he was faced with a difficult decision. He could not support the ruler who had shown little willingness to accept the political awakening among his people and who regarded the National Conference as well as the Muslim Conference as a threat to his throne. He could not give a lead on the issue of accession because as he explained at the time what the State needed first was political freedom without which any consideration whether Kashmir should accede to India or Pakistan would be futile and purposeless. The immediate problem was liberation from the chains of slavery in which the ruler held them captive. In these circumstances neither India nor Pakistan, he argued, should expect the National Conference to waste its time over the question of accession. His party needed help in its struggle against an autocratic ruler and if the Congress and Muslim League were prepared to join the Kashmiris in their crusade for freedom, there would be time enough for taking a decision on the State's ultimate relationship with India and Pakistan.

In his approach to the problem India agreed with Abdullah. Right since the days of people's struggle under the leadership of Abdullah and the National Conference, an overwhelming majority in the Valley had been wanting to be with India.[21] During the days of national struggle in Kashmir the Congress led by Mahatma Gandhi and Jawaharlal Nehru had always stood for the oppressed people of the States against their rulers in the same way as Sheikh Abdullah had championed the cause of the people of the Kashmir valley against the Dogra ruler. In the light of the visits undertaken by Gandhi and Nehru to Kashmir after partition, *The Times* commented, 'The Union of India has been taking a lively interest in the subject and indications are that the Hindu Maharaja of Kashmir, Sir Hari Singh, has lately been much influenced by the representations made by Gandhi who visited Kashmir three months ago and by other Congress leaders'.[22]

Thus, the turn of events after partition showed that liberating Abdullah was not a princely whim on the Maharaja's part ; it was presumably done at the behest of the Indian government. Abdullah had long associations with Nehru and the latter had fully utilised their close personal relationship. Although Abdullah was opposed to the Maharaja's tyrannical rule and had contributed to the political awakening of Kashmir, at the critical moment of his country's history he played the role of an opportunist.[23] Without perhaps fully realising the whole situation, he came to the aid of the Maharaja's design to join Kahmir to India against the wishes of the people. Immediately after his release he went to Delhi, where Nehru persuaded him to support the Dogra ruler whom he had hitherto opposed, and he made a number of speeches which were markedly pro-Indian and anti-Pakistan.

It was not impossible that Sheikh Abdullah had done so by personal factors. To his misfortune the issue of partition of the Indian subcontinent on religious grounds assumed the greatest importance in Kashmir politics; Muslims were heavily swayed by Pakistan ideology ; the ship of National Conference cracked and was sinking; the rank of Sheikh's adversaries swelled. The momentous event tried Abullah's mettle and brought out the salient features of his character; unreliability and proneness to betrayal of followers, friends and associates. Even after having closely associated himself with Congress leaders for a number of years, as the partition loomed large on the horizon, Sheikh consulted wisdom in making friendship with

Mohammad Ali Jinnah, the arch enemy of Çongress Party and Indian nationalism. He entertained the feelings of fear, distrust and repugnance with Jinnah. But he opposed State's accession probably that if Kashmir joined Pakistan his political rivals would come to power ; since this might well mean his political death, he threw his lot with India. Even on the issue of plebiscite, the strongest opposition came from Sheikh Abdullah himself. His contention was that he alone represented Kashmir and whatever he decided was good enough for the Kashmiris and it was not necessary to have a plebiscite to find out what the people wanted.[24] As he had opted for India, that was enough for his people.

Abdullah seemed anxious actually for the future of Jammu and Kashmir which was in danger at the time he was released from jail. The accession of the State to either of the dominions was a secondary matter. But on the otherhand, Pakistan was impatient to put pressure on the State from many sides. The Pakistan Radio and newspapers incited the Muslim population of the State to rise against the Hindu ruler who, they said, was a threat to Muslims and Islam. The appeal was openly religious, directed to the baser elements of human naturè, namely those of lust, loot and murder. Consequently, as Abdullah had himself described the crisis which overtook the State, 'Soon after my release I heard of preparations along the Western borders of Kashmir for some kind of invasion or raid. Armed people infilterated into the State territory and in many places there were armed conflicts. These raiders created havoc and looted Muzaffarabad and other places. It was obvious also that this invasion was meant to coerce and compel the people of Kashmir to act in a particular way, namely, to accede to Pakistan. Every Kashmiri was shocked by the raid and the ruin in the trail of this raid. Every Kashmiri resented the compulsion on his will. Every Kashmiri was ready to defend his motherland against the intruder. They refused to be compelled to accede to Pakistan in this way. Abdullah, having explained the critical position in Kashmir to members of the Government of India and, in the light of Maharaja's request to get rid of the State from raiders, decided to stand shoulder to shoulder with the people of Kashmir in defending the heritage and to share with them the perils and sorrows that may be in store.[25]

The heritage as well as Abdullah's own convictions were being put to the test. Two things, as he felt, were at stake–religious and cultural tolerance and a democratic structure in which social legislation designed to reduce the pressure of the few on the many could be undertaken. Abdullah dealt with these two points again and again over the years. As in British India, so in Kashmir, the national forces were democratic and secular, but found themselves, because of British mechinations, struggling against anti-national and theocratic currents which were feudalistic and determined to maintain past privileges that had abridged the freedom of the common man. The struggle was not superficial but deep and in a sense all-pervasive. The people had broken the teeth of the invaders. At least for the time being secular nationalism had triumphed over bigotry and religious expansionism. This was fully demonstrated by the resistence put up by the people when the Pakistani army, under the garb of unorganised raiders, invaded Kashmir in 1947-48.

Sheikh Abdullah, on his part, left no one in doubt about his own dedication to them, his uncompromising opposition to Pakistan which had rejected the urges for which India stood, and about Kashmir being inseparable from India. On one occasion he said, 'Our relationship with India is not a product of sentiment. We have contracted this relationship after giving it ample thought and deliberation. We have taken this step because our ideal and our path is common and one. Those who want to weaken these relations are not only playing a traitor to the sacred principles of humanity but also indulging in a dangerous game with the independence and freedom of their country'. He repeatedly criticised Pakistan and at the same time praised India for being a secular and democratic character : In fact India belongs neither to Hindus nor to Muslims nor to Sikhs. In India there is complete freedom and equality for everyone. In this very India we are terminating today the 106-year old ruling dynasty of Kashmir. If India were a Hindu country, how could it had supported us in doing away with a Hindu Maharaja ?

Although Abdullah's long association with Gandhi and Nehru persuaded him to join India, but he needed a constitutional buffer to convince his people that they would not be dominated by Hindu-majority India. It is true that the Kashmiris have an individuality of their own; in certain respects they differ from the rest of Indians, essentially cultural, emotional and sentimental. It had been deliberately ignored that the Muslims in the Valley have a distinct culture of their own, with a beautiful language and Sufi tradition and customs, which they proudly call 'Kashmiriyat'. They have nothing in common with the dominant Punjabi culture of Islamabad. The 'Kashmiriyat' or 'Kashmiri Identity' had played a far more important role in its politics than the Muslim identity. Before 1947, the political support by Indian leaders - in particular by Gandhi and Nehru to the struggle of the people of Kashmir against an autocratic rule, and later at the time of partition to their right to choose between India and Pakistan attracted them to Hindu-majority India instead of what was called the homeland of Muslims.[26] As Kashmiri Muslim felt that their Kashmiri identity was threatened by the Muslim raiders from Pakistan who tried to annex them to that country forcibly, they sought Indian help and cooperated with the Indian Army.

Perhaps to defend this Kashmiri identity the Kashmiri leaders sought special status under Indian Constitution. The Article 370 of the constitution which conferred a special status on Kashmir State was specifically meant to be a temporary provision. At the time of partition extremism was rated high ; moderation, balance and common sense were at a discount; a psychosis had been generated by horrible bloodshed and religious hysteria in both India and Pakistan. The constitution-makers were fully confident that the close association of the people of Kashmir with free democratic India would convince them of their bright future by becoming an integral part of the Republic. The Indian leaders had to prove not only by their words but also through their deeds that the Muslims could live like free, respectable and equal citizens of India as envisaged in the constitution, convinced that their fears entertained at the time of partition were mostly unfounded. On the otherhand, the leaders of Kashmir had to satisfy the people that through secularism alone they could achieve political and cultural freedom as well as economic progress within India than by forming part of Muslim Pakistan.

In the post-accession period between 1947 and 1951 Sheikh Abdullah in his speech to the National Conference and address to the Constituent Assembly assured the Indian leaders and public as well that Kashmir is a part and parcel of the Indian Union. In May 1949 he said to Nehru, 'I want you to believe that Kashmir is yours. No power in the world can separate us. Every Kashmiri feels that he is an Indian and that is his homeland.[27] However, the autonomous status could not be utilised for the advantage and benefit of the State people from the highest to the humblest as was sagaciously envisioned by the farsighted Constitution-makers. It did not take them long to understand that in the name of democracy they could enrich themselves and fulfil their own ambitions by means, fair or foul. Therefore, to keep people in darkness and not to make them politically conscious and socially awakened became a vested interest of Kashmir politicians. A policy was evolved to make Kashmir Muslims feel perpetually in terror of the hostile Hindu majority and depend upon the local co-religionist leaders for protection against it.

The Indian leaders and Jawaharlal Nehru in particular continued to entertain the hope that the Sheikh would not only remain with India but would take an active part in the political, economic and social development of this country. But towards the end of 1952 it became manifest that the public resentment against Abdullah's authoritarianism was mounting; corruption, nepotism and high-handedness were assuming intolerable proportion. He, in his moments of vanity even forgot the fact of Kashmir being a constituent unit of a federal republic. Abdullah flatly denied that the State people had finally or irrevocably decided to accede to India; they had, he stressed, yet to make their choice and should be provided with an opportunity through a free referendum what they desired to do. He began to appreciate the views of Pakistan leaders and saw sense in their policies and doings.[28] Belately, the Government of India realised that the policy of depending on one man in disregard of the feelings of the State people in general was unwise and it is incumbent that it should curb the undemocratic, antipeople activities of the Sheikh. When some measures were taken to this end Abdullah reacted overly resulting in his deposition from the chair, arrest and imprisonment on August 9, 1953.

India

As soon as the plan for the partition of the Indian subcontinent was announced, on June 3, 1947, the leaders of the Indian National Congress became active. The party, from its foundation, was organised along democratic lines. Its resolutions were publicly debated and then voted upon in its periodic decisions. It allowed dissent and tolerated and even encouraged different and minority opinions to be openly held and freely expressed. Some of its important decisions were taken after heated debates on the basis of public disagreement and open voting.[29] Its attitude towards religion particularly in its relation to the State pervaded the thinking of many top leaders of the Indian National Congress which adopted a resolution on fundamental rights in Karachi in 1931, 'Every citizen shall enjoy freedom of conscience and the right freely to profess and practice his religion, subject to public order and morality'. More specifically it asserted : 'The State shall observe neutrality in regard to all religions.

When in October 1947, the Congress Government of India accepted the accession offer of Kashmir jointly made by Maharaja Hari Singh and the National Conference leadership, it was fully aware of the tremendous difficulties which it was sure to encounter in integrating the State with Indian Union; it realised that constitutional and legal accession would be meaningless if it was not followed by emotional integration of the Kashmiris in the mainstream of India's social and political life. It is true even today and will remain so in future. Jawaharlal Nehru and India's first Prime Minister, who piloted the entire scene, while replying in a heated debate, said to the opposition in Parliament on August 7, 1956, 'The strongest bonds that bind will not be your armies or even your constitution to which so much reference has been made, but bonds which are stronger than the constitution and laws and armies-bonds that bind through love and affection and understanding.'[30]

As the Indian National Congress was at the helm of affairs, it inherited all responsibilities regarding accession of the Indian states. For the purpose the Government of India set up the States Department on July 5, 1947, in the charge of Sardar Patel who worked in consultation with Abdul Rab Nishtar, a member from Muslim League Party. The day it was set up, Patel in an inaugural address, defined the Government of India's policy and invited the States to accede to the Dominion of India.[31] Later Lord Mount–batten while speaking at a Conference of the Rulers and Representatives of Indian States on July 25, 1947, said, 'the Indian Independence Act releases the States from all their obligations to the Crown. The States have complete freedom–technically and legally they are independent. Viewing the urgency of the situation, he declared, 'If you are prepared to come, you must come before the 15th August'. Since the majority of the States were geographically situated in such a way that they could not make their link with the Dominion of Pakistan, the only alternative left before them was to make a link with the Dominion of India.

The Instrument of Accession was prepared by the States Department. It was of two types. First, that which was to be signed by the Rulers of fully empowered States, numbering one hundred and forty and another which was to be signed by the Rulers of States in respect of which the Crown exercised certain powers and jurisdiction.[32] The number of States was over three hundred. Apart from these two forms, there was a third form of Instrument of Accession which was to be signed by 'intermediate Rulers, who were higher in status than the Rulers where the Crown exercised certain powers and jurisdiction, but did not possess 'full powers'. The number of such states was seventy. Except the State of Jammu and Kashmir all Indian States were acceded to the Indian Union before August 15, 1947.

For Jawaharlal Nehru and Mahatma Gandhi, Kashmir's accession was a timely response to the two-nation theory on which Pakistan is based. They felt the need to counter protagonists of the two-nation theory in India, who were and still are trying to convert India into a religious state, a Hindu version of Pakistan.[33] However, the difference between Nehru and Gandhi, though they tended to the same conclusion, was of interest. Gandhi's approach of religion was based on his intense belief in its truthfulness. His starting point was of a religious man who, believing all religions to be true, accepted the theory of a state which fitted in with this belief; hence the secular State. Nehru's starting point was that of a practical political thinker and leader who, while personally believing all religions to be mostly untrue, had to provide for their freedom to function peacefully without prejudicing the democratic system; hence the secular State. To Nehru the secular State was the cardinal doctrine underlying modern democratic practice.[34] When the political struggle against the British ended and India attained freedom, these ideas were given a practical shape. It was made clear by Nehru when he said in the Constituent Assembly, 'So far as India is concerned we have very clearly stated both as Government and otherwise that we can not think of any State which might be called a communal or religious State. We can only think of a secular, non-communal, democratic State, in which every individual to whatever religion he may belong, has equal rights and opportunities ?

When the curtain rose in October, 1947 the future of secularism in India was in doubt. Jawaharlal Nehru scripted the accession of Jammu and Kashmir to demonstrate that; despite the horrors of partition, the people of a Muslim-majority princely state could be persuaded to link their future with the secular and democratic India. This is why that Maharaja Hari Singh's offer of accession was not accepted until it was endorsed by Sheikh Mohammad Abdullah, leader of the National Conference. Nehru even insisted that he be made head of the State Government to make the accession meaningful and acceptable to the majority of its people. The National Conference was also a united body and had complete control in the Valley. In this state, the people's movement was more pro-Indian than pro-Pakistani and the leaders of the movement acknowledged their allegiance to Gandhi and Nehru. Pandit Nehru's prestige amongst the Kashmiri was very high. They remembered that he was the leader who had gone to Kashmir in support of the people's liberation struggle and had courted arrest by the Maharaja.

In the task of accession, the Indian leaders were helped by Lord Mountbatten and the Hindu rulers of Patiala, Kapurthala and Faridkot, who all paid visits to the Maharaja during June and July 1947. In the month of June Mahatma Gandhi and Jawaharlal Nehru had requested Lord Mountbatten to visit Kashmir as both of them wanted to study the political situation of the State. They were anxious that the Maharaja of Kashmir should make no declaration of independence. Lord Mountbatten refused to oblige them but said that he would much prefer seeing his old acquaintance with Maharaja first. He visited the State on June 19, 1947, and remained there for four days. As revealed by Alan Campbell-Johnson, his press attaché, that one of the reasons for the visit was to dissuade Gandhi and Nehru from going to Kashmir. Despite this, Gandhi took a visit to the state in early August and other Congress leaders went there, including the President of the Congress, Acharaya Kripalani. However, the role of Mountbatten at the time of accession seemed dubious. A person who could persuade and cajole nearly 600 ruling princes when sitting in New Delhi, could not even discuss the future of Kashmir during his four days' visit to Maharaja. It would argue an incredible indifference on Mountbatten's part towards a very large and strategically important state.

As a result of the visits undertaken by the important Indian leaders to the State of Jammu and Kashmir, there were a number of developments which were greatly influential in promoting the State's subsequent accession to India. For example, soon after Gandhi's visit the Prime Minister of Kashmir, who was known for his pro-Pakistan attitudes and had made a 'standstill agreement' with Pakistan, was replaced by a militant Dogra, Janak Singh and later by Mehar Chand. Both of them were definitely in favour of Kashmir's accession to India. Further, as a follow up of Gandhi's talks with the Maharaja, negotiations started with the Government of India to build a direct road between India and Jammu. The object of these negotiations was to create an alternative route between Kashmir and India so that essential supplies, and troops, could pass from one to the other without crossing the territory of Pakistan.[35] It was clear from these negotiations over the road, and from the speed and secrecy of its construction, that the Maharaja had agreed with Delhi that his state should join to India.

Sheikh Abdullah, in a significant development but perhaps at the behest of the Government of India, was released on September 29, 1947, and extended full support to the Maharaja. He had close and long associations with Nehru that the latter had fully utilised. Abdullah's full and timely support to the accession issue of the State helped India to a large extent that Indian leaders owed sincerely. However, Abdullah's compulsions and his dubious character kept the two important Indian leaders-Nehru and Sardar Patel apart. Nehru was a humanist and an optimist and he had hoped that, seeing the secular and democratic forces at work in India and the progressive trends which even Muslim countries like the UAR and Turkey were following, Sheikh Abdullah would be able to get over his basic trait of communalism and become a national leader, not merely a leader of Kashmir but a leader of the whole of India. But no amount of good example, no amount of persuasion, no amount of friendship and even exhortations by such highly respected Muslim leaders like Maulana Abul Kalam Azad and Rafi Ahmed Kidwai could eliminate the basic communalism in Sheikh Abdullah, and this is what ultimately prevailed.[36]

Sardar Patel's assessment of Sheikh Abdullah was more correct than that of Nerhu. He suspected that the Sheikh was not genuine and was misleading Nehru. Patel disagreed with the assessment of B.N. Mullik, the then Deputy Director in charge of Internal Affairs (Intelligence Bureau), about the situation in Kashmir in general and of Sheikh Abdullah in particular. Patel gave his views about Abdullah to the Deputy Director and apprehended that Sheikh Abdullah would ultimately let down India and Jawaharlal Nehru and would come out in his real colours; his antipathy to the Maharaja was not really an antipathy to a ruler as such, but to the Dogras in general and with the Dogras he identified the rest of the majority community in India. Events, as they turned out subsequently, proved that Sardar Patel was right because it was only after three years that the Indian leaders found themselves fighting against Sheikh Abdullah.

Once the State of Jammu and Kashmir acceded to the Union of India and Abdullah became the head of the government his original colour came out. He, along with his co-workers, at the cost of people's interest tried to create and keep up tension. Sheikh poses to be firm believer in secularism and yet his actions continue to keep the suspicions of the non-Muslims alive because he demands a special status for Kashmir only because the Muslims form the majority in one part of the State. It is this Kashmir pot which Sheikh Abdullah has kept boiling for serving his self-interest, which has been directly or indirectly responsible for much of the communalism which has raised its head in India. His idea of democracy too was somewhat different where there would be an elected parliament filled by people selected by him and with no opposition or only a nominal one, which would give sanction to whatever he desired and thus give the stamp of democracy to his dictatorial will.

India considered the State of Jammu and Kashmir an integral part of and recognised Kashmiris as one of the national languages of India and gave the population of Jammu and Kashmir all the rights and privileges which the people of other states of India possessed under the Constitution, and yet made important exceptions in favour of Jammu and Kashmir. Abdullah had been able to take advantage of Article 370 to inaugurate Jammu and Kashmir's own Constituent Assembly in November 1950. However, the difference between Nehru and Patel was significant here. The former was concerned more with gaining the allegiance of the people that with securing territory. But Patel did not share the democratic ideal of rule by consent if it threatened national unity. As Home Minister he inherited the colonial belief that the primary responsibility of the centre is to hold the country together; that demands for autonomy represent centrifugal forces that could tear it apart if encouraged. He was unhappy when shown the draft of Article 370 which would give effect to the pledge to confer special status on Jammu and Kashmir. The differences were too fundamental to be reconciled. Nehru took Jammu and Kashmir away from Patel and created a Ministry of Kashmir Affairs under Gopalaswami Ayyangar. A quarrel over ministerial jurisdiction led to sharp exchange of letters followed by Patel's resignation. This occurred a few days before Gandhi's assassination on January 30, 1948. The leaders resolved to work together over his body, but differences remained.

Pakistan

When the British government in 1892 introduced the principle of election and representative institutions, the Muslims expressed their apprehension of being dominated by a majority with whom they differed in every sphere of life. The Muslim leader of the period, Sir Syed Ahmed, warned the Muslims against the dangers of majority-rule in India contending that 'the larger community would totally over-ride the interests of the smaller community'. This fear of domination by the Hindu governed the Muslim policies and actions; the Muslim minority in undivided India considered itself to be in perpetual danger of domination. The fear led to the formation of a Political Party named Muslim League. The party, since its inception, had championed the Muslim cause and in 1940 when the dawn of independence was near, it formally proclaimed the vision of a separate Muslim state under the leadership of Mohammed Ali Jinnah. The new state, Pakistan, was claimed as a homeland for Indian Muslims on the principle of the right of self-determination. For the Muslims, the cry for Pakistan became a struggle for survival. When the British government decided to grant self-rule to India in 1946, the two communities were engaged in a bitter struggle involving violence and communal riots on a vast scale. In the circumstances it became almost impossible to keep the country united and finally partition of India was accepted by the parties concerned, dividing the subcontinent into two Dominions – India and Pakistan.

As the responsibility of Muslims of the whole of India became the natural duty of Muslim League, Pakistan and Jinnah respectively, they all began to take a lively interest in Kashmir affairs. As a result of the split in the National Conference, in 1941, a section led by Ghulam Abbas formed the new Party, Muslim Conference. Three years later in 1944 Mohammed Ali Jinnah visited the Kashmir and lent his support to the Muslim Conference. By the time the pattern of politics between the Indian National Congress and the Muslim League had begun to affect the political movement in the State. The Muslim Conference drew inspiration from the Muslim League and began to poison the mind of the Kashmiris. And so a section of the people of Kashmir started to look at political, social and economic problems through the distorting lens of religion. The party, fully supported by the Muslim League, was busy in planting seeds of violence and conflict in the State, and in a sense, seeking to destroy the soul of the people. Further in May 1947, the Acting President of the Muslim Conference along with Ram Chandra Kak, the then

Prime Minister of Jammu and Kashmir, even pleaded for the independence of the State and assured the Maharaja of the support and cooperation of the Muslims forming eighty per cent majority in the state as represented by their organisation. Ghulam Ahmad, the Deputy Leader of the Muslim Conference, on May 21, 1947, made an appeal to the Maharaja to declare Kashmir as an independent state.

Unfortunately the State of Jammu and Kashmir failed to take any decision of the accession of State to either of the Dominions before August 15, 1947 and a new chapter in Indo-Pak relations began that cast a dark shadow on the future relations of the two countries. After independence India was in no hurry for an immediate solution of the question. Pakistan was. Accordingly Pakistan put pressure on the State from many sides. The Pakistan Radio and newspapers incited the Muslim population of the State to rise against the Hindu ruler who, they said, was a threat to Muslims and Islam. The appeal was openly religious, directed to the baser elements of human nature, namely those of lust, loot and murder. On September 22, 1947, a Convention of Muslim Conference workers formally asked for the State's accession to Pakistan. The only claim of Pakistan, right since the day of independence, has been that because the majority in the Kashmir Valley are the followers of Islam, they and the region occupies by them must automatically come to Pakistan. This is the well-known 'two nation theory on the basis of which Pakistan was formed. While the National Conference, another Political Party of the State was against the accession of the State to Pakistan. Its leader, Sheikh Abdullah, wanted that the decision of the Maharaja in regard to this question should be independent. According to him, quick decision on the issue would be incorrect and unwise. In the situation of indecisiveness, none of the leaders but Sheikh Abdullah was released on September 29, 1947.

In an effort to create chaos and anarchy the Government of Pakistan refused to abide by the terms contained in the Standstill Agreement, which it had concluded with the State of Jammu and Kashmir. Its non-cooperation resulted in the total failure of the state machinery in the State, raising the temperature of people's mood. On October 18, 1947, the Government of Kashmir, in a communication to the Prime Minister of Pakistan protested against the violation of the Standstill Agreement and hoped that he would personally look into the matter. In response of the request, a well-organised tribal invasion was made which compelled the Maharaja to send an offer of accession and of military help to the Government of India. The latter had accepted the offer and send its armies to the State of Jammu and Kashmir, when it became an integral part of the Indian Union.

The Government of Pakistan contested the validity of the accession and declared it to be "based on fraud and violence[37] and on a "conspiracy".[38] They cited, in this connection, the release of Sheikh Abdullah by the Maharaja as against the continuing imprisonment of the leaders of the Muslim Conference, the landing of the Indian troops in Srinagar on the very day of the acceptance of the State's accession by India, and the visits of the Indian leaders to Kashmir before accession. It felt offended at the accession. Jinnah,, on the very next day on October 28, 1947, ordered his troops to march into Kashmir but as a result of the intervention of Field Marshal Auchinleck, the then Supreme Commander of the Indo-Pakistan Army, that it was soon cancelled. Further Liaquat Ali Khan, the Prime Minister of Pakistan, in a telegram to the British Prime Minister on October 29, 1947, said, 'There is no doubt that the State troops attack Muslims at Poonch. Women and children took refuge in Pakistan, and burning villages could be seen from our border .... later they set out to massacre Muslims of Jammu'. Liaquat revealed that the Dogra brigadier in command of Jammu had admitted that his orders were to drive out Muslims from a belt of territory three miles wide.[39] Pakistan held the view that even without the use of force, Kashmir's accession to India would have been a flagrant denial of the principle determining the division of the subcontinent between the Indian Union and Pakistan.

The validity of the accession of Kashmir to the Union of India was always on the card for Pakistan. It did not, and does not accept as its representative made this plaint to the Security Council in 1948: The Pakistan Government have not accepted and cannot accept the accession of the State of Jammu and Kashmir to India. In their view, the accession was based on violence and fraud. It was fraudulent in as much as it was achieved by deliberately creating a set of circumstances with the object of finding an excuse to stage the accession. It was based on violence because it furthered the plan of the Kashmir Government to liquidate the Muslim population.[40] It questioned the entire process that the two party had adopted and declared that the existence of Standstill Agreement, which had never been repudiated, was a bar to the subsequent accession of the State to India. Further, the acceptance of accession by India was conditional, and there was no provision for conditional acceptance under the Indian Independence Act, 1947. But above all, the most important fact was that the ruler of the state had no authority left to make any decision : his people had disowned him and the Azad Kashmir organisation was by that time exercising control over a large part of the territory of the state. The 'Maharaja's State' had virtually disintegrated ; its ruler had fled, and the forces leading the popular revolt against his tyrannical rule had established themselves successfully in various parts of Kashmir.

Pakistan's design to get the State of Jammu and Kashmir by force, for the first time, frustrated by India. After the occupation of Kashmir by the Indian army, Liaquat Ali Khan, the Prime Minister of Pakistan, in a press statement on November 16, 1947 stated : 'It is quite clear now that what the Indian Government are after its permanent occupation of Kashmir. The Indian Government's whole conduct is based on "might is right" and on the belief that Pakistan is unable to fight them. .... If the Indian Government are allowed to follow their imperialist land-grabbing policy, this will have repercussions not only in Asia but throughout the world'.[41] Apart from this, India's attempt to present the world with a *fait accompli* in Kashmir was regarded in many quarters as a serious breach of the international morality of which Pandit Nehru had always been a foremost advocate, and India's attitude was seen to be governed by a militant nationalism. While Pakistan appealed to moral law and mobilised the principle of self-determination, India buttressed his arguments with 'reasons of state'. They wondered that Nehru, who had championed the cause of the Hindu people of princely states, put his democratic principles in cold storage when sanctioning the use of troops against the Muslim people of the princely state of Kashmir. His claim in the Indian Parliament on March 8, 1949, that he had Gandhi's 'blessing in the steps we took in Kashmir', was protested by Prem Nath Bazaz when he asks, could Mahatma Gandhi, the apostle of non-violence, bless the Indian armies to occupy the state and to defend the Hindu princely state against the obvious desire of the Muslims.[42]

Social

Plebiscite

'Plebiscite'is a method of ascertaining the general desire of the inhabitants of a given territory or area on some specific question. This method was first used in the French Revolution to defend the wholesale annexations of territory made by the conquering French republic. It is distinguished from referendum which is a normal method or procedure of voting applied on a general system to certain clauses of legislation.[43] Regarding inhabitants the State of Jammu and Kashmir, in 1947, was guided under the appropriate Acts and Regulations of the State. The subject is dealt with in Part VI of the Constitution of Jammu and Kashmir. According to a State Act of 31 January 1927 thc hereditary subjects of the State are defined as follows : 'All persons born and residing in the state before the commencement of the reign of Maharaja Gulab Singh Bahadur and also persons who settled therein before the commencement of Samvat 1942, and have since been permanently residing. This definition of a hereditary State subject affects the Muslims more who had suffered as a result of Pakistan aggression and had migrated across the cease-fire line in 1947. Although the Government of Jammu and Kashmir offered land, for example in Jammu, to industrialists to set up factories with a view to creating employment for State subject the rights of hereditary State subjects are, for all practical purposes remained intact. It was only in 1969 that an official bill on permanent settlement of refugees in the Jammu and Kashmir Legislative Assembly sought to confer on Government the right to acquire land after paying compensation in terms of the Land Acquisition Act.[44] The bill fell this time on technical grounds, but was reintroduced and passed on April 5, 1971.

On August 15, 1947, after the British left the subcontinent, 562 princely states became sovereign to make their choice between India and Pakistan or remain independent. All the obligations arising from the treaties and agreements signed hitherto by the princes and the Crown were to come to an end and the States were free from any control or influence after the lapse of paramountcy. This constituted a case of total succession.[45] As the whole subcontinent was divided on the basis of religion, where the ruler of a state and his subjects were of the same religion, no dispute ordinarily arose. It was different where the ruler was Hindu and the population mainly Muslim, or where the ruler was Muslim and the population mainly Hindus. Relations between the two Dominions approached boiling point over the fate of three princely states : Junagardh, Hyderabad and Kashmir.

On the issue of the right of the ruler to choose either of the dominions, the Indian National Congress and the Muslim League had different interpretations. Contrary to the British view, the Congress Party had always claimed paramountcy for the people. The sovereignty of the people was an article of faith with the Congress and it could not deviate from it. Even from the tactical point of view, it was only by upholding the sovereignty of the people that India could justify her action of sending troops to Junagardh and Hyderabad in support of the people. The issue of both these territories had been taken to the Security Council, which, however, did not take up the complaints seriously as the outcome of the decision of the vast majority of the people was never in doubt. If India had accepted the British view then the entire history of India after independence might have been different, with each ruler exercising his individual judgement as to whether he should accede to India or to Pakistan or even remain independent. But taking the initiative out of the hands of the rulers meant that so far as the Indian portion of the subcontinent was concerned, all the States except Kashmir, which had a majority Muslim population, would automatically accede to India, and this is what actually happened.

But the Muslim League supported the British view that paramountcy in a State would revert to the ruler. It, therefore, favoured ruler's prerogative in the matter and contended that

Junagardh's accession to Pakistan was complete as also Hyderabad's declaration of independence. However, all the three cases-Kashmir, Junagardh and Hyderabad, had to be considered together and not in isolation. If India could claim Kashmir purely by virtue of the Maharaja signing the instrument of accession, then she would have to concede Pakistan's claim over Junagardh's for the same reason and also tolerate Hyderabad as an independent State. Both Junagardh and Hyderabad were more vital from India's security and prosperity than Kashmir and it was obvious that the rulers of these two territories were acting contrary to the wishes of the people, the overwhelming majority of whom were Hindus. Ultimately, the State of Hyderabad and Junagardh were acceded to India.

Lord Mountbatten, the then Governor-General of India, visited Kashmir on June 19, 1947, with a view to study the political situation of the State and remained there for four days. During his stay, it is believed, that the unfeasibility of the independence proposition was conveyed by him to the Maharaja and his Prime Minister Ram Chandra Kak. He apparently persuaded the Maharaja to make up his mind for accession with either of the Dominions. He was also quoted as having told the Maharaja that he may accede to Pakistan if he wished in which case the State's Department would not take it as an unfriendly act.[46] He himself revealed in June1948 at a meeting of the East India Association at London that in course of the meeting with the Maharaja, on everyone of these four days, he persisted with the advice, ascertain the wishes of your people by any means and join whichever Dominion your people wish to join by August 14, this year. However, his failure to persuade the Maharaja to join either of the Dominions before the set deadline (August 14, 1947), was not without doubt and only showed an incredible indifference on Mountbatten's part towards a very large and strategically important state. As Professor Nicholas Mansergh has observed, 'There was no state in the subcontinent the future of which, if left undecided when the independent impartial authority withdrew, was more likely to occasion dissent between the two Dominions. The failure to concentrate more closely on the problem it presented was destined to prove an oversight fraught with grave consequences'.[47]

Still, it is not clear what inspired Lord Mountbatten to give such advice as to 'ascertain the wish of the people' to the Maharaja and his Prime Minister. It can in no way be appreciated. It was on his instructions that the same advice was repeated by the British Resident in Kashmir and by Lord Ismay who was holidaying in Srinagar immediately after the transfer of power. Although the Maharaja himself was not in favour of submitting his Hindu Monarchy to Muslim supremacy. But he was confused by the suggestion that he could accede to the new Dominion of Pakistan because of the composition of the population of the State. It is pertinent to note here that the same advice of ascertaining the wish of the people was not given in other princely states, such as Hyderabad and Junagarh, where the issue was much more complicated. Perhaps he was knowing that in the Sate of Jammu and Kashmir it was not an easy task to ascertain the wishes of the people as they were divided between two different political organisations–the National Conference and the Muslim League. It is also notable that as Mountbatten himself had paid a visit to the State and discussed the matter with Maharaja and his Prime Minister, the State Department of India failed to visualise the seriousness of the problem and had not made any approach to the Maharaja at all in the fashion it did in the case of other Indian States. All these facts indicate that the attempts of Lord Mountbatten was a part of larger imperial design which the British hoped while determining the legal framework.[48]

Events took a forward turn and in a very critical situation, on October 26, 1947, the Maharaja sent his offer of accession to the Indian Union which was accepted, the next day. As he had also signed the Instrument of Accession, the Defence Committee at its meeting on October 27, had decided to accept the offer. The Governor-General, while accepting the Instrument of Accession wrote a separate letter to the Maharaja, which *interalia* provided :

In the special circumstances mentioned by Your Highness, My Government have decided to accept the accession of Kashmir State to the Dominion of India. Consistently with their policy that, in the case of any State where the issue of accession has been the subject of dispute, the question of accession should be decided in accordance with the wishes of the people of the State, it is my Government's wish that, as soon as law and order have been restored in Kashmir and her soil cleared of the invader, the question of the States' accession should be settled by a reference to the people.[49]

The Instrument of Accession was signed and accepted in the same manner as was executed in the case of other Indian States, i.e., according to the provisions of Section 6 of the Government of India Act, 1935, as adopted by the Indian Provisional Constitutional order 1947. The contents and the form of the Instrument of Accession was the same as was adopted by the Rulers of fully empowered States.

The British in general and Lord Mountbatten in particular took a lively interest in Kashmir affairs that not only marred Indo-Pak relations but made it a hot cake for world powers. True, Nehru, at the suggestion of India's last viceroy, Lord Mountbatten, agreed that the people of Kashmir should have an opportunity to express their views about the accession. Again it was on the advice of Mountbatten and Clement Atlee, the British Prime Minister, and against his own instincts that Jawaharlal Nehru took the issue to the UN and offered a referendum / Plebiscite in that State. Once the matter reached the UN, the British converted it into a territorial dispute between India and Pakistan. Even Josef Korbel, a member of the United Nations Commission for India and Pakistan found the role of Governor-General as dubious and in 1948 observed, 'Mountbatten's attitude and advice in this case raise critical questions. Why, for example, did he advice that Indian military assistance to the Maharaja must be covered by the legal technicality of accession? .... He must have known that if war over this issue were to develop between these two Dominions it would not be on the basis of the legality of such a method of accession but rather over the fact itself ...... it is most difficult to understand why no one, particularly Mountbatten, advanced the most obvious idea—that of immediately getting into intact with the Karachi Government for consultation.[50]

If a Plebiscite as committed by Mountbatten and agreed by Nehru had been held in Jammu and Kashmir some time in 1949, there was good chance that majority of the people would have voted for India, because the wounds inflicted by the Pakistani raiders on the peaceful people of Kashmir were still fresh in their minds and India was held in much respect as their saviour. The leaders of the Indian National Congress had opposed the tyrannical rule of the Maharaja and had supported the movements launched by the National Conference. They also remembered that it was Pandit Nehru who had courted arrest in support of the people's struggle. Even the assessment of the British at that time was that there was an even chance for India to pull off the plebiscite. Hence, there was every reason at this time to hold that the plebiscite if freely held, would be overwhelmingly in India's favour. But now there is every chance that if given the choice, most Kashmiris would opt for independence and not for India or Pakistan.

Views of India

For India the case of Jammu and Kashmir was just a reverse in comparison to the issue of Junagardh and Hyderabad. It had a Hindu ruler and a majority of the Muslim population whose desire to accede to India could not be taken granted. Even the Maharaja had vacillated for a fairly long time and had signed the Instrument of Accession only after the Pakistani invasion. Therefore, having taken the stand all through that people's sovereignty was paramount, India could not make an exception in case of Jammu and Kashmir and base her claim on the strength of the accession by the ruler. If at that time India did not agree to the plebiscite in Jammu and Kashmir, the Junagardh case could be re-opened and India's position in Hyderabad could also be questioned. Hence, both from the moral as well as from the tactical point of view, India's decision to accept the plebiscite formula was correct. However, India, while accepting the principle of plebiscite, had made three conditions which, in her view, could create conditions favourable to winning the plebiscite.

According to a separate communication to the Ruler of Jammu and Kashmir, the Governor-General of India, on October 27, 1947, made it clear that as soon as law and order have been restored in

Kashmir and its soil cleared of the invaders, the question of the State's accession should be settled by a reference to the people. The suggestions of the Governor-General was accepted by the leaders of India. Further, Jawaharlal Nehru in a speech from All-India Radio on November 2, 1947, confirmed this acceptance by saying, 'We have declared that the fate of Kashmir is ultimately to be decided by the people. The pledge we have given and the Maharaja has supported it, not only to the people of Jammu and Kashmir, but also to the world. We will not and cannot back out of it. We are prepared when peace and law have been established to have a referendum held under international auspices like the United Nations. We want it to be fair and just reference to the people and we shall accept their verdict. I can imagine no fairer and juster offer'. India had committed on its own accord to hold a plebiscite in the State of Jammu and Kashmir in order to decide the future of the State. But this offer was to be ascertained only after the invaders had vacated the State. This condition was imposed so that the people of the state may exercise their right freely and without any fear.

On January 1, 1948, India took the matter to the UN. Its representative P. P. Pillai in a letter addressed to the President of the Security Council stated the situation existed between India and Pakistan. He also referred to the holding of plebiscite in the State and requested the Council to make situations conducive so that a fair and fearless opinion of the people could be ascertained. The Security Council met to discuss the issue on January 15, 1948, and Gopalaswami Ayyangar, the Indian representative, had laid down that the Government of India had accepted the accession on the understanding that the will of the people regarding it could be made clear in a plebiscite or referendum when law and order had been restored. In order to ensure complete impartiality in this regard, it might be held under international auspices.[52] The explanation meant to impress upon the Security Council the urgency of taking action first for the vacation of the territory of the State of Kashmir by the raiders in view of the fact that the plebiscite was not possible unless the occupied territory was vacated. The only point which was to be decided was of plebiscite after the vacation of occupied territory. The Security Council's action was sought only to achieve this end.

In course of the discussion, the Security Council resolved on August 13, 1948. The resolution is in three parts having several paras. Part I mainly dealt with ceasefire agreed upon by both India and Pakistan. But parties agreed to ensure that all forces under their command shall refrain from taking any measures that might augment the military potential of the forces under their control. After the implementation of Part I, they would workout on Part II whose important sections are sub-paras A, B and C. Sub-para 'A' of Para 1 stated that the Government of Pakistan has agreed to withdraw its forces from the State of Jammu and Kashmir. Para (2) states that the Government of Pakistan will use its best endeavour to secure the withdrawal of tribesmen and Pakistani nationals from the State of Jammu and Kashmir. Para (3) states that the territory so vacated, pending a final solution, shall be administered by the local authorities of Jammu and Kashmir. Thus, it is clear from the specific language that unless steps and conditions are carried out and met, further measures as required by the resolution cannot be taken. Part III is the concluding part of the resolution which states, 'The Government of India and the Government of Pakistan reaffirm their wish that the future stature of the State of Jammu and Kashmir shall be determined in accordance with the will of the people and to that end, upon acceptance of the truce agreement, both governments agree to enter into consultations with the commission to determine fair and equitable conditions whereby such free expression will be assured.'[53] The Commission, on its part, had specifically given assurance to India that the plebiscite proposal would not be binding on India if Pakistan does not implement part I and II of the resolution – that is, the total vacation of occupied territories and its restoration to the authority of the Jammu and Kashmir government.

Of the 562 princely states, the State of Jammu and Kashmir was single where Nehru agreed to a plebiscite. The assurance is regarded as a political mistake, not only in India but also by some outside observers. Situations too had changed rapidly. Sheikh Abdullah, once a trusted friend, who by that time was the actual ruler of Kashmir, was deposed and jailed in August 1953. It was justified on the ground that he had shown his favour to an independent Kashmir which, New Delhi feared, might have gone over to Pakistan. Conditions in the subcontinent and in the world have changed and now a plebiscite in Kashmir would become a new test of the two-nations theory which Nehru had vigorously opposed in 1947. He feared that if it favours Pakistan, would lead to renewed turmoil and bloodshed among Muslims and Hindus in both Pakistan and India.[54] However, this view, strongly held by the Prime Minister whose family are of Kashmiri origin and who has an emotional attachment to Kashmir. Further it is disputed by some leading Hindu experts, who say that the assumptions would maltreat Muslims in India because Kashmir is a libel on Hinduism.

The 'Plebiscite' or 'reference of the people' has of course, never been held. Usually three arguments are cited by Indian officialdom for this. The first, that Pakistani forces failed to vacate those parts of Jammu and Kashmir under their control – a pre-condition, under the UN resolutions, for the plebiscite. The second is that the territory's 'lawful' ruler had acceded to India, thereby automatically confirming the validity of such accession, is acceptable, but problematic. It is to be noted here that Nehru's government had committed itself to a plebiscite despite the legality of Hari Singh's accession. It is also unbelievable for a country like India that absolute sovereignty vests in the person of a corrupt and despised autocrate, a stand which sharply contradicts the ethos of the democratic struggle in Kashmir, and presumably, that of the Indian national movement as well. The third and last contention is that Kashmir is 'an integral part of India.' This argument holds that the people of Jammu and Kashmir, acting through their democratically elected representatives, have repeatedly and freely ratified the moral and legal validity of accession to India in free, competitive elections, and that India has in return, honoured its part of the 1947 bargain by conferring on Jammu and Kashmir the privilege of regional autonomy, to an extent not enjoyed by any other constituent unit of the Indian Union, and formally enshrining it in the Indian Constitution.[55]

The Security Council, although recognised the urgency of the situation, passed many resolutions from time to time but never acted upon it. Despite resolutions and recommendations made to India and

Pakistan, the problem remains unsettled as far as Security Council is concerned. The Security Council has failed to find out any workable solution mainly because of the pulls and counter pulls among the two great powers and their associates. When this fact was made known to the people of Jammu and Kashmir, they decided to take the issue out of the court of the Security Council and decide their own future. They were getting impatient and resented the fact that forces in the Security Council, which did not have the interest of the people of the State at heart but were guided only by their own imperialistic interests, were thwarting the attempts of the people to find their own salvation and thus defying their wishes.

In response to the requisition made by the main political organisation of the State, the Supreme Head of the State issued a proclamation convoking a Constituent Assembly consisting of representatives of the people elected on the basis of adult franchise for framing a constitution for the State of Jammu and Kashmir. In 1956, Kashmir's Constituent Assembly, under the Muslim Prime Minister Baksi Ghulam Mohammed, voted to make Kashmir a state of the Indian Union, thereby officially confirming the existing situation. This vote is regarded by many Indians as a consultation of the will of people, tantamount to the plebiscite. Earlier, when Security Council heard the proposal to call a Constituent Assembly it feared that it was going to be bypassed. The imperialists found that their game was up and they hastily introduced a draft resolution in the Council disapproving the idea of a Constituent Assembly. Council's move was vehemently opposed by Sheikh Abdullah, who issued long statement asserting the right of the people of the State to decide their future through the instrument of the Constituent Assembly. Actually, India was embarrassed, but the people of Kashmir were determined to end their state of continued uncertainty and to find their own salvation.

The question of plebiscite in the State of Jammu and Kashmir as committed by Indian leaders and as provided in the Security Council's resolution of August 13, 1948 and January 5, 1949, does not arise at the present stage. It has now become time-barred, outdated, impractical, absolete and bear only historical importance.

However, apart from the 'irrelevance and inappropriateness of the plebiscite demand and the doubtful political viability of an independent Jammu and Kashmir, the urge for self rule in Kashmir's popular consciousness is remarkable. The idea of self-determination is the transformed version of the notion of plebiscite. Despite the coercive and manipulative of both the Indian and Pakistani authorities, mass opinion in the valley is not only confused but by and large unambiguous and unequivocal in the belief that only independent statehood would constitute genuine emancipation.[56] But the Government of India ruled out any possibility of holding plebiscite. A Foreign Ministry release in January 1994 states, 'The question or need for ..... plebiscite in any part of India, including Jammu and Kashmir, simply does not arise. The people of Jammu and Kashmir have exercised their democratic rights repeatedly as people in other parts of India. Thus it is not feasible in the present day circumstances due to India's implacable opposition to any notion of plebiscite, and Pakistan's manifest lack of interest in the idea except for propaganda purposes.

Pakistan

The decision of the Maharaja in 1947 that the state should accede to India has never been accepted by Pakistan, for whom the overwhelming preponderance of Muslims in the valley dictated that the state should become part of Pakistan. It took the stand that the predominantly Muslim population of Kashmir was not consulted in Maharaja's decision and that because the majority in the Kashmir valley are the followers of Islam, they and the region occupied by them must automatically come to Pakistan. The Government of Pakistan did not, and does not, accept the validity of the accession of Kashmir to the Union of India and its representative made this plaint to the Security Council in 1948 :

The Pakistan Government have not accepted and cannot accept the accession of the State of Jammu and Kashmir to India. In their view, the accession was based on violence and fraud. It was fraudulent in as much as it was achieved by deliberately creating a set of circumstances with the object of finding an excuse to stage the accession. It was based on violence because it furthered the plan of the Kashmir Government to liquidate the Muslim population.[57]

Right since the beginning Pakistan called it a 'dispute' and had repeatedly asserted that there could be no peace in the Indian subcontinent until the Kashmir problem was resolved. While India is of the view that the Instrument of Accession was just like a treaty concluded between two states. After the cessation of British authority over princely states, the decision of the King or Prince, as the head of the state, was final. Both signatories were competent to sign the Instrument. All the principles of International law applicable to treaties were to apply to the Instrument of Accession and even no ratification was required.

India took the issue to the Security Council under Article 35 of the UN Charter, who after discussion passed the resolution, through the Security Council on August 13, 1948, and whose part III called upon India and Pakistan to reaffirm their wish that the future status of the State of Jammu and Kashmir would be determined in accordance with the will of the people. It also provided that the Pakistani forces should be withdrawn first from the state. It clearly meant that the entry of Pakistani forces in the state was illegal. Indian forces were to be withdrawn subsequently after the commission had notified that the withdrawal of the Pakistani forces had begun. Hence, in terms of the UN resolution, Pakistan has no right to even talk about Kashmir till it first vacates the Pak-occupied Kashmir (PoK) and hand it over to India, who is its rightful owner.

From the deliberations at the UN and charges and counter-charges levelled by representatives of India and Pakistan it became clear that the two states basically different from each other in relation to the issue of Plebiscite in Jammu and Kashmir. A series of mediators were appointed one after the other during 1949-1951. The thrust of the proposals of all mediators was the demilitarisation of the state, to be followed by a plebiscite. In an effort to settle the problem of Kashmir the Prime Ministers of India and Pakistan met in New Delhi, in August 1953 and the communiqué issued on the occasion stressed : (i) it was their firm opinion that this dispute would be settled in accordance with the wishes of Kashmir........

the most feasible method of ascertaining the wishes of the people was by a fair and impartial plebiscite; (ii) the plebiscite administrator should be appointed by the end of April 1954; (iii) previous to that, the preliminary issues that had held up progress towards a plebiscite so far should be decided and actions in implementation thereof be taken, and with this object in view committees of military and other experts should be appointed to advise the Prime Ministers; (iv) Progress 'can only be made in this direction if there is an atmosphere of peace and cooperation between the two countries.[58] The meeting was followed by exchange of letters between the Prime Ministers and revealed ultimately a failure to reach an agreement even on most of the preliminary issues.

After an interval of five years, the issue was brought back to the Security Council in 1957. By that time the regional power balance had been changed due to US military aid to Pakistan and its joining of Western military alliance. Although Mohammad Ali, the then Prime Minister of Pakistan, gave an explanation and said in Parliament in 1954 : 'it is extraordinary that Pakistan should decide to accept military aid from the USA in order to strengthen her defences should be regarded by the Indian Prime Minister as a ground for postponing or abandoning the efforts for an amicable settlement of the Kashmir dispute.[59] On the otherhand, in order to make India her friend and punish Pakistan for joining the Western Bloc, the Soviet Union came out with support for India on Kashmir. In course of discussions to the Security Council Pakistan complained of India's annexing Kashmir with the help of the so-called' constituent assembly. Like earlier resolutions, it again reaffirmed that final disposition of the State of Jammu and Kashmir should be made in accordance with the will of the people, expressed through the democratic method of a free and impartial plebiscite conducted under the auspices of the United Nations. The resolution also urged the parties to maintain for the time being the *Status quo* of the state. Super power involvement in respect to Kashmir had cast a dark and ominous shadow of the East-West cold war over the dispute between the two Commonwealth countries of the subcontinent. It receded any further hope of peaceful solution of the dispute through the United Nations. In 1957, through a fresh resolution, Gunnar

Jarring, the then President of the Security Council, was requested to consider any proposal likely to lead to a settlement and for that purpose to visit the subcontinent. Even he, in his report of April 30, 1957, did not fail to take note of the changing political, economic and strategic factors surrounding the whole of the Kashmir question, together with the changing pattern of power relations in West and South Asia. He also expressed his awareness of "the grave problems that might arise in connection with and as a result of a plebiscite."[60]

On the part of Pakistan, its demand for plebiscite in Kashmir was hypocritical. She demands the right of plebiscite for the people of Kashmir, she denies the same right to Sind and Baluchistan. At best, issues settled in terms of the Indian Independence Act cannot be reopened at random. And if one issue is opened, many more will open up. In 1947, the North-West Frontier Province was not given the choice of independence. Many Pathans boycotted the plebiscite because they had no choice. Their province, not being contiguous to India, could not possibly accede to India. Likewise, the fate of Sindh was sealed by a divided anti-League vote. The Province was 70 per cent Muslim and 30 per cent Hindu. In the general elections held in early 1946, 30 per cent Hindus voted for the Congress; 30 per cent Muslims voted for the parties of nationalist Muslim leaders G. M. Syed and Maula Bux; and 40 per cent Muslims voted for the Muslim League. In any plebiscite Sindh would have opted for India. Baluchistan's future was decided by just the municipal committee of quetta.[61] Even today, there are independence movements in the two states which are being described as (PoS) Pakistan-occupied Sindh and (PoB) Pakistan-occupied Baluchistan.

After the failure of mediation through the UN and direct negotiations between the Prime Ministers of India and Pakistan, the latter had started all forms of infiltration, propaganda, subversion, sabotage, outrages and murder. By raising the false bogey of India's alleged oppression of the Muslims of Kashmir it continued to denigrate India before the Muslim world and foster a spirit of hatred against India among her own people. Undoubtedly the state of Pakistan is based on religion and the religious appeal which it continues to make to the Muslims of Kashmir has an important bearing on the issue, for it is an incitement to bigotry and intolerance which can only breed violence and disruption. Since 1947 it has described its aggression in Kashmir as jehad or holy war. Now, of course, it has been joined by China who supports the Plebiscite or the right of self-determination for Kashmir. Pakistan is not likely to vacate the occupied portion of Kashmir. It had concluded a treaty with China which provided for the demarcation of the border of the northern area of Kashmir, giving to China a part of the territory of the State of Jammu and Kashmir. Under an agreement an area of about 5,180,59 sq. km. has been ceded by Pakistan to China.[62]

It appears that the idea of self-determination is a transformed version of the original notion of Plebiscite. From the very beginning the Security Council's approach to the problem was neither realistic nor suitable to the context of the problem. The Council overemphasized the Plebiscite issue and avoided to consider, in all its attempts, the legal aspect of the issue, viz., the accession of the State of India. The result was that it could not find out the aggressor, and avoided looking into question of the respective claims of the parties. Mainly on account of Council's incompetence Aziz Ahmad, the representative of Pakistan, made a statement on September 28, 1976, before the General Assembly and urged that the dispute could be taken up at an appropriate time and 'resolved in accordance with the right of self-determination of the people of Kashmir as recognised by the Security Council resolutions of August 13, 1948 and January 5, 1949. A similar statement was made again in 1978 before the General Assembly by Agha Shahi, the representative of Pakistan.[63] However, in the case of Kashmir, the question of self-determination as raised by the representative of Pakistan, is a misnomer. In it, the question involved was not that of the right of self-determination of the people of Kashmir, but whether the people should be given the right to ratify the Maharaja's accession or to opt out to join Pakistan. In the matter of the right of self-determination as adopted in the U.N. Charter, it applies only to colonial peoples, i.e., the people of trust and non-self governing territories.[64] Thus the Security Council in the resolutions of August 13, 1948 and of January 5, 1949, did not at all recognise the right of self-determination of the people of Kashmir as invoked by Pakistan.

These all having failed, Pakistan had put another plan into operation from 1989 in the name of Kashmiris right to self-determination. It has now continued till date and involves extensive training and financing of exfiltrated Kashmiri youth, Jehadi militants from PoK, Pakistan and other countries, masterminded by organisations based in PoK and Pakistan and culminating in a series of jehadi and Fidayeen attacks. Tens of thousands of Indian citizens in the state as well as security personnel have perished as a result of militant activities and anti-insurgency operations.[65] Because of the Pakistan factor, the insurgency in Kashmir has always had to be handled with greater firmness than those elsewhere. Having permitted conditions within Kashmir to deteriorate to the level that they had reached, the Indian state had little option but to fight hard to break the insurgency within Jammu and Kashmir and the external support it was receiving from Pakistan. As a result, grievous damage was done not only to the volitional connection of the State with the rest of the country, but also the concept of Kashmiriyat that linked the 36 per cent non-Muslims of the State with the 64 per cent Muslims in the valley and elsewhere.[66] Far from helping Kashmiri Muslims in the name of Islam, Pakistan has brought them nothing but death and destruction, shattering the social order, disrupting the tourism upon which they largely depend and resulting in a human tragedy of massive proportions.

The People of Jammu and Kashmir

Several developments of immense importance took place in October 1947, and in a very difficult situation created by Pakistan, the Maharaja of the state decided to accede to the Union of India. Lord Mountbatten, the then Governor-General of India, at the time of acceptance of the Instrument of Accession wrote a separate letter to the Maharaja which provided that in consistent with the Policy of the Government of India where the question of accession has been subject of dispute : it should be decided in accordance with the wishes of the people of the state. As soon as law and order have been restored in Kashmir and her soil cleared of the invaders, the question of state's accession should be settled by a reference to the people. Accordingly, Jawaharlal Nehru, the then Prime Minister of India, in his historic declaration at Lal Chowk in Srinagar in

October, 1947, said that after the raiders had been thrown out and peace had been re-established, the people of Jammu and Kashmir would be given an opportunity to decide their future.

From India's point of view, the promise has been kept and Kashmir has decided its future through the Constituent Assembly and through general elections. In response to a requisition by the main political organisation of the State, the Supreme Head of the State issued a proclamation convoking a Constituent Assembly consisting of representatives of the people elected on the basis of adult franchise for framing a constitution for the State of Jammu and Kashmir. The people of the State had elected a sovereign Constituent Assembly which met for the first time on October 31, 1951. Sheikh Abdullah, the President of the National Conference and at that time the undisputed leader of the Kashmiri Muslims, on several occasions said that the accession of the State of Jammu and Kashmir was final and irrevokable. He stated before the Constituent Assembly of Jammu and Kashmir on August 11, 1952 : "It was also made clear that the accession of Jammu and Kashmir state with India was complete in fact and in law to the extent of subjects enumerated in this Instrument."[67] Earlier in October 1948 a Special Convention of the National Conference was held and it, in a resolution passed, expressed fullest support to a final accession to India and hoped that the Indian Government and the people of India would lend the people of Kashmir all material, moral and political support in completing this task and in achieving our goal of economic and political freedom. The whole world would acknowledge that in 1948 the National Conference with its united leadership under Sheikh Abdullah represented 95 per cent of the Muslim population of the Kashmir Valley. Through this Special Convention, the vast majority of the people of the valley had unreservedly decided in favour of a permanent accession of Kashmir to India. This unanimous decision of the Convention was enough and could be regarded as the fulfilment of the pledge that Nehru, on behalf of India, had given earlier.

However, as to the issue of plebiscite and its substitutes, Abdullah himself was not clear and did not know whether to follow suit or not. Sometimes Plebiscite is "only a method". There could be alternatives, for example, "free elections on this issue." Another was to get a vote from the State Assembly "provided elections to it are absolutely free". Later in a public meeting he explained that he did not mean that elections could be a substitute for a plebiscite. He added that until a plebiscite was held, there should be a people's representative government for which a fair and free election should be held.[68] As a result of the political developments, Sheikh Abdullah was arrested in August 1953 and it was found that contacts had been established by his supporters with Pakistani agents. An underground organisation named War Council had been formed shortly after Sheikh's arrest. Further Mirza Afzal Beg, a close associate of Abdullah cleverly changed the name of the War Council to Plebiscite Front. Thus, the Plebiscite Front was born on August 9, 1955. Its ostensible object was to secure for the people of Kashmir the right to an impartial plebiscite which had been promised to them by India and also the Security Council ; but the Front was only a camouflage; and henceforward the work was carried on both openly and underground in the name of the Plebiscite Front and the War Council respectively. Thereafter, Pakistan started financial aid to the Plebiscite Front.

After all, it was for the people to decide whether they wanted to have a formal plebiscite to decide their future or they considered that they had already properly exercised their option and no further ascertaining was necessary. The general people of Kashmir felt the delaying tactics of the Security Council in finding an equitable solution of the Kashmir problem in accordance with the wishes of the people of the state. The United Nations Organisation had repeatedly failed in its attempts to arrive at a peaceful settlement of the Kashmir problem. Under the pretext of referring the question of the State's future disposition to the will of the people, the Security Council tried novel and as to unending methods which were not connected even remotely with the basic issue of accession.[69] They also resented the fact that forces in the Security Council, which did not have the interest of the people of the state at heart but were guided only by their own imperialistic interests, were thwarting the attempts of the people to find their own salvation and thus denying their wishes.

Actually India was embarrassed, but the people of Kashmir were determined to end their state of continued uncertainty and decision was taken unilaterally to settle their future through a democratically elected Constituent Assembly. However, the pro-Abdullah forces had kept the issue alive with the help of Pakistan and other subversive elements, although in the name of Kashmiris right to self-determination. The idea of self-determination is the transformed version of the notion of plebiscite.

Legal Bases

With the termination of the British rule in India on 15 August 1947, the princely states had the choice to join either the Dominion of India or Pakistan. A large majority of them acceded to either India or Pakistan without creating any big problem for the two states. The day on which suzerainty of His Majesty over the Indian states lapsed, all treaties and agreements betweem the Crown through treaty, grant, usage, sufference or otherwise came to an end. The state became independent and sovereign in the full sense of International Law. The Maharaja became the uncontrolled and absolute sovereign in all spheres from that date. After enactment of the Indian Independence Act, Lord Mountbatten, the then Governor-General of India, in a press communiqué of July 25, 1947, stated that the Act had released the states from all their obligations of the Crown. The States have complete freedom-technically and legally they are independent.[70] Even the Supreme Court of India in Prem Nath vs. State of Jammu and Kashmir confirmed the view and described the position of Maharaja of Jammu and Kashmir as follows, "... Maharaja Hari Singh continued to be an absolute monarch of the State and in the eyes of International Law, he might conceivably have claimed the status of a sovereign and independent state."[71] Some writers have relied on the Report of the Indian States Committee and held the view that the State of Jammu and Kashmir did not have any international status after the lapse of paramountcy. Although the said report had very correctly asserted that the 'Indian States have no international life', but it should be kept in mind that the Report was prepared during the time the Crown was the Paramount Power. The Report did not say anywhere that the state shall have no international status even after the lapse of Paramountcy. Thus, when the paramountcy lapsed, the States which did not sign the Instrument of Accession were independent and sovereign.

To determine the international status of a state, particularly the State of Jammu and Kashmir, two aspects should be carefully examined, First, provisions of the Indian Independence Act, and secondly, whether the State, after the lapse of paramountcy, possessed all the attributes which are essential in order to call it a state under International Law. As to the first the Rulers had been given an absolute discretionary power regarding the accession of their states to either of the new Dominions. Section 2 para 4 of the Act clearly provided 'that they were not prevented from doing so.' The British Prime Minister also made a similar statement on July 10, 1947, in the House of Commons. He said that with the ending of treaties and agreements, the states regain their independence.[72] Because Maharaja of Jammu and Kashmir did not accede to any of the Dominions by August 15, 1947, the day on which the paramountcy lapsed, the state became independent and sovereign in the full sense of International Law. An entity in order to be called a State must have a permanent population, a defined territory, a Government and a capacity to enter into relations with other states. The State of Jammu and Kashmir had this capacity on equal footing after the lapse of paramountcy. Its Ruler had concluded a Standstill Agreement with Pakistan and offered similar agreement to the Government of India. These attributes clearly show that the State of Jammu and Kashmir, like other states of the international community possessed all the essential attributes of a sovereign state.

Events moved fastly on account of Jammu and Kashmir not joining either of the Dominions. Keeping in view the geographical and strategic importance both India and Pakistan were vitally interested in the decision that the state would take. It announced its decision to negotiate Standstill Agreements with both India and Pakistan and three days later signed an agreement with the latter.

When Pakistan failed to comply with treaty obligations, a panic-like situation prevailed in the State of Jammu and Kashmir. Between August and October, a major local revolt was conspired against the Maharaja's authority among the Muslims of the North-Western Poonch area of Jammu and as claimed by Hari Singh, Pakistani government was actively aiding this revolt. The climax of the growing crisis came in the fourth week of October when a large number of tribesmen from the North-West Frontier Province and Pakistani nationals invaded Kashmir valley to which Maharaja's forces proved no match for them. In this context of confusion and chaos when whole of the Kashmir was in turmoil, Maharaja acceded to India on 26 October and thereupon requested the Government of India for military aid to defend the State. The Indian troops rushed quickly. After a fierce battle the invaders were pushed out of the valley. The war between the two terminated on 1 January 1949 as a follow up of a proposal of the UN Commission. The ceasefire left India in control of almost two-thirds of Jammu and Kashmir, including almost the entire valley. In course of fighting Pakistan occupied a part of the State of Jammu and Kashmir. These parts comprised two-fifth of the state, possessed and administered by Islamabad under the name of 'Azad Kashmir'. This possession by Pakistan may be regarded as belligerent's occupation of enemy's territory in International Law. The occupied areas of Kashmir were simply placed under the authority of the army of Pakistan eversince the cessation of hostilities. Consequently, Pakistan is not entitled to treat the occupied part as its own territory nor its inhabitants as its own subjects. The State of Jammu and Kashmir, including those parts which are occupied by Pakistan, is legally, an integral part of India.

The Instrument of accession, signed by the parties concerned, under para 3 laid down that the Diminion on legislature may make laws for the State only in those matters which are specified in the Schedule appended to the Instrument. The Schedule mentioned Defence, External Affairs and Communications as the law-making subjects. It read with Section 6 of the Government of India Act would leave the residuary sovereignty of the state entirely unaffected. The Maharaja of the State, even after the execution of the Instrument of Accession enjoyed all the rights and powers, as a Head of the State, in all the spheres subject to reservations contained in the Instrument of Accession. However, the liberality of the Government of India has been misunderstood and misinterpreted in interested quarters, we cannot overlook the legal implications of the Accession of the State of India. The first thing to be noted in this regard is that the Instrument of Accession signed by Maharaja Hari Singh on the 26th October, 1947, was in the same form as was executed by the Rulers of the numberous other states which had acceded to India following the enactment of the Indian Independence Act, 1947. The legal consequences of the execution of the Instrument of Accession by the Ruler of Jammu and Kashmir cannot, accordingly, be in any way different from those arising from the same fact in the case of the other Indian states. The legal basis as well as the form of Accession were same in the case of those states which acceded to Pakistan and those which acceded to India. There is, therefore, no doubt that by the Act of Accession of the State of Jammu and Kashmir became legally and irrevocably a part of the territory of India and that the Government of India was entitled to exercise jurisdiction over the State with respect to those matters to which the Instrument of Accession extended. Despite this sound legal position, the Government of India had given an assurance to the effect that the constitutional relationship between India and the State would be subject to confirmation by the people of the State. So far as the issue of Plebiscite in the State is concerned, it is a separate communication to the Ruler on October 27, 1947, and does form a part of the Instrument of Accession. It contained merely an expression of wish and did not create any binding obligation upon India. International Law does not require that a treaty concluded by the Head of the State or the Ruler thereof would be subject to any reference to the will of the people (Plebiscite). It also does not require that the parties to an agreement should look to whether the agreement has been arrived at by prior consultation with the people. The Instrument being a treaty cannot be abrogated by the State or its Constituent Assembly unilaterally.

References

1. As quoted in M. J. Akbar, India, The Siege Within : Challenges to a Nation's Unity, Penguin, 1985, pp. 221-22.
2. Premnath Bazaz, Inside Kashmir, Mirpur, 1987 (Orig. edn. 1941), pp. 252-53.
3. Jawaharlal Nehru, Discovery of India, London, 1960, p. 387.
4. Alastair Lamb, Crisis in Kashmir, 1947 to 1966, London, 1966, p. 31.
5. B. L. Sharma, Kashmir Awakes, Delhi, 1971, pp. 69-70.
6. Congress Working Committee's Resolution on Kashmir on 25 September 1946.
7. Cf. Mohammed Ayoob, 'The Indian Ocean Littoral : Intra-Regional Conflicts and Weapons Proliferation, in R.J.O' Neill (ed.), The Spread of Weapons in the Indian and Pacific Oceans, Canberra, 1978, p. 188.
8. Ian Stephens, Pakistan, p. 234.
9. For the full text of the Act, See Select Documents on Asian Affairs, India 1947-50, Vol. 1, Internal Affairs, S. C. Poplai (ed.), Oxford, p. 24.
10. Vera Micheles Dean, New Patterns of Democracy in India, Delhi, 1961, pp. 191-92.
11. V. P. Menon, The Story of the Integration of the Indian States, p. 376.
12. Alan Campbell-Johnson, Mission with Mountbatten, London, 1952, p. 120.
13. Sisir Gupta, Kashmir : A Study in India-Pakistan Relations, New Delhi, 1966, p. 95.
14. For detail See, *Ibid.,* p. 265.
15. Constituent Assembly of India (Legislative) Debates, Vol. 1, No. 7, 25 November 1947, Col. 593.
16. William, Jennings Bhyan, The Old World and Its Ways, 1907, p. 308.
17. Constituent Assembly of India, (Legislative), *op. cit.,* Col. 593.
18. B. L. Sharma, *op. cit.,* p. 103.
19. *Ibid.,* pp. 102-4.

20. Balraj Puri, "A question of Semantics : Freedom Vs. Independence in Kashmir" The Times of India, 25 November 2002.
21. Vasant Sathe, "The Pride of Kashmiriyat," The Hindustan Times, 31 January 2002.
22. The Times, 25 October, 1947.
23. G. W. Choudhury, Pakistan's Relations with India, Meerut, 1971, pp. 64-65.
24. B. N. Mullik, Kashmir : My Years with Nehru, Bombay, 1971, p. 8.
25. The Hindu, 28 October 1947.
26. Balraj Puri, "Many Faces, One Image," The Hindustan Times 20 September 2001.
27. B. N. Mullik, *op. cit.,* p. 195.
28. Premnath Bazaz, Democracy Through Intimidation and Terror, New Delhi, 1978, pp. 16-17.
29. Bipin Chandra, "Tryst with Tyranny," The Hindustan Times, 22 December 1999.
30. Prem Nath Bazaz, *op. cit.,* p. 2.
31. For the text of the speech See, White Paper on Indian States', Published by the Government of India, Ministry of States, 1950, p. 157.
32. For the Form of Instrument of Accession, See, *Ibid.,* p. 169.
33. Ajit Bhattacharjea, 'Kashmir : The Actors Change, But the Show Must Go On", The Hindustan Times, 3 July 2000.
34. M. C. Setalvad, Patel Memorial Lectures on Secularism, 1966.
35. G. W. Choudhury, *op. cit.,* pp. 62-63.
36. B. N. Mullik, *op. cit.,* p. 197.
37. Alan Campbell-Johnson, *op. cit.,* p. 277.
38. Michael Brecher, The Struggle for Kashmir, Newyork, 1953, p. 33.
39. Security Council Official Record, Nos.1-15, 1948 (meetings 228-29).
40. *Ibid.,* No. 646 of January 15, 1948.
41. The Dawn, 17 November 1947.

42. Premnath Bazaz, The History of Struggle for Freedom in Kashmir, New Delhi, 1954, p. 343.
43. Edwin R. A. Seligman, ed., Encyclopaedia of the Social Sciences, Vol. II, Newyork, 1954, pp. 163-66.
44. The Times of India, 6 April, 1969.
45. H. O. Agarwal, State, Succession and the Indian States, Vol. 5, 1977, p. 156.
46. V. P. Menon, *op. cit.,* p. 376.
47. Quoted in G. W. Choudhury, *op. cit.,* p. 62.
48. J. N. Dixit, "Three is a Crowd, Always", The Hindustan Times, 23 December 2001.
49. For the text of the letter See S. C. Poplai (ed.), Select Documents on Asian Affairs, India-1947-50, Vol. I, Internal Affairs, Oxford University Press, pp. 373-74.
50. Josef Korbel, Danger in Kashmir, Princeton, 1954, pp 79-80.
51. B. N. Mullik, *op. cit.,* p. 5.
52. SCOR., 3rd Year, No. 1-15, p. 10.
53. Vasant Sathe, 'Unwrapping Kashmir," The Hindustan Times, 7 July 2001.
54. Vera Micheles Dean, *op. cit.,* pp. 193-94.
55. Sumantra Bose, The Challenge in Kashmir-Democracy, Self-Determination and a Just Peace, New Delhi, 1997, p. 28.
56. Newberg, Paula, R., Double Betrayal : Repression and Insurgency in Kashmir, Washington D. C., 1995, pp. 72-74.
57. Security Council Document 646 of January 15, 1948.
58. See, The Negotiations Between the Prime Ministers of India and Pakistan Regarding the Kashmir Dispute (June 1953-September 1954), Karachi.
59. The Dawn, 20 April, 1954.
60. Vera Micheles Dean, *op. cit.,* pp. 195-96.
61. K. R. Malkani, "Agra's Bitter Aftertaste, "The Hindustan Times 18 August 2001.
62. H. O. Agarwal, *op. cit.,* p. 150.
63. The Times of India, 21 October, 197 8.

64. Prakash S. Sinha, Has Self-Determination Become a Principle of International Law Today ? International Journal of International Law, Vol. 14 (1974), p. 347.
65. Karan Singh, "A Catastrophe Averted," The Hindustan Times, 6 July 2002.
66. Verghese Koithara, *op. cit.,* pp. 113-14.
67. M. C. Chagla, Kashmir, 1947-1965, p. 48.
68. The National Herald, 15 April 1968.
69. B. N. Mullik, *op. cit.,* pp. 184-85.
70. For the text of the Speech See 'White Paper on Indian States,' (1950), p. 160.
71. All India Radio (1959), Supreme Court, p. 749.
72. House of Commons, Official Report, 439, H. C. Debate, C. 2451.
73. For detail See Sections 5-6 of the Government of India Act, 1935, read with section 7(1) (b) of the Indian Independence Act, 1947.

4

Diplomatic Deadlocks on Kashmir

Complexities of the Problem

India and Pakistan have been in a state of war over Kashmir ever since 1947. India is fighting for Kashmir as proof of its adherence to the secular way of life. Kashmir should be with India as it proves that a Muslim majority area can be part of a predominantly Hindu secular state. This is the great value of Kashmir being a part of India, the country with the second largest Muslim population in the world. Pakistan wants Kashmir because it is a Muslim majority area and thinks that it belongs to it by right. Islam, whether as a separatist force that had not aligned itself with the mainstream anti-colonial movement or as a movement that sought to create a national state for its people, has always been at the root of the conflict between India and Pakistan. The matter is more evident in Kashmir because Kashmir, unlike the rest of undivided India did not follow the logic of partition based on religion. The first Indo-Pak war of 1947-48 ended in a ceasefire with Kashmir being divided between the two countries. Pakistan has always looked at this situation as an unfinished task that would be complete only after Kashmir becomes an integral part of Pakistan. But the Government of India has, no doubt, a good legal reason of the view : The Ruler of Jammu and Kashmir had unconditionally acceded to the Indian Union; the accession was accepted by a freely-elected Constituent Assembly of the State of Jammu and Kashmir in 1951; and was reaffirmed in the State's Constitution in 1956. Thus, the whole of Jammu and Kashmir becomes an integral part of the Indian Union. Kashmir is vital to us from many points of view. Kashmir is also vital to Pakistan and so there is an inherent conflict in the situation.

Solution of the Kashmir problem is important not because it is a Muslim majority area but because it has the key to normalisation of relations between India and Pakistan. At New Delhi and Islamabad the presence of a deeply ingrained conflict mentality, not to say a culture of mistrust, seemed to have made any initiative towards cooperation and accommodation unacceptable to domestic public opinion in both the countries. There was hardly a country which did not carry its ghost about with it and, for India, it was the ghost of Pakistan. Behind that ghost lay the history not only of the recent past but also of the many years preceding freedom. Relations with Pakistan appeared to be a continuation of the old communal conflicts, and there could be no real solution till that basic conflict in the minds of the people in Pakistan and India was resolved. Jawaharlal Nehru, the then Prime Minister of India, in his letter to Chief Ministers, on 1 November 1957, did not claim that India was free from this communal temper, but it did not dominate everything else as in Pakistan. No Government in that country had any policy except of fear and hatred of India and, till that ceased, the future was dark [1] He, however, accepted his failure to win the goodwill of the Government of Pakistan.

As the subcontinent was partitioned on the basis of religion and in the background of communal riots, it became the single determinants that govern Pakistani action. For India this jingoism did not last long. In those days when Kashmir became part of India emotions were high, and quite legitimately so. India was still a very young nation-state and threats from neighbouring Pakistan loomed large in the post-partition national psyche. The nation-state is popular endorsement of territory. This implies that in all authentic nation-states territory is sacralised. Territorial acquisition are not just a matter of geography, there is a profound sense of cultural attachment to them. It is quite useless to look for rational reasons behind this sentiment.[2] However, jingoism differs from patriotism and the latter goes a step further. Patriotism is also concerned with people who live on the soil, and puts people on a par with the soil, Jingoists are never happy with it. Jingoism is dismissive of people and of cultural diversities. It is solely besotted by considerations of territory. A patriot is also devoted to the soil but realises that the best way of firming up national boundaries is by paying attention to the people who live within it.[3] In both instances territory is critically important.

It was this cultural attachment of the people of India that looked to Kashmir as its integral part. The territorial bond that unites and vivifies the Indian nation-state is not just a subcontinental characteristic. In the relative placid environment of Canada too there is an equal feeling regarding territory. It was seen when a section of English Canadians started considering the possibility of letting Quebec go it met with an interesting response. Unfortunately we have become to use thinking of every problem or most of the problems in terms of communalism, of Hindu versus Muslim or Hindu and Sikh versus Muslim and so on. That has been unfortunate legacy of ours, and the extent to which it took us cannot be forgotten by us nor the tragedies that it has led to. Even at this juncture, the case of Kashmir stands apart, because Kashmir is not a case of communal conflict. It may be a case of political conflict or a case of any other conflict, but it is essentially not a case of communal conflict.[4] We have cast eyes on Kashmir not for any gain but because of old bounds, because of old sentiments and new sentiments also. Kashmir is very close to our minds and hearts and if by some decree or adverse fortune Kashmir ceases to be a part of India, it would be a wrench and a pain and torment for us.[5]

In this connection it is worth assessing that whether Kashmir is a symptom or a disease. The two would have found some other reason to stay distant because they have not yet overcome the religious differences, which led to the partition of the subcontinent. After the constitution of Pakistan on the basis of the two-nation theory, the rulers or political parties have been at pains to run down secularism in India. It is a secular state, as is clearly and unambiguously stated in its constitution, in contrast to the theocratic states of Pakistan, Bangladesh and Sri Lanka and unlike all its unitary neighbours India has inherited a quasi-federal state structure. Pakistan has been insisting on describing India as a Hindu country. On being influenced from the approach there have been serious suggestions from Pakistan to divide the state on the basis of Hindu and Muslim, the formula used at the time of partition. Such proposal have never been taken into consideration as it would harm the Indian polity as well as the Muslim population in the country. The two countries, if arrayed as Muslim Pakistan and Hindu India can hardly find a solution to the problem of Jammu and Kashmir, which demands a secular approach, transcending religion.[6] The ground has to be prepared from where the nettle of communalism must be uprooted.

Accession of the state of Jammu and Kashmir to the Union of India was followed by an invasion on the part of Pakistan and a fighting had taken place on a large front along almost the entire border of the Kashmir State and Pakistan. In the post-accession phase the state of Jammu and Kashmir became an integral part of Indian Dominion territory which had thrust upon the latter a constitutional duty to defend the state with the active support of Kashmiri army and the public as well. There arose an urgency about these matters, for the first step that must be taken was to put a stop to the fighting and this could only be done if the invaders returned across the border in Pakistan. Since Pakistan was unwilling to cooperate with India in this matter, the alternatives left with India was to send its Armed Forces across Pakistan territory to deal effectively with the invaders, or to request the United Nations to ask Pakistan to do so. Any resort to the first course would have involved armed conflict with Pakistan.

New Delhi, in an effort to avoid a full-fledged war with Islamabad and to try every available method to find a peaceful solution, made a reference to the Security Council on January 1, 1948. Our making a reference on this issue to the Security Council of the United Nations was an act of faith, because we believe in the progressive realisation of world order and a world government.[7] In regard to Kashmir, Nehru was pained because it had got entangled in external politics, in the relations between India and Pakistan. He added that it got entangled was not odd, but the manner of its entanglement was odd. The problem became all the more complicated because of the involvement of the Great powers, particularly the USA. Since it was taken up in the Security Council in January 1948, India had hoped that the United Nations would uphold India's genuine cause. But it did not happen as the attitudes of the United States and the United Kingdom were very much favourable to Pakistan rather than to India. The extremely partisan attitude of the United States on the issue of Kashmir was absolutely anti-Indian and suicidal to her interest and also for maintaining peace in the subcontinent.[8] This is another heavy burden which we have to bear. Our experience of international politics and the way things are done in these higher regions of the United Nations, has been disappointing in the extreme.

In the light of the then prevailing international context, if not militarily, but diplomatically, we have reached almost a crisis over the Kashmir issue. This development on Kashmir owed quite a variety of factors, connected with everything except the merits of the Kashmir issue. The Americans who voted for the partition of Palestine and thereby alienated the sympathies of the Arabs seemed anxious to win back Arab support which was essential for them in view of the oil situation and the possibility of war in the Middle East. The Arab League in February 1948, threatened withdrawal of oil concessions if the United States continued to support the partition of Palestine. Both, the USA and the UK also seemed to be a fear in mind that if Pakistan becomes weak internally the situation might be exploited by Soviet Russia. But above all, the achievement of independence and a desire to maintain our own foreign relations, free of attachment to blocs, had brought us sharply against the ugly forces of power politics.[9] India held the pro-Pakistan position of the USA and this belief grew in when we saw that there was not only substantial change in the Security Council's attitude to Pakistan. The United States neither took any stern action against Pakistan nor criticised the presence of its troops in Kashmir since October 26, 1947. Though it had no doubt regarding the legal validity of Kashmir's accession to India, it accepted the position that the accession should be chalked out in the light of a plebiscite to resolve the issue finally.[10]

First of all, this 'reference of the people' was mentioned in a letter written to the Maharaja of Kashmir by the then Governor-General at the time of accession and later the pledge was accepted by the Indian leaders. Though it did not form a part of the agreement made between the Maharaja and the Government of India, in the phase of cold war and mainly due to power politics of Great Powers, thc issue of Plebiscite overshadowed the accession of Kashmir to the Union of India. As per the spirit of the accession the Indian government tried to fashion its actions and honour the pledge it gave to the people of Jammu and Kashmir. Its responsibility was two-fold: To protect them from invasion, rape, loot, arson and everything that accompanied that attack. The second was given unilaterally to the state's people to decide finally what their future was to be. But the last one was more important. There seemed to be a good deal of misunderstanding about Kashmir's accession in people and in some newspapers, mostly abroad that something had happened in last three weeks that had made this accession complete.[11] In the circumstances India made a declaration that it would abide by the will of the people of Kashmir as declared in a plebiscite or referendum. However, it could not held because the Plebiscite was conditional upon Pakistan pulling out all its troops, regular or irregular from the state.

Later on India began to face a challenge within the state of Jammu and Kashmir itself. The problem of Kashmir took a new turn with the commencement of internal struggle for self-determination by the people of Kashmir. It covered the area of Kashmir valley and specially in Srinagar. The new idea projected the entire, territory of the pre-1947 princely state of Jammu and Kashmir as some sort of timeless, sacred geography and the sole political unit for the exercise of the 'right to self-determination. This stance was in utter disregard of all territorial units and borders, forgetting the fact that the erstwhile princely state ceased to exist in 1947 and that its disparate territory have been divided decades ago between two hostile states. The idea even overlooked the differing situations prevailed in three different regions – Kashmir Valley, Jammu and Ladakh, with which the state is composed of. This new element had made the problem more complicated and served as a great catalyst for war and conflagration between India and Pakistan with the active involvement of regional actors, such as, China and the Islamic world.

Over Idealistic Approach

It is a general feeling of the people in India that excessive idealism, its lack of experience in diplomacy at the time of independence, and an overly accommodative trait of Hindu culture, led India to make one mistake after another in handling the Kashmir question. Our policy on Kashmir has never been full-proof from strategic and tactical points of view while negotiating Pakistan on Kashmir issue. The overall objective was neither clear nor consistent. India adhered strictly to the certain ideals which had shaped its thinking and action during our freedom struggle. It even did not care to ponder over its opposite number Pakistan which had a different gospel. They were not for unity but disunity, not for construction but for destruction, not for peace but for discord, if not war.[12] But many who thought that practising a good neighbourly policy is a purely one-sided affair with the responsibility for it to be borne entirely by this country have now become sadder and wiser and realise that such a policy needs the willingness and cooperation of the two parties to be developed satisfactorily and cannot be implemented on unilateral basis, though unilateral steps may help on appropriate occasions. In most mature countries, this would need no special emphasis and would be taken for granted.[13] Unfortunately, this basic flaw pervades not only in our security policy but also in our economic planning and in various other aspects of our national life.

Keeping in view the struggle for freedom fought by the people of Jammu and Kashmir in pre-accession phase, the leaders of India, including Jawaharlal Nehru held the view that in Kashmir there was a straight fight between communalism and the ideal that we have hold for the last several decades. India viewed it as its primary objective to provide the democratic social economic and political rights for a secular Jammu and Kashmir. After the state acceded to India, Nehru's immediate aim and policy was to ensure its political economic and social integration with the rest of the country. This was the basis of the Delhi Agreement of 1953. By this a previously autocratically ruled princely kingdom had to be given the protective cover of a democratic dispensation in terms of rights for the people.

At the time the measure of Nehru's relative success was that Sheikh Abdullah, the undisputed leader of Kashmir came to unequivocally repudiate 'theocratic Pakistan. The Indian Prime Minister was sure for the mass support and informed the Parliament that if any sympathy for the invaders had existed among the people, the whole Valley would have been offered on a silver platter to the invader. When people talked of plebiscite and accuse India of imposing itself on Kashmir, he had not the shadow of a doubt that a plebiscite in Kashmir could only result in the victory of the present Government.[14]

India, while attributing the state of Jammu and Kashmir a democratic look made the world to believe that the province was not an integral part of India to the same extent as the other states were. To start with, Sheikh Abdullah was installed in Kashmir as its first Prime Minister and not as another Chief Minister, thus placing him on par with the Prime Minister of India. This was followed by a special status granted to Kashmir under Article 370 of the Constitution to provide for its traditions and 'susceptibilities' which were said to be peculiar to it. As if this was not enough, in the beginning India went to the extent of allowing Kashmir to have a separate constitution, a separate flag, and also a separate anthem.[15] On economic front, ever since independence we have kept pouring crores of rupees in that valley in the hope that we could win over its people to our side. We have waged four wars, the last one on Kargil in 1999, with Pakistan over it, and an entire army formation is located there in a constant state of readiness. We have experimented with different political systems and have changed Governors, in the hope of seeing even a small flicker of light in that Vale's dark tunnel. But so far there has not been even a glimmer of that hope.[16] Now the time has come to understand and appreciate how and when things went wrong and how the present empass came about.

Initiation of Direct Talks on Kashmir

The predominantly Muslim state of Jammu and Kashmir has been a bone of contention between India and Pakistan which witnessed four wars since the days of the partition of the subcontinent. After the invasion on Kashmir in the last quarter of

1947, India took the issue to United Nations Security Council to call upon Pakistan to desist from it. It did not ask the world body to adjudge the validity of State's accession or to determine where sovereignty lay. The Government of India went to the UN to complain about aggression by Pakistan which might jeopardise world peace. But this body took advantage of the initiative in referring the matter to the UN and thus enlarged the scope of their enquiry. Throughout the year 1948 the United Nations investigated the matter and passed two resolutions in April and August 1948, respectively. Its resolution dated August 13, 1948 consisted three part of which the first relating to the cease-fire had come into effect by January 1, 1949. However, the rest two parts of the resolution relating to a truce agreement and holding of a plebiscite after the first two parts were implemented, remained a deadlock point till date. Further the Security Council appointed mediators and commissions for the settlement of dispute but was of no use as both the sides took diametrically opposite stand. At last, the Council appointed Frank P. Graham of the US as new mediator in April 1951, who, after failing to break the deadlock suggested in the first quarter of 1953 for direct negotiations between India and Pakistan.

Willingness to discuss the Kashmir question with Pakistan without preconditions was clearly a demonstration of India's faith in peaceful methods of settling international differences. Each time the Government of India expresses its earnest desire to discuss this bottleneck with Pakistan but it had to play into the hands of that country so far as the issue of secular democracy versus theocracy was concerned. India has to face a nation whose very foundation is based on religion and religious fundamentalism.[17] Even the efforts to centralise the Pakistani administration was, to a large extent, influenced by the partition. Jinnah's assumption of the Governor-Generalship was to ensure that the sovereignty of Pakistan did not go by default. The tortuous negotiations in days to come over the division of assets and the conflict over Kashmir confirmed the correctness of this decision. The question of having a viable armed forces acquired new significance as the dispute over the princely states, particularly Kashmir. Thus, the dispute over assets and territory reinforced the perception that the establishment of a strong centre was crucial to Pakistan's survival as an independent state.[18] In foreign affairs too, Pakistan initially refused Clement Atlee's repeated offers of an alliance because they did not include Kashmir. By 1951, its opposition had softened slightly and premier Liaquat was willing to discuss defence without Kashmir on the agenda. However, he refused to commit any troops towards a regional alliance as long as the Kashmir problem was outstanding.

Graham, the new UN representative covered much on the issue but jumped on the conclusion that it would be unrealistic to ask for the withdrawal of forces from the areas held by India and Pakistan. Keeping in view the main resolution of the Security Council that the dispute should be settled by a plebiscite, he proposed that the parties should come together and devise means by which this could be done. It was in this background that Mohammad Ali Bogra who became the Prime Minister of Pakistan in April 1953, made an impassioned appeal to Nehru to settle all outstanding disputes between India and Pakistan. He said in the Parliament of Pakistan, 'I consider that the maintenance of peace and establishment of friendly relations between India and Pakistan are essential to the peace and stability of Asia'.[19] He stressed the need for the settlement of Kashmir without which no permanent peace or friendship in the subcontinent was possible.

The first ray of hope was followed by several round of talks between India and Pakistan and they reached at an understanding when both the Prime Ministers had met in London in June 1953. Exchange of visits were took place by the Prime Ministers of India and Pakistan to each other's country and the two decided that the best way to ascertain the people's wishes would be to hold an impartial and regional plebiscite, and that the Plebiscite Administrator should come from a small country and not from a big country like the USA or the UK which had political interests in the region.[20] The meeting of the two Prime Ministers from 17 to 20 August 1953 resulted in a communiqué which stressed : (i) it was their firm opinion that this dispute would be settled in accordance with the wishes of Kashmir....the most feasible method of ascertaining the wishes of the people was by a fair and impartial plebiscite; (ii) the plebiscite administrator should be appointed by the end of April 1954; (iii) previous to that, the preliminary issues that had held up progress towards a plebiscite so far should be decided and actions in implementation thereof should be taken and with this object in view committees of military and other experts should be appointed to advise the Prime Ministers; (iv) Progress 'can only be made in this direction if there is an atmosphere of peace and cooperation between the two countries. [21] However, further talks between India and Pakistan were marred by some developments in their relations with Great Powers, particularly on defence–related aspects. This was an unfortunate development since the understanding had brought very close to each other in settling the outstanding dispute.

The last quarter of 1953 witnessed certain significant developments on the foreign policies of India and Pakistan. India had experienced the cold attitude of the United States towards itself in relation to the proposal for its participation in the efforts for Peace in East Asia following the Korean war. It came rather close to the USSR with the economic agreement signed with them early in December. But the developments, that took place on Pakistan's side, was not only different but explosive as well. As the negotiations for US arms aid to Pakistan was in progress early in November and again a month later Nehru wrote to the Prime Minister showing his concern that such a development would undermine the prospects of friendly settlement of issues between the two countries by making their foreign and defence policies "diametrically opposed." [22] His letter of December 9, 1953, in particular, mentioned the Kashmir context and said that the US military aid to Pakistan would "completely" change the aspect of the Kashmir problem and that the question had now become "one of militarisation and not of demilitarisation.

Apart from this Pakistan also joined the Middle East Pact sponsored by Great Britain and the US. It became a member of the South East Asian Treaty Organisation (SEATO) in September 1954, and Bagdad Pact, later known as Central Treaty Organistaion (CENTO) in July 1955. Though these alliances were directed against the Communist Russia and China, Islamabad failed to conceal her own motives and openly declared that this would strengthen her hands against India in Kashmir, and even help in solving the issue. Its posture at the moment led India to conclude that Pakistan wanted to settle the issue by force of arms. Indeed, the US-Pak Aid Pact as well as Pakistan's entry into CENTO and SEATO so changed the situation that it was impossible to create a suitable atmosphere any longer for successful talks on this disputed issue. It also brought the US on the side of Pakistan and latter's membership of other alliances brought several countries at its call. Naturally these all introduced the cold war in the Indo-Pakistan subcontinent.[23] Thus, it was the beginning of a definite change in the Indian stand of the readiness for a partial plebiscite as agreed earlier because it made Pakistan ambitious and encouraged the latter to press India for concessions.

Side by side the other developments that cast a dark shadow on the issue were on the rise. Viewing the decision of the Kashmir Constituent Assembly which ratified Kashmir's accession to India, Nehru told the Pakistani Prime Minister in February 1954 that the delay in holding the plebiscite owed to the non-agreement on the conditions "which would ensure a fair and peaceful plebiscite". He also made this point clear in the middle of May 1954 which stated the change of circumstances and the compulsion of events that were beyond India's reach. It became evident when Mohammad Ali Bogra talked with Nehru and his colleagues from 14 to 18 May 1955 in New Delhi. The Joint Communiqué issued on the occasion confirmed that the two side had gathered fresh differences though they agreed to continue these talks at a later stage. Further at the close of 1955 the Soviet Prime Minister N. A. Bulganin and First Secretary of the Communist Party of the USSR N. S. Khruschev visited India and the latter had declared in Srinagar on 10 December that Kashmir was part and parcel of India. He made it clear that in view of Russia the question of Kashmir as one of states of the Indian Republic had been decided by the people of Kashmir.[24] The statement gave a clear relief to the Government of Jammu and Kashmir and to the millions of the people of India. Hereafter, Russia's attitude in the Security Council had changed and the Soviet representative vetoed every resolution which the Council tried to push through with the weight of the Anglo-American bloc and which was adverse to India's interest, was not acceptable to that country.

As India and Pakistan were busy to get support for their Kashmir cause, Pakistan, perhaps in retaliation, succeeded in persuading the meeting of the SEATO held in Karachi, in March 1956, to declare that the UN resolutions on the issue remained unchanged. India reactly sharply to the views expressed by the SEATO and Nehru told the Parliament that 'all talk of a plebiscite was completely beside the point", though India was still willing to discuss the question of Plebiscite as he feared it would led only to "a blind alley".[25] A little later, on 13 April 1956 he was eager enough for the settlement of Kashmir question and said in a public meeting in New Delhi, "I am willing to accept that the question of the part of Kashmir which is under you should be settled by demarcating the border on the basis of the present cease fire line. We have no desire to take it to fighting".[26] But unfortunately it was acceptable neither to Pakistan nor to the Great Powers, supporting the former.

The year 1956 was a significant from the view points of events affecting the Kashmir question. Throughout the summer of 1956, India's relations with Pakistan remained in the background. Nehru refused to discuss Kashmir even informally at the Commonwealth Prime Ministers, Conference, and thereafter Suez and Hungary monopolised attention. Both the countries began to pay the price of cold war going on among the Great Powers. At the bilateral level too notes and exchange of letters took place between the two Prime Ministers alleging each other regarding harassment of minorities in the two countries. [27] The general atmosphere was worsened further by the change of regime in Pakistan Suhrawardy replacing Choudhuri Mohammad Ali as Prime Minister, resulting in Firoze Khan Noon, as the new Foreign Minister. Dislike of India was the main driving force of the new dispensation and they, once again, raised the question of Kashmir at the Security Council. Other developments favouring Pakistan was also occurred and at the close of 1956 China declared that it supported the principle of self-determination by Kashmiris for the settlement of the issue. Pakistan moved again to the Council in the light of several developments but mainly due to the adoption of the Constitution for Kashmir by its Constituent Assembly that came into being from 26 January 1957. In practical and technical terms India assumed the chapter of Plebiscite being closed with this. It made the matter known to the Council that it would not any longer agree to the Plebiscite being held in the state of Jammu and Kashmir.

Deepening of the Crisis

In the background of Pakistan's request along with several allied developments the Security Council of the UN took the issue of Kashmir at the beginning of 1957 and passed two resolutions on 24 January and 21 February respectively for the settlement of dispute between India and Pakistan. Earlier, the latter had urged the Council to call upon India to refrain from accepting any change in the new Kashmir Constitution and to spell out the obligations of the parties under the terms of the international agreements for a plebiscite. Pakistan was well aware of the fact that its legal position on Kashmir is unviable. That is why it has been acting in desperation. Its dilemma is explained by its knowledge that a genuine plebiscite in Jammu and Kashmir will not lead to that state joining Pakistan. At the Council India again raised the question of aggression by Pakistan and held that the promise of a plebiscite was given to the people of Kashmir and not to Pakistan, and it referred the first two parts of the UNCIP of August 1948, without whose implementation no plebiscite could be held in the state.

The Security Council adopted a resolution on 24 January 1957 that reaffirmed that the future of the State could only be decided by a plebiscite and the steps taken by the Constituent Assembly of the State in this regard would not constitute a disposition of the State. In February 1957 the Soviet Union used its first veto in India's favour on a Western resolution moved in the Council which provided for the State's demilitarisation and for the use of a UN force there in order to establish conditions for a plebiscite in Kashmir. As the new situation warranted, Council, on 21 February adopted an amended resolution asking its President, Gunnar Jarring of Sweden to examine with the Governments of India and Pakistan any proposal likely to promote settlement of the Kashmir issue having regard to the previous resolutions of the United Nations. Gunnar jarring in his report submitted to the Council in April 1957, maintained that the holding of plebiscite in Kashmir might raise 'grave problems and secondly he mentioned the changing political, economic and strategic factor surrounding the whole of Kashmir question.'

At the bilateral level too, neither India nor Pakistan was hopeful of finding a solution of the problem and sought the help of delegation, other than political. Jawaharlal Nehru, on April 6, 1953, had warned his Cabinet Secretary, "Nothing substantial can come out of a discussion of the Kashmir issue on official level."[28] He preferred parleys at the summit. Between those Parleys he favoured an alternative. At a later stage Mohammed Ali, the Prime Minister of Pakistan, suggested Nehru for secret representatives of the two Prime Ministers meeting to explore possibilities under a fresh approach, on March 13, 1955, Nehru responded to India's high commissioner by saying that it would be better if some private representatives of Pakistan came here quietly for talks and later someone on our behalf went equally quietly to Karachi for talks. He suggested both the High Commissioners not to participate directly in these talks as this was likely to prove embarrassing. [29] In Pakistan Ayub Khan was the first who had plainly indicated that he is prepared to consider alternatives to the UN resolution or the plebiscite. He was so eager and anxious to solve the problem that Manzoor Qadir, his Foreign Minister, announced in a major policy statement on March 12, 1960 : "If somebody has a solution other than ours, let him suggest it. We can at least start thinking about it."

Initially the regime of General Ayub Khan gave a new look to its understanding with India that culminated in Nehru's visit to Pakistan and the signing of Indus-Waters' Treaty in September 1960. In the Joint Communiqué issued at the end of the visit the two leaders also agreed to discuss a number of Indo-Pak issues including Kashmir. They favoured a careful consideration to give further thought with a view to finding a solution. At the moment the team that ruled Pakistan was of the view that a strong India is in its interest and stated that India could be the pivot of economic collaboration among the less developed countries of Asia.[30] However, this spirit of goodwill was soon replaced by a bitter attitude on the part of Pakistan. In fact it was done at the behest of several internal and external developments that happened during the period. First, the slogan for a jehad for Kashmir was raised in Pakistan leading to equally strong reaction in India. Pakistan started criticizing the softening of the US attitude towards India and asked the US Government to exercise pressure on India with regard to Kashmir. Thirdly, attempts were made in Pakistan to come closer to Communist China. In January 1961 an indication had been given of the continuance of Sino-Pakistan talks regarding the demarcation of the border between the two countries despite the fact that Pakistan, by itself, had no common border with China and that only Azad Kashmir had a common frontier with China. The two governments had announced on 3 May 1962 their decision to enter into negotiations regarding the demarcation of the boundary.[31] Finally Pakistan took an opportunity to raise the issue of Kashmir at the UN Security Council when on December 18, 1962, India launched military action against Portuguese and liberated Goa.

However, in the circumstances nothing was more ominous than the deterioration of India-China relations. The problem of the boundary had become a major one was made clear by Chou Enlai's reply to Nehru on 23 January 1959 in which he stated that the boundary between the two had never been formally delimited and laid claim to a large areas of Indian territory. It put at stake approximately 85,000 sq. km.in the NEFA, 38,000 sq. km. in Ladakh and 500 sq. km in the middle sector, which India considered was its but shown as China's on their maps. It was followed by just a later development in which the Indian Government granted asylum to Dalai Lama at the end of March 1959 and admitted several thousand Tibetan refugees who accompanied him. A top level conference between the two countries held in New Delhi in April 1960 failed to cut much ice and five years of diplomatic and public soft-pedalling seemed to be over. Meanwhile, China had also improved its relations with India's immediate neighbours, such as, Nepal, Sri Lanka and Pakistan.

In the autumn of 1962, when India's relations with China was at the lowest ebb, Ayub Khan probably attached more importance to his grand strategy of applying pressure on India through better relations with China and influence with the United States than to bilateral discussions. China launched a major attack in October 1962 and Pakistan made no secret of its bias against India. It criticised Nehru for not accepting China's term and accused of pursuing expansionist and atavistic policies.[32] The Chinese inflicted several humiliating reverses on India for a month and then unilaterally declared ceasefire. In between the period on 27 October the Indian Prime Minister addressed communications to Ayub Khan of Pakistan, President Kennedy of the USA, Premier Macmillan of the United Kingdom and heads of some other friendly Governments. Of them, the reply of Ayub Khan was more disappointing. He regretted that the Sino-Indian dispute "should have led to intensified military activities and induction of new war potential, thus endangering the peace and stability of the region, hoped for a peaceful resolution of the conflict, but added that "various outstanding disputes between India and Pakistan can also be resolved amicably, should the Government of India decide to apply these principles with sincerity and conviction.[33] Ayub counted two dangers to Pakistan's security, communalism and Hinduism but he considered the latter to be more alarming.

As the crisis in Sino-Indian relations deepened early in 1959, Pakistan felt the need to take advantage of the situation. While latter's growing understanding with China was a cause of concern for India, it made Pakistan ambitious who now believed to extend beyond Kashmir. At the Conference of Commonwealth Prime Ministers in March 1961, Ayub said to Nehru that Kashmir was a burden on the armies of both countries and, if that were settled, relations would be very friendly with no problems remaining. He proposed that Kashmir be made into a separate unit like Switzerland. The Indian Prime Minister showed no interest and simply said that he was anxious to settle the problem. Thereafter, Pakistan's attitude on the issue became harder and Ayub was reported to have said to the editors in a private meeting that his country would take advantage of India's difficulties with China and that, in any dispute between India and China, Pakistan would be on China's side. On the other hand Pakistan was also anxious over massive arms assistance given to India by the Western countries. The members of Pakistan's National Assembly with Z. A. Bhutto, in particular, criticized India for creating a war hysteria throughout the world in order to create national cohesion in the country and to get Western help.

But the prevailing situation affected Western countries in a different way. They kept their global strategy alive as applicable to the subcontinent and considered two points uppermost. First, that India and Pakistan should unitedly face the Chinese menace or that at least Pakistan should help India in its defence against China; and two, that India must make some concessions to Pakistan on Kashmir to obtain the latter's support against China. In the background of Nehru's appeal for support and sympathy for India attempts were made for an Indo-Pakistan rapprochement by W. Averell Harriman of the USA and Duncan Sandys of Britain. The Kennedy administration of the US also took a lively interest in solving the issue of Kashmir with India's reiteration that it would never attack Pakistan. Having been persuaded by Kennedy Nehru wrote to Ayub, 'Whatever the differences between India and Pakistan, Chinese expansion was a matter of common concern. The idea of any conflict with Pakistan is one which is repugnant to us, and we on our part will never initiate it. I am convinced that the future of India and Pakistan lies in their friendship and cooperation for the benefit of both.'[34] Harriman and Sandys argued that public opinion in their countries would only favour generous aid to India if it were linked with a settlement on Kashmir and in situation it became near impossible for India to refuse a talk with Pakistan.

Thus, it was on the basis of a situational evidence that India agreed to start talks to reach an honourable and equitable settlement on the outstanding differences on Kashmir and other related matters. Consequently a joint statement was issued simultaneously by President Ayub Khan and Prime Minister Nehru on 30 November 1962. It stated that the two sides had agreed that a renewed effort should be made to resolve the outstanding differences between their two countries on Kashmir and other related matters and "decided to start discussions at an early date with the object of reaching an honourable and equitable settlement" which would be "conducted initially" at the ministerial level and "at the appropriate stage" directly by Nehru and President Ayub.[35] 'This is an historic moment,' was the remark of Nehru and fresh hopes had been raised of a solution to the Kashmir issue which had bedevilled relations between the two countries since independence.

Mere declaration of joint statement was not sufficient and both sides were less than happy over this new understanding. By 1962 the Kashmir issue had become dead and buried but the joint talks were forced upon them by the UK and the USA. Both sides moved on the dotted line of talks with utmost caution. Nehru while searching genuinely for a solution on Kashmir, let it be known that he had no great hopes of the talks being successful. Kashmir was not the cause but the result of Pakistan's ill-will and Nehru believed that even if a settlement on Kashmir were reached, it would be followed by another demands. At this time the question of plebiscite did not arise because it would revive communal feelings; and India could not consider any settlement on Kashmir which directly impeded her handling of Chinese aggression.[36] In Pakistan, though official opinion appreciated the declaration, the press was hostile to it. Even *The Pakistan Times*, which was not so hostile warned editorially on 1 December 1962 that a settlement of the Kashmir dispute should in no case be allowed to jeopardise our relations with China; and they must remain above suspicion. In the post–ceasefire phase Pakistan was adopting an attitude of blackmail and the Western Powers, perhaps unknowingly, were to some extent parties to this.

Series of Talks in a No-talk-situation

As a follow up of the joint statement issued at New Delhi and Rawalpindi on 30 November 1962, delegations of the two countries held six rounds of talks beginning from 27 December 1962. Ministers from both the countries were appointed as leaders of the respective delegations. Sardar Swaran Singh, India's Minister for Railways, headed the Indian delegation while Pakistani delegation was under Z. A. Bhutto, Minister for Industries, Natural Resources, and Works. In the talks which started on 27 December the leaders of the two delegations merely restated their old positions. Bhutto suggested the speedy implementation of the August 1948 and January 1949 resolutions of the UNCIP,[37] while Swaran Singh, leader of the

Indian delegation laid emphasis on peaceful solution of the problem and that it must not affect stability and progress in Kashmir. He also referred to unsettled issues and urged that the two countries should agree on a "moratorium on criticism and abuse. The two delegations merely restated their old positions as it was contained in the joint communiqué issued at the end of the talks on December 29, 1962, "the two sides discussed various aspects of the Kashmir problem in a spirit of cordiality and understanding and exchanged their views freely and frankly and that they agreed to make a joint appeal to leaders, officials, the press and the radio and other media of publicity in the two countries for a moratorium on abuse.[38] But they decided to continue their discussions in New Delhi from 15th of January 1963.

Despite the fact that leaders of the delegations expressed satisfaction and claimed "some progress," the timing of their talk was clouded with the announcement on the night of 26 December that Pakistan had reached an agreement with China concerning the alignment of the boundary between China and Azad Kashmir. Though for the last two years the said agreement was in the offing its confirmation at the moment was fatal for the talks from India's points of view. The Chinese declaration clearly stated that the two sides hoped to sign the agreement on this as soon as possible, and added that it would be a provisional agreement to be replaced by a final treaty after the Kashmir problem had been settled.[39] The Indian delegation present at Rawalpindi to start talks expressed at once its surprise and regret but the positive roles played by the British High Commissioner and the American Ambassador in Rawalpindi prevented the talks from breaking. With a single stroke of the pen, Ayub Khan succeeded in allaying the Western apprehension about his policy of befriending China. It convinced the Western capitals that the emerging Sino-Pakistan entente was primarily tactical, designed to bring pressure to bear on India to negotiate a settlement of Kashmir and other disputes with Pakistan. Ayub Khan came to be regarded as an Asian statesman who was genuinely averse to the spread of Chinese influence and who could be expected to play a robust anti–Chinese role if only Nehru reciprocated and accepted his proffered hand of friendship.[40]

In the series of talks India's position seemed much weaker than ever before. It was prepared to discuss any issue that was raised by Pakistan, but on Kashmir was willing to go no further than modifying the ceasefire line to give Pakistan an extra 1,500 square miles and to treat the new alignment as the international boundary. This, of course, did not satisfy Pakistan whose appetite had grown in the changed circumstances and it treated India as a defeated nation. Additionally, if there was any race between the United States and China for Pakistan's allegiance, Peking had won the first round, particularly after signing the border agreement with Pakistan in March 1963.The American dream of Indo-Pakistan joint efforts to ensure the security of the subcontinent was shattered and Ayub Khan was prompt enough to put its blame on India saying that her intransigence had wrecked his efforts for bringing the two countries together against China. Going a step further it sent its Foreign Secretary on a lengthy tour of European countries urging them not to grant military assistance to India as she was building up her army, utilising the excuse of Chinese aggression in order to be better prepared to fight Pakistan.

The latter's reaction to the changed situation was to shift from a policy of alliance to a policy of bilateralism, aimed at maintaining simultaneous good relations with the USA, USSR and China.[41] The Sino-Indian war and Pakistan's boundary agreement with China made Kashmir an important component in the power equation between the two countries. As attitudes hardened they began to view Kashmir as an essential condition of security. Its loss was perceived by both as entailing a relative loss of security. 'Even if one leaves aside the intricate details of the psychological and historical differences, if one omits the religious and economic considerations and if one forgets the psyche and the sentiment, one is still left with the Kashmir dispute. To a great extent all these differences, and more, are channelised into the Kashmir dispute.'[42]

The New Delhi Talks by the appointed delegations of India and Pakistan held between 16-19 January 1963 and it, apart from several other important matters, discussed the various aspects of Plebiscite in Kashmir. During the talks the Pakistani delegation made it perfectly clear that they could not even hear a reference to an agreement along the present ceasefire line with or without minor adjustment. Over-emphasis was given on the Plebiscite issue which was denied by India as it would gave a rise to communal elements. The Indian side was not ready even to respond a Pakistani request for alternative proposals for an overall plebiscite in Kashmir. In January Ayub accused India for being tricky and short-sighted and demanded a commitment to hold a plebiscite in Kashmir within a year.[43] The Great Powers, USA and UK, were particularly interested in the talks, were agreed to the Indian position that a plebiscite was no longer feasible, however, on the other, they suggested that India should make some public gesture to show that New Delhi was serious about the talks. And the first such goodwill gesture must come from India because Ayub was weaker than Nehru and Pakistan a lesser power than India. In other words, in their larger global aim to contain Communism, they wanted to exploit India in the background of its humiliating defeat at the hands of China.

The situation at the talks became so complicated that the talks were likely to break. But at the last moment they could evolve a procedure for the third round. They formulated a common working paper which accommodated the approaches of the two sides for a political solution of the Kashmir problem.[44] In this formula India favoured a settlement based on territorial adjustment, taking into account administrative and geographical factors and the least disturbance to the people, whereas Pakistan wanted a territorial division which would take into account the composition of the population control of rivers, the economic and strategic interests of Pakistan, and the wishes of the people of the state.[45] The Joint Communique issued at the end of the talk on 19 January stated that the two sides had discussed 'various aspects of the Kashmir problem', that the 'attitude of the two sides was constructive throughout' and that the further discussion would resume in Karachi in the early part of February 1963.

Unlike the New Delhi Talks which was focussed on the issue of Plebiscite in Kashmir, the Karachi Talks that took place between 8-10 February 1963 laid emphasis on partition of Kashmir with a view to provide headwaters of the Jhelum and the Chenab to

Pakistan. The plan, as put forward by India, was rejected by Pakistani delegation on 9 February and stated by its leader Bhutto in the National Assembly that the Indian plan 'involved nothing more than a re-adjustment of the existing ceasefire line'.[46] Then Bhutto put forward his own partition plan which in effect would have given the whole of Jammu and Kashmir to Pakistan, barring, a small area comprising more or less the district of Kathua in the north-east tip Jammu. In fact the Pakistani side asked for the transfer to Pakistan of the whole state of Kashmir 'in a forgotten moment of generosity'.[47] As the two sides adhered strictly to their approaches, serious deadlock was reached on the last day of the talk. Bhutto suggested that only a concession by India could sustain the negotiations, however, the intervention of Walter McConaughty, the American Ambassador in Karachi, was able to make Pakistan agreed to continue the talk, perhaps, in the hope of securing third-party mediation. The Joint Communique issued on 11 February referred to their consideration of various aspects of the Kashmir issue and said that 'a further exchange of views on these aspects was necessary and that the two delegations would continue the talks in Calcutta in the second week of March 1963. The talks had obviously lost all meaning and Pakistan probably hoped that India would break them off. But India agreed to continue the talks further because it was not its turn to complain that Pakistan was not wholly serious and not anxious to come to an agreement. The problem, as Nehru viewed it, was not that of Kashmir but of Pakistan's basic attitudes; even if there were a settlement on Kashmir, as long as these attitudes continued, differences between India and Pakistan would develop in some other shape.

The Calcutta Talks of 12-14 March 1963 was preceded by the signing of Sino-Pakistani border agreement on 2 March. Nehru expressed his 'shock' at it in the Lok Sabha and termed it not as 'fortuitous or accidental' but 'deliberate' and added that the signing of this agreement has been timed to prejudice the outcome of the ongoing talks on Kashmir.". The whole affair is a warning that it is wrong to take the identity of Indian and Pakistani interests for granted and a reminder that the Indian Government must guard against the danger of collaboration between the two aggressors."[48] Even before the initiation of the talk the Indian Government sent protest notes to the Chinese and Pakistan Government on 2 and 5 March respectively against the signing of the agreement.

It was in this background that the talks started on 12 March 1963. After the initial discussion on Sino-Pakistan border agreement, the Kashmir talk was resumed in which the two sides had reiterated the positions taken in Karachi. Differences between the two were so deep that at the time of the conclusion of the talks on 24 March, they were reported to be discussing their partition scheme. Apart from the Kashmir problem they discussed the border issue and treatment of minorities but to no avail. The Joint Communique issued on 15 March simply noted the two delegations had discussed Kashmir and other related matters and that they would take up these issues in Karachi from 21 April 1963.

Continuous failure of Indo-Pak talks for resolving the Kashmir problem had disappointed the Anglo-American group who hoped that the settlement would pave the way for their influence in the subcontinent, apart from containing the Chinese dominance in the region. As they had helped India in the wake of Chinese aggression at the cost of their good relations with Pakistan, throughout the talks they favoured Pakistani side and expected a 'substantial gain' for Islamabad. In pursuance of a well-thought plan in the intermission of talks an American partition plan for Kashmir, supported by Britain had presented to both the parties under 'Rostow Plan'. It was originally proposed by Walter W. Rostow, top adviser on policy planning of President Kennedy. According to it, the dividing line would run north-west of the Srinagar-Leh road, giving a small portion of the Valley and Ladakh to Pakistan and keeping the major portion, including Srinagar, with India.[49] The Western Powers also took the opportunity to suggest that Pakistan as well as India should have a substantial partition in the valley with freedom of access to civilians and armies of both sides, and that the Indus water treaty be reopened in order to provide Pakistan with facilities on the Chenab river for the storage of water. These proposals, though unacceptable to India, encouraged Pakistan to demand that the Valley being indivisible, it be transferred to the latter as a whole. India not only refused to consider its transfer to Pakistan, but conveyed its objection to the third power intervention, which had only worsened the situation, 'I am convinced that these ill-considered and ill-conceived initiatives, however well-intentioned they may be, have at least for the present made it impossible to reach any settlement on this rather involved and complicated question.[50] The development had widened the gulf between the two countries.

At this stage, Pakistan was in favour of internationalisation of the Valley for a limited period, to be followed by a plebiscite, while India was of the view that still there was no real desire on the part of Pakistan for a settlement and the latter only wished to take advantage of India's poor relations with China. It was clear from the discussions held between the two delegation at second Karachi talks that happened to be in April 22-25, 1963 and ended on a very disappointing note. In the talks Bhutto claimed literally the whole of Jammu and Kashmir state saying that it comprised the catchment areas for Pakistan's rivers, the Chenab and the Jhelum, that the population in the Valley was predominantly Muslim, and that the merger of the State with Pakistan was imperative for the protection of the Pakistani Grand Trunk Road and the railways. This claim was summarily rejected by India on the ground that it was opposed to any communal approach for resolving the issue. It resulted in issuing of a routine joint communique which stated that the two sides had discussed the various aspects of Kashmir and announced that they would continue the talks in Delhi on 15 May 1963. However, the Pakistani perception had hardened Indian attitude, otherwise, India had been in a mood to make some concessions.

The sixth round of talks, which was known as the Second New Delhi Talks 15-16 May 1963, was started to declare the end of further talks. On the very first day Bhutto proposed Pakistan's proposal for six months international control over the Valley and it, at once, was rejected by India. In response to it Pakistan rejected India's offer of a no-war Pact between the two countries and declined disengagement on the ceasefire line with both sides pulling back their troops. As no concrete result came out of the talks, the joint communique noted that they held their talks in six sessions which "were frank and cordial" and "recorded with regret that no agreement could be reached on the settlement of the Kashmir issue." The whole exercise had received a fatal end. In the press conference which the two leaders addressed separately, blaimed each other for the failure of the ongoing talks. At this Swaran Singh revealed India's liberal attitude during the talks and said that it was prepared to offer 34,000 square miles to Pakistan out of the total area of 84,471 square miles of the State of Jammu and Kashmir but Pakistan was ready to concede to India hardly 3,000 square miles of the total area of the state. He also expressed his intention to continue these efforts and said that India would not be adverse to utilising good offices of a mutually acceptable personality for resolving the Kashmir problem. He held Pakistan's unrealistic attitude of rejecting India's generous offer of a political settlement as the main cause of its failure. But, on the other Bhutto attributed it to India's traditional hostility to Pakistan. He termed the breakdown not merely the end of the first phase of Indo-Pakistan negotiations, but the final breakdown. After the failure of Indo-Pak talks on the status of Kashmir relations between the two became increasingly tense. Bhutto showed his personal frustration and ably represented his countrymen's aspirations while in reply to Nehru said in a statement at Lahore, 'Let it be known beyond doubt that Kashmir is to Pakistan what Berlin is to the west, and that without a fair and proper settlement of this issue, the people of Pakistan will not consider the crusade for Pakistan complete.[51]

From India's points of view too, the impasse was a great disappointment. Nehru expressed his abiding anxiety to reach a settlement with Pakistan as it had been for long a part of India and not politically but emotionally linguistically, culturally, in every way there was more affinity between India and Pakistan than any other two persons or countries. He had a sincere desire and larger design as well for a general improvement in relations with Pakistan and was searching for a long-term settlement encompassing all matters and not just Kashmir. He was serious about the formation of a confederation that comprised India, Pakistan and their neighbours and the idea was disclosed while talking to a Delhi Correspondent of *Washington Post* on the eve of the first round of talks between the Ministers of the two countries. His plan came as a suggestion that a confederation relationship between India and Kashmir could lead to a similar arrangement between the two halves of Pakistan and enable in due time a large confederation.[52] But the failure of talks on Kashmir had evaporated the cordial sentiments expressed by the leaders of the two countries as the close of the fifties. It was an issue over which both the sides found it difficult to budge from their original positions. They adopted too rigid an attitude to make any solution possible. About a year later when communal virus began to raise its ugly heads, Nehru in a major speech in the Lok Sabha on 24 April 1964 urged the country to adhere to Gandhi's approach and force Pakistan 'psychologically' into friendship by evincing goodwill and providing an example of decent behaviour. India was not free from wrong-doing and should not become too self-righteous.

The series of talks which were initiated with high hopes in India and Pakistan revolved around Plebiscite, Partition, internationalisation and Political settlement. All these text book solutions for a territorial dispute proved fruitless. In the talks India had agreed to the discussion with an open mind and was willing to make fairly large concessions, but it was not possible to concede all of Pakistan's demands. They had failed because the deadlock proved unbreakable. From the outside the issue might seem unintelligible and interminable, but inside the subcontinent all discussions of the future, of world affairs, of economic development, come back to this unfortunate and miserable dispute which poisons the whole life of the two countries.

Cry of Kashmir at Tashkent

After the failure of direct talks on Kashmir between India and Pakistan their relations entered a further bitter phase. The Anglo-American initiative to solve this ruinous dispute came to nothing and the deadlock continued with all its dangerous implications. It witnessed the differing approach of the two apart from sporadic disturbances in the State of Jammu and Kashmir itself. China's support to Pakistan had encouraged the latter to press India for concessions, and even to use force first, in the Rann of Kutch in April 1965 and, later that year in September, in Kashmir, to change the *status quo* in its favour. In fact Pakistan was preparing for the seizure of Kashmir by force. From 5 August 1965 Pakistan sent infiltrators across the border into Kashmir on a large scale. In response India reacted by sending its security forces into Azad Kashmir. The first conflict, which occurred in April was a limited border engagement but in latter's case the two went on an undeclared full-fledged war that lasted for about three weeks. Lal Bahadur Shastri and Ayub Khan admitted that their country faced an actual war and blamed each other for attack. With the outbreak of war efforts for mediation and ceasefire had gained momentum by UN Secretary General U Thant and the Security Council but especially by the Soviet Union. It was due to Soviet Union's active intervention and initiation that President Ayub Khan and Prime Minister Shastri agreed for a ceasefire with effect from September 23, 1965.

When the outbreak of the hostility was almost sure, on 4 September 1965, Alexi Kosygin, the Soviet premier dispatched his identical letters to Indian and Pakistani heads of Government calling for "immediate cessation of hostilities" and reciprocal withdrawal of troops behind the ceasefire line. He invited Ayub and Shastri to hold talks on Soviet soil and offered to take part in such a reconciliation meeting 'if both sides wished it'. A Kremlin statement of September 8, renewed the offer to use the Soviet good offices and called on the leaders of the two countries to display realism, restraint and understanding of the grave consequences of the development of the armed conflict.[53] Fortunately, both the countries accepted the Russian offer 'in principle' and once the ceasefire was effected the prospect of the offer became brighter. However, the diplomatic view of New Delhi never overlooked the idea behind the offer which came in the form of international opinion. The Indian Prime Minister told the Lok Sabha on November 22, 1965; "Almost every country wants that we should somehow settle the question of Kashmir peacefully.[54]

Since 1965, India's negotiating position has improved markedly in some respects, but deteriorated steeply in others. Not one country advocates plebiscite in, or independence for, Kashmir, or questions the legality of its accession to India. None recognises it to be a domestic matter either. The legality of the accession is as incontestable as the existence of a political dispute, involving the two countries and the people of the state, in whose settlement the world is interested.[55] But not to talk of others, the Constitution of India itself explicitly records the future of Kashmir as a matter yet to be decided, and Pakistan, tacitly as a party with which an accord on the issue is to be reached. Article 253 confers on Parliament full legislative power 'for implementing any treaty, agreement or convention with any other country'. As applied to Kashmir, it has a proviso : "No decision affecting the disposition of the State of Jammu and Kashmir shall be made by the Government of India without the consent of the government of that state." It follows three inferences – a decision affecting the "disposition" of Kashmir is yet to be taken by an international agreement between India and "another country", and with the consent of the people.[56]

With a view to ease the situation and as the more dynamic and constructive effort was made by the Russians, it seized the opportunity and launched a big offensive in the subcontinent. However, at the juncture sudden Soviet interest was not out of context and marked by two developments – Pakistan's deepening collusion with China and its brewing up military tension with India. It seemed that in the wake of the three weeks' undeclared war of 1965 between India and Pakistan, they adopted the policy of continuing to retain India's friendship intact while making use of that war for drawing Pakistan also to the Soviet influence.[57] After Khruschev, the Russians under their new South Asian policy, began to take interest in Pakistan. The first Soviet overtures to Pakistan were made in 1963-64, and these were probably related to the boundary agreement signed between China and Pakistan in March 1963, which gave China direct access to strategically important areas in Kashmir. This understanding between them was not one-sided and Pakistan also made conscious efforts to normalise her relations with the Soviet Union and other Communist countries. It began with the visit of Z.A. Bhutto in February 1961 during which an oil agreement between the two was signed. The process of normalisation witnessed culmination in April 1965 when President Ayub visited Soviet Union and sought healing for past wounds along with exploration of new avenues of cooperation.

But, above all, the Soviet Union took note of Pakistan's growing dissatisfaction with the United States. Pakistani leaders could not reconcile themselves to the changed situation under which non-aligned India had taken precedence in American thinking over allied Pakistan. Pakistani leaders saw US Policy in South Asia in the early sixties as a case of over-reaction to an imagined Chinese threat to India's independence and integrity. In post 1962-phase America too faced a policy dilemma in the subcontinent because it wanted to maintain a balance of power, which, in this situation, was difficult to achieve. "Everything we give to India adversely affects the balance of power with Pakistan, which is much smaller country. So, we are dealing with a very complicated problem, because the hostility between them is so deep."[58] However, it was just a chance that US policy in the region had generated a periodic arms race between India and Pakistan. The US maintained a neutral instance in Indo-Pakistani disputes, and their arms assistance to Pakistan was given on the specific understanding that these arms were not to be used against India. And even though the Soviets came to the support of India on the Kashmir issue eventually, there was an element of superpower collusion in the arms assistance given to India in the aftermath of the India-China war of 1962. At this juncture too, the US had fully supported the Soviet initiative which led to the cessation of hostilities in the 1965 Indo-Pakistan war. Moscow and Washington took almost identical stands on the Indo-Pakistan war. Both wanted the fighting to end as quickly as possible and both were most anxious that China should not intervene in it.

After some initial hesitations, on 8 December 1965 simultaneous statements were issued at Karachi, Delhi and Moscow announcing a summit meeting in the Soviet city of Tashkent for 4th January 1966. The discussions at Tashkent began under the guidance and vigilance of the Soviet Premier, who was the chief actor of the peace talks. In the summit India was represented by Prime Minister Shastri, External Affairs Minister Swaran Singh, Defence Minister Y.B. Chavan, Ambassador T.N. Kaul and Foreign Secretary C.S. Jha. The

Pakistani delegation included other than Ayub Khan and Bhutto, Information Minister Khawaja Shahabudin, Commerce Minister Ghulam Farooq, Air Marshal Asghar Khan, the Air Force Chief, Foreign Secretary Aziz Ahmed and several other prominent diplomats. All through the talks Russia played a leading part in these negotiations and it was premier Kosygin's devoted effort that led to the conclusion of Tashkent Agreement on 10 January 1966. The signed declaration expressed their firm resolve to restore normal and peaceful relations between the two countries and to promote understanding and friendly relations between their peoples. Under the agreement the two leaders committed themselves to exert all their "efforts not to have recourse to force and to settle their disputes through peaceful means. It created an image for Russia as a peacemaker in Asia.

Before the declaration was signed, the two sides exchanged their views on Kashmir. At Tashkent the prime consideration for Pakistan was a settlement on Kashmir. Any agreement without Kashmir would be meaningless and it was made clear by President Ayub Khan before the commencement of the summit on 19 December 1965 that his country would agree to sign a no-war pact with India if the latter would settle with Pakistan the dispute over the state of Jammu and Kashmir. But India favoured step by step approach and manoeuvred for an acceptance of its occupation of the Valley together with, if possible, a no war agreement.[59] If past experience carried any message for Pakistan it was the futility of this hackneyed formula because Islamabad had firm belief in sustaining the tempo and degree of tension, particularly in case of India-Pakistan dispute. For the first four days the two delegations faced each other at the negotiating table thrashing out the phrases and minutiae of their proposal draft. Pakistani side first wanted the settlement of Kashmir dispute and no war agreement thereafter, while India preferred no war agreement to be taken before any progress on Kashmir could be made. No fruitful result was in sight in this atmosphere of futility and the deadlock was strong enough to kill a solution. However, there was always a great stress on the right atmosphere for fruitful discussions – a vacuous phrase meaning a winding down of tension in exchange for the promise of further talks.

It was at this stage that Russia came forward and began to intervene directly. The crucial meeting between Kosygin and Ayub Khan took place on January 9, 1966, in which the latter had agreed to shelve the Kashmir issue. A beginning for the talks on Line of Control was also made at the summit, with Lal Bahadur Shastri giving his consent to Kosygin putting it to Ayub Khan that the then existing ceasefire line with some adjustments might be made the permanent India-Pakistan boundary. Shastri gave his consent although he was aware that some minor adjustments might be needed to make the boundary conform to certain physical features and that there might be some consequent loss of territory to India.[60] But neither India nor Pakistan could resile from the respective positions they had taken, and the greater the effort made to find a solution the more it pained. It seems that in case of Kashmir the third party role can be relevant under two conditions. One, the parties concerned are not on talking terms, which is not the case between India and Pakistan. Two, the parties concerned can be persuaded to compromise on basic positions in response to certain incentives or rewards which may be offered by the third party. In the case of India and Pakistan they value their basic positions so much that no incentive would be enough to lead them to a compromise.[61]

In the circumstances a Soviet draft was quickly prepared and presented to India and Pakistan for acceptance. Because neither the Soviet Union nor India wanted to rock the boat by haggling too much and were happy with the reconstituted draft. Objections as regard to the several provisions were raised by Z.A. Bhutto, the then Foreign Minister of Pakistan and President Ayub who insisted on various changes, the most important being to strike out a specific no war clause. He was adamant that any agreement must include a settlement of Kashmir and when he continued to rail about Kashmir's plebiscite, Foreign Minister Gromyko had to remind him that since Pakistan had failed to achieve its case by war, Bhutto should not expect the Soviet Union to deliver Kashmir to Pakistan on the conference table. On the other hand, in addition to the Soviet Union Ayub Khan was under considerable pressure from the Western powers to come to a settlement with India. The Soviet peace initiative was strongly backed by the United States and Lyndon

Johnson had unequivocally told Ayub when he visited Washington in previous December that his country could not influence India on Kashmir and advised the former to get it out of the system.[62] The Soviet Union and the United States were anxious to continue with détente and the situation in the subcontinent was an unnecessary source of friction.

The Tashkent Declaration was signed on January 10, 1966. It was a peculiar document that covered barely two typewritten pages laying down a list of generalities which were intended to govern the complex relationship between India and Pakistan. But what made the declaration a political dynamite was the manner in which it treated the vexed question of Kashmir. In the final agreement it was stated that "the interests of the peoples of India and Pakistan are not secured by the continuance of tension between the two countries. It is against this background that Jammu and Kashmir were discussed, and each of the two sides put forth their respective positions."[63] It made no reference to Kashmir as an 'issue', 'dispute' or Problem. Considering that the two countries had twice gone to war over the Kashmir issue, it seemed a sorry response. The Kashmir problem, of course, remained far from being resolved at Tashkent. At least, it opened a way out of the terrible impasse created by the war of September 1965. It certainly eased the explosive situation that the war followed.

The agreement was hailed in many parts of the world. *Pravda* welcomed it as it opened a new chapter in Indo-Pakistan relations. The declaration was a success for the peace living peoples of India, Pakistan, and the Soviet Union who constituted almost a quarter of the world population. India also explained the agreement to its people as favouring one and Swaran Singh, India's Minister for External Affairs considered the renunciation of force by both the sides as "the central point of the whole declaration. It was similar to a no-war pact and added that both sides had agreed not to recourse to arms over Kashmir or any other question and emphasised that the declaration kept the seeds for normalisation of relations and discussion of various other problems. In nutshell, the Indians were understandably satisfied at the signing of the agreement. They had wanted an acceptance of the *status quo* in Kashmir and the removal of a war threat. *The Times of India* in its editorial, on January 17, 1966, endorsed the Indian point of view,' nothing can now be gained by questioning the Kashmir's status as an integral part of India.[64]

However, after signing the Tashkent document President Ayub Khan stood helpless before the people of Pakistan and opposition parties as well. For eighteen long years the people of Pakistan had been fed on the day that they would liberate Kashmir. Massive appropriations of the nation's wealth to the war chest had been justified on these grounds. Acceptance of the declaration evoked a sharp reaction at home and violence erupted even before the Pakistani delegation returned. The people fed on fairy tales of Pakistani military victories began to feel that what the heroes had own on the battle fields had been lost by the leadership at the negotiating table. Mobs ran amok cursing Ayub and his government and shouted slogans like "hume khoon ka jawab do." The war had reached a stalemate on the ground which was regarded as amounting to victory for Pakistan as the longer the confrontation continued the greater the pressure on India to reconsider its approach on Kashmir. The whole country stood united and resolved to carry on the struggle. President Ayub had signed the document when he could have refused to accept any agreement which did not include a settlement on Kashmir.[65] From the summit, the nation as a whole, had pinned high hopes to have a settlement on Kashmir in Pakistan's favour.

The ruling establishment of Pakistan tried to explain the public at large the benefits of the agreement. As the people were agitated over the issue of Kashmir President Ayub Khan stated on 14 January 1966 that 'we also impressed upon the Indian Prime Minister that peace could not be lasting unless the Kashmir dispute was amicably settled," that Pakistan was not prepared to consider Jammu and Kashmir as part of India and added : "The Indian Prime Minister wanted us to sign a no war pact, but we made it clear to him that we would never be a signatory to such a pact unless the Jammu and Kashmir dispute was settled honourably and equitably. As Foreign Minister Bhutto attributed his share of responsibility and, though, unwillingly, defended the agreement on occasions. At the juncture Bhutto's explanation to the nation was supplementary, who not only defended[66] the agreement on the floor of the National Assembly on March 14, 1966, but said that "the states can be spunged clean only when the people of Jammu and Kashmir have exercised their inherent right of self-determination" and that the Declaration was only the dialogue between India and Pakistan for a permanent solution of the "tragic dispute". The movement against the agreement was subsided, but a little later Bhutto began to condemn the both – Tashkent Declaration and President Ayub's regime with a view to gain political benefit emerged as a result of people's dissatisfaction. The Declaration and its acceptance by Ayub was based on a realistic appraisal of the prevailing military and diplomatic situation. No change of heart or attitude occurred on either side, with major problems including Kashmir unresolved, no miracle could be expected from just by one declaration, made at Tashkent.

Sweet and Sour at Simla

Pakistan's military option on Kashmir began to decline after 1965 and that with passing of time, the military advantages reversed, along with the growing disparities in strength. The war that the two had fought in 1971 entailed a reappraisal by Pakistan of its hard-line stand on Kashmir. This time Pakistan was forced into such a reappraisal since after the war India had held all the trump cards at the negotiating table. It left India with more than 90,000 Pakistani prisoners of war and almost 6,000 square miles of Pakistani territory. Fighting in Kashmir had also enabled India significantly to redraw the ceasefire line to its advantage. It qualified India to ignore the UN ceasefire line of 1949, and discuss directly with Pakistan the new one, which incorporated certain territorial gains during the war in the Kargil sector.[67] Thus, unlike Tashkent, the agreement at Simla committed itself to something more substantial than that by agreeing to the principle of settling differences peacefully and bilaterally.[68] In the past also there were several transitory phases in India's relations with Pakistan when mutual goodwill and spirit on conciliation could be seen and, at times, some acute bilateral problems could be tackled on that account. But such instances were few and far between and not of much effect in causing any basic improvement in the prevailing unhappy relations.

The Kashmir issue is likely to resolve only after the full normalisation of Indo-Pakistan ties and in an atmosphere of goodwill and trust between the two states. The Simla Summit was definitely the first and the most important step in this direction. The new beginning made in the subcontinental relations was a major achievement as the two leaders could meet, so soon after a war which had changed the face of the region, not as victor and vanquished but as equals, and not through the meddling intermediacy of great powers but by themselves to grapple directly with their differences.[69]

Z. A. Bhutto, the Prime Minister of Pakistan led the delegation for Simla and with him was a huge entourage of about ninety including a large press contingent, politicians, diplomates and others. The team included his principal negotiators; the veteran Aziz Ahmed; aide Rafi Raza; Party stalwarts like Mustafa Jatoi and Hayat Sherpao; National Awami Party leader Arbab Sikandar Khan, his daughter Benazir and host of others. While the Indian side had lined up a powerful negotiating Party. Apart from Indira Gandhi who headed the delegation and had arrived in Simla a few days before to supervise the arrangement, with the team was Congress brass-Finance Minister Y.B. Chavan, Defence Minister Jagjivan Ram, Fakhruddin Ali Ahmed, and External Affairs Minister Swaran Singh. However, the real working caucus was led by the suave D.P. Dhar, and included the Principal Secretary to the Prime Minister P.N. Haksar and Foreign Secretary T.N. Kaul.

For Bhutto to go to Simla was a forbidding experience. In fact, he was sandwiched between his own people's exaggerated expectations and the Indian position. For the benefit of his countrymen he maintained his military posture and in his more direct dealings with India. One of the reason for this was that he had come to power through the support he enjoyed in the Punjab which had a history of anti-Indian militancy. He was also the man who, in the United Nations Emergency Session in Newyork in 1965, had promised to fight for a thousand years. Indeed, a great part of his career had been founded in trumpeting and exploiting the anti-Indian cause, and in some moods he seemed reluctant to face the need to have to make peace. As the date of Summit approached Bhutto became increasingly conciliatory on several issues except the Valley and refused persistently to relinquish Pakistan's claim to Kashmir. Bhutto left for Simla on 27 June 1972 and seemed to recover some of his customary enthusiasm when addressed the crowd, 'there shall be no Tashkent under any circumstances; and on Kashmir no compromise on the issue of the right of self-determination'. Though, years ago, Bhutto propounded bilateralism as a central principle of Pakistan's policy, it was not intended to be applied to its relations with India.

Bhutto's adherance to Kashmir had always annoyed Indira Gandhi and both were suspicious of each other's view. Impressions gained from the war did not go in Pakistan side with Indian Prime Minister's remark about Bhutto that he was not a balanced man, confirmed Indian delegation that he could not be trusted either. In addition the right wing in India was clamouring for an end once and for all to the Pakistani threat. If India had won the war there was no reason why she should not extract a victor's price at the coming conference. This sentiment had a clearing meaning that all claims to Kashmir should be finally renounced by Pakistan; and a no-war pact signed. A large army of prisoners of war, large tracts of occupied territory, and all the psychological advantages accruing from a great military victory made India's position weighty in comparison to Pakistan.

The talks at Simla was preceded by an official level meeting of India and Pakistan at Murree, the latter's hill resort. D.P. Dhar, a Kashmiri confidante of Indira Gandhi and chairman of the Foreign Policy Committee was chief of the Indian team, while Pakistani delegation was led by Aziz Ahmed, head of the Pakistan Foreign office. At the meeting which was aimed to discuss the preliminaries of the Simla, the Indian side pressed for an overall settlement of all outstanding questions and even sought a no-war pact with Pakistan. Well aware of the fact that such demands, if conceded, would only compound political difficulties at home, the Pakistani delegation rejected it and reminded India of the violation of the Geneva Convention in holding on to the prisoners of war. As the discussions at Murree was not made public, the group of journalists who came to witness the final agreement at Simla, were not known to the previous position.

The intense negotiations at Simla started in the afternoon of 28th June 1972. There were press conferences, working dinners, state banquets, briefings and hard negotiating sessions where drafts were discussed and revised. Everyone knew the major issues at stake, but how close the two sides were coming to each other remained a mystery. With the advancement of the talks both sides adhered strictly to their views and it seemed on 2 July, the last day of the conference that there was no agreement in sight. However, the development that took place in the evening of the same day, saved the big show from being a disaster. The assurance held out by Bhutto in private made it a success. When the talks were stated to have failed Bhutto met Indira Gandhi prior to the farewell banquet and told her that she must trust his assurance that he would have the line of actual control recognised as the international border between India and Pakistan.[70] The two leaders dispensed with all aides, talked in an informal atmosphere in which Bhutto referred to their mutual problems and linked it to the chain of history. As disclosed by Bhutto in November 1976 while talking to a journalist, that he spoke to her of their great cultural heritage; Mughal heroes and emperors like Aurangzeb and Ashoka and the judgement of generations to come if they failed at Simla.

Of the logics given by Bhutto in favour of an agreement at Simla, the most appealing were deteriorating India–Pakistan relations and emergence of democracy in Pakistan after 14 long years of military rule. He talked sadly of the sorry affairs in relations between the two countries, regretted the tragedy in human suffering that the war had brought about, and expressed hope of a bright future for both countries if there was a lasting peace in the subcontinent. He went on to say that his was the first democratically elected government in Pakistan's history, and unlike the dictators of the past, was directly answerable to the people of Pakistan. Bhutto made it carefully a point that if an agreement could not be reached, or if he was forced to accept a humiliating settlement, he was at risk of being overthrown by the army. He also took the opportunity to remind Indira Gandhi that she would emerge from this a statesman of world status if she could be responsible for a lasting peace in the subcontinent.[71] The net result of the talks held between the two leaders was positive. After he finished Indira Gandhi smiled and agreed to resume the conversation. By around 11 p.m. on the night of 2 July the two parties emerged smiling because an agreement had finally been reached. In the early hours of the 3rd July the historic Simla Agreement was signed.

The text of the Simla Agreement contained six main clauses, of which maximum provisions incorporated several sub-clauses. The general provisions of the Agreement had touched the basic principles which had been in contention between the two governments ever since the partition. The First Clause of it states, "The Government of India and the Government of Pakistan are resolved that the two countries put an end to the conflict and confrontation that have hitherto marred their relations and work for the promotion of a friendly and harmonious relationship and the establishment of durable peace in the subcontinent, so that both countries may henceforth devote their resources and energies to the pressing task of advancing the welfare of their peoples."[72] This opening clause was pronounced as the heart of the agreement and in order to achieve this objective the two governments expressed their determination in sub-clause two of the said clause which followed that the two countries are resolved to settle their differences by peaceful means through bilateral negotiations or by any other peaceful means mutually agreed upon between them. It adds further that pending the final settlement of any of the problems between the countries, neither side shall unilaterally alter the situation and both shall prevent the organisation, assistance or encouragement of any acts detrimental to the maintenance of peaceful and harmonious relations.[73] These far–reaching provisions witnessed the abandonment of the policy of confrontation and the acceptance of bilateralism which was, in principle, a real departure in Pakistan approach to its relations with India.

The expression that the two would resolve their long pending problems bilaterally and through peaceful means was directly related to the issue of Kashmir. However, sub-clause two of the clause four was with regard to the Kashmir conflict and stipulated that "in Jammu and Kashmir, the Line of Control resulting from the ceasefire of December 17, 1971 shall be respected by both sides without prejudice to the recognised position of either side. Neither side shall seek to alter it unilaterally, irrespective of mutual differences and legal interpretations. Both sides further undertake to refrain from the threat or the use of force in violation of this line.[74] The actual document covered three small pages but most of them laid down the general intentions to put an end to conflict and normalise relations. In this context what was more important was the manner in which the document was drafted and the flexibility of its language which allowed both sides to interpret its clauses to suit their individual position.

In the Simla Agreement the Kashmir question had been left over for future settlement, but the provision to respect the Line of Control together with the general commitment to bilateralism and peaceful methods amounted to a significant acquiescence in the *status quo* in Kishmir. In broader perspective in accordance with the Simla the following factors were agreed upon :

(i) Responsibility for the security of the State of Jammu and Kashmir rests with the Government of India.

(ii) The sovereignty of the Jammu and Kashmir government over the entire territory of the state shall not be brought into question.

(iii) There shall be no recognition of the so called Azad Kashmir government.

(iv) The territory occupied by Pakistan shall not be consolidated to the disadvantage of the state of Jammu and Kashmir.

(v) The administration of the evacuated areas in the north shall revert to the Government of Jammu and Kashmir and its defence to the Government of India, which will, if necessary, maintain garrison for preventing the incursion of tribesmen, and for guarding the main trade routes.

(vi) Pakistan shall be excluded from all affairs of Jammu and Kashmir-especially a plebiscite, if one should be held.

(vii) If a plebiscite is found to be impossible for technical or practical reasons, the commission will consider other methods of determining fair and equitable conditions for ensuring a free expression of people's will .

(viii) Plebiscite proposals shall not be binding upon India if Pakistan does not implement part I and II of the UN resolution of August 13, 1948.[75]

Flexibility of the language at Simla provided an opportunity to both the parties to interpret the clauses in ways, they liked. The provision that India and Pakistan would settle their differences bilaterally and their wish to respect the redrawn ceasefire line as the Line of Control in Kashmir were viewed by them as opposite to each other. As to the negotiation through bilateral method, Indira Gandhi's interpretations of this part of the Accord ran counter to Bhutto. From there onwards, India always emphasised the spirit of bilateralism in India-Pakistan relations, perhaps, to exclude third party involvement and it was made clear by her while addressing a press conference on 13 July, 1972. She stressed that the stationing of United Nations observers in Kashmir was entirely an Indian matter. It was intended, in a way, to have the effect of burying Pakistan's claim for a special status for Kashmir as well as Pakistan's call for the implementation of past UN resolutions on a plebiscite. On the other, Bhutto meant it differently when, in his speech to the National Assembly, categorically denied that advocating bilateral settlements precluded the United Nations or outside intervention. A few days later he went on to quote, in this connection, Article 103 of the United Nations Charter which states that in the event of a conflict between the obligations of the members of the United Nations, and their obligations under any other agreements, the United Nations Charter prevails.

Though India and Pakistan agreed to accept 17 December 1971 ceasefire line as the Line of Control in Kashmir, they took the meaning opposite to each other. For India, acceptance of the 1971 ceasefire line meant that the old 1949 ceasefire line had now disappeared and the partition of the State was a *fait accompli* in practical terms. But, Bhutto considered it as a gain for Pakistan : 'By bifurcating and delinking the international boundary from the ceasefire line in Kashmir, the Valley has been acknowledged as a disputed issue. Earlier, at the negotiating table at Simla the Indian side proposed that "the *de facto* line of control was to be graduated to the level of the *de jure* border" but Pakistan was not agreeable. Later on the night of July 2 Bhutto agreed that the LoC would be gradually endowed with the "characteristics of an international border." All this was unwritten and everything was repudiated by Pakistan. Surprisingly, with 96,000 prisoners of war of Pakistan and a few hundred kilometres of occupied territory of Pakistan, India had failed to get a written commitment from Bhutto about the LoC becoming the international border.[76] India could have held on to the captured PoWs and the territory until something concrete had emerged on those lines.

The story of ceasefire line which later converted into Line of Control as per its changed nomenclature begins in January 1949 as a ceasefire line between the Indian and Pakistani armies at the end of their first war over Kashmir. For decades, Indian leaders have sought to convert the border drawn in blood through Jammu and Kashmir in 1947-48 into a legal, permanent, international frontier. Jawaharlal Nehru, the Prime Minister of India, on number of occasions, had suggested his Pakistani counterpart that the idea was liable to be considered as a solution to the problem. Converting the LoC into the judicial boundary between India and Pakistan is not former's official stand, however, for practical purposes, official India kept no illusion about the possibility of getting these territories, and would ideally like the *de facto* territorial *status quo* to be given the stamp of permanent, judicial legitimacy.[77] But Pakistani leaders from Liaquat Ali Khan to Mohammed Ali Bogra to Pervez Musharraf have always rejected the suggestion vehemently. Without doubt, LoC is one of the most important and difficult issues in the Kashmir conflict.

Viewing Pakistan's position as very weak at the conference table, Bhutto was unwilling to negotiate on Kashmir, but agreed at last with the condition that if any solution is provided, it would be implemented in a piecemeal manner and in step with the overall improvement in India-Pakistan relations. The Prime Minister of India insisted on a simultaneous settlement of all India-Pakistan disputes, including Kashmir. President Bhutto suggested that Indo-Pakistan disputes should be settled step by step and not in one stroke. He further suggested that the Kashmir dispute should be considered after the other disputes and differences had been resolved.[78] Though the Indians wanted an all-embracing settlement, this was impossible for Bhutto as the political temperature at home prohibited him from making any final settlement on such sensitive matters. By persuading India to accept a step by step settlement, Bhutto gained an important victory, for he needed time to win over internal opposition in Pakistan.

Bhutto's disagreement to incorporation of the Indian proposal in the Simla Agreement did not devalue the idea. Elaborating its merit Indira Gandhi said, "Neither country would be gaining or losing territory; it would not involve any transfer of population; and Kashmiris as an ethnic community would be left undivided. The line of control was thus to become an ethnic and linguistic frontier. At the time of the Kashmir division it was also an ideological frontier, being the limit of Sheikh Abdullah's influence. The line is also broadly a cultural divide. What is known as "Kashmiriyat"[79] does not extend to Pak-occupied Kashmir. Bhutto had also concluded that the Indian proposal was the only feasible one, but did not want the dark shadow of the Kashmir problem to continue to loom over Indo-Pak relations and was, thus, personally inclined to accept the *status quo* that is the line of control as a permanent solution.

From Simla, Bhutto returned to his country as a victor as he lost nothing in concrete and evaded tactfully any final settlement of the Kashmir problem. He had emerged with Pakistan's territory intact, to start a dialogue and above all, convince the people of Pakistan that Simla was not a sell-out. Pakistan had gone to Simla a defeated country and yet came away with an agreement that involve no further compromise. This was Bhutto's achievement. His first speech on his arrival at Lahore airport was typical, "It was never my intention to agree to another Tashkent. Another Tashkent can only be signed over my dead body.....on the vital question of Kashmir too, we have made no compromises. We told them categorically that the people of Kashmir must exercise their right of self-determination." But when some Indian political parties criticize their government on the agreement, Bhutto defended Indian cause by saying that this is the success of principles for which he paid compliments to the Prime Minister of India because she had accepted Pakistan's point of view by agreeing to the principles.

Despite the success at Simla, the domestic opposition did not spare Bhutto and charged him with agreeing to form a confederation of India and Pakistan while the rightist Jamaat-e-Islami said that it was far worse than the Tashkent Declaration. When he was taunted in a debate on the Agreement in the National Assembly for going back on his talk of waging a thousand-year war against India, Bhutto said frankly, ".....I cannot do it in the 5,10,15 years .... I will not do it because I know it will be the end of my country." At one point the proceeding turned to the talk of the futility of war and he did not miss the occasion to remind the members, "we may not have gained anything by peaceful means, but how much have we gained by war ? The gain by way of war is that even we have lost half the country .....Let us forget the past, let us forget our follies, let us forget all the wrongs we have done. We live in the same geographical area, we cannot get out of the subcontinent.......... Since we live here, let us find some way of living together.

At least the mutual understanding prailing at the moment did not last long. It was felt that the Simla Agreement of July 1972 failed to yield the expected and desired results. Pakistan's traditionally anti-India forces had not yet reconciled. Finding encouragement from the United States and the PRC Pakistan continued with its intransigence and the normalisation of relations which was expected under the Agreement did not progress.[80] There would seem to be a case for resolution of this question on the basis of mutual adjustments of the existing Line of Control, but the political will to bring about such a consummation has been lacking on both sides. Not different but almost opposite interpretations of the Simla

Agreement had marred the relations between the two countries for a number of years to come. While India adopted to the view that all outstanding issues between India and Pakistan are in purview of bilateralism the latter had ruled it out. A little later Bhutto himself went to say, "Pakistan is incomplete without Jammu and Kashmir both territorially and ideologically.[81] He asserted that Simla was 'to his mind irrelevant as far as Kashmir is concerned" .... no matter what was written on a piece of paper he may have signed; he had not accepted Indian position, Indira Gandhi's position[82]. The principled position of Pakistan on Jammu and Kashmir was that the Simla Agreement that the two countries had signed in 1972, recognised this as an outstanding dispute which remained to be settled. Even potentially it continues to be an explosive issue, as seen in the clashes which have taken place between the two in recent past.

Continuation as a 'Core Issue'

Once, in Pakistan's view the problem of Jammu and Kashmir was accepted as a "dispute", it began to consider the same as 'core issue'. In yester years, whenever, Indian over-cautiousness had taken the form of hedging after agreeing to discuss the problem of Jammu and Kashmir along with other issues which need to be resolved between the two countries, Pakistan had joined the offer of talks to the condition that the core issue of Jammu and Kashmir be settled first of all. On the dispute they failed to present any concrete suggestion officially except the context of outdated UN resolution. Over the years Pakistan has fashioned the terms of reference for discussion on Kashmir in the following concepts: Self-determination, the Muslim identity of the people of Kashmir, violation of human rights, the denial of representative government in Jammu and Kashmir[83] etc. There is no doubt that we had to contradict these pakistani arguments to establish the validity of our views on the status of Kashmir.

First of all, Pakistan needs to get rid of the imprisoned mindset that far from being "Core" the issue of Jammu and Kashmir is one of many, and certainly not central to Peace talks. There is socio-economic and socio-cultural growth to consider. However, over the years, India has also developed a duality of approach in case of Kashmir. Right from the period 1977 till 1996, on the onehand we have said that the Kashmir issue should be discussed and resolved "bilaterally with Pakistan", on the other, we connived from discussing the substance of the issue on the basis of the argument that the status of Kashmir as an integral part of India, cannot subject to any negotiations. Instead of adopting this contradictory logic we could have boldly agreed to discuss the Kashmir issue with Pakistan, emphasising that the substance of the dispute is Pakistan questioning the legality and constitutionally valid status of Jammu and Kashmir as an integral part of India. Our refusing to discuss the Kashmir issue specially and in substance has affected the credibility of our stance in the international community of which Pakistan has taken full advantage.

With the change of guards in New Delhi and Islamabad the talks between the two revived during 1996-97. It was for the first time since 1972 that New Delhi agreed to have talks with Pakistan on Kashmir. Earlier India pledged its support to the Simla Agreement but did not discuss the future of Kashmir. We made ourselves believe that there was no need to have talks with Pakistan. But Islamabad continued to treat the issue as a dispute between India and Pakistan and always emphasised on the third party mediation/intervention and wished its solution as per the UN resolution. No Indian government can accept the secession of Jammu and Kashmir and no Pakistani government can accept the LoC. At Simla in 1972, the LoC was sought to be imposed in the wake of a military defeat. It failed as such attempts do eventually. It is worse than pointless for a leader to embark on a peace process unless he is clear and realistic about the product he seeks, the concessions that are on offer and the one's he is himself prepared to make.[84] Both must be ready for a compromise and then only move forward.

Three round of Secretary–level talks were held between the two countries, the first followed, when the two Prime Ministers met at Male on 12 May 1997. In the talks, right from the beginning, Pakistan insisted that unless the "core issue of Kashmir" was solved, bilateral relations would never improve. It also implied that the Indian approach of normalising relations in other spheres would only serve to provide a cosmetic touch and would not materially alter the relations. While India continued to insist that it was ready to discuss Kashmir, normalisation of relations in other spheres, especially commercial, economic and people to people would help accelerate the process of normalisation.[85] The new dispensation was, no doubt, hopeful of solving the issue of Kashmir, was cautioned, 'The Gujral doctrine should not become a mantra. It is a commendable policy and has worked well in Sri Lanka, Bangladesh and Nepal. But in the case of Pakistan it must be applied to the extent that we get the right response from the other side. The doctrine's success will depend on matching deed for deed'.

The second round of Foreign Secretary–level talk was held in Islamabad in June 1997. As a proof of good gesture, New Delhi in haste, to achieve forward movement, agreed to constitute six working groups to discuss as many as problems it had identified. Islamabad's allegation was that there was no separate group constituted on Kashmir. The Government of Nawaz Sharif would have been satisfied if only a separate group was constituted to resume talks on kashmir as disclosed by the Pakistani premier in conversation with Kuldip Nayar, a visiting Indian journalist, 'I do not mind how long time it take provided we begin to discuss Kashmir'.[86] However, discussing Kashmir as a separate subject in a separate working group does not automatically imply that India would compromise in any manner on the status of Kashmir. Pakistan always discussed Kashmir as the first item on the agenda, but moved on to discuss other subjects in a practical manner. The eight point charter of priorities chalked out by the Foreign Secretaries during the talks also included confidence–building measures.

In the third round of talks that started in New Delhi, in the middle of September 1997, they did not succeed in breaking their earlier position. The Foreign-Secretary-level talks ended with no forward movement on outstanding bilateral issues, particularly a mechanism for discussing Kashmir due to the apparent lack of desire on Pakistan's part to show any progress. The deadlock on Kashmir issue continued as a Pakistani foreign office spokesman quoted,

"Pakistan considers Kashmir as the "Core Issue" which must be addressed urgently and effectively and a resolution on this contentious issue found in accordance with the UN resolutions. In the circumstances, the talks failed and even the opportunity provided by the President of the US in Newyork, where the Prime Ministers of India and Pakistan were meeting with the former, could not procure any concrete result as Islamabad missed no time to clear that the talks with India would continue only after the 'core issue' of Jammu and Kashmir was given "due place" and discussed and negotiated in a "substantive and specific manner."

The Political relations between the two was charged in March 1998 when a Bharatiya Janata Party-led coalition took over in New Delhi under the premiership of Atal Bihari Vajpayee. It culminated soon by explosion of nuclear devices by India on 11 and 13 May 1998, followed by Pakistan on 28 and 30 May. The nuclear tests done by them have introduced a new sense of urgency in Indo-Pak relations and unfortunately refocussed attention on Kashmir as a focal point of the dispute between the two countries. It meant the linkages between Kashmir and the possibility of the use of nuclear weapons took a more serious dimension. The nuclear game in South Asia now requires mature handling by both countries if they are to demolish that the argument of non-nuclear weapons state that the developing countries are too irresponsible to handle such weapons of mass destruction. At least, the explosion has made Kashmir an international issue. Since Kashmir was where the conflict was occurring, the world demanded that India and Pakistan either denuclearise themselves or settle the Kashmir dispute.

As indicated by the world opinion, they are bound to change the *status quo* or to accept it. It provided Pakistan an opportunity to internationalise its dispute with India, especially Kashmir. While expressing for a dialogue with India, Islamabad has also indicated its wish for an international guarantor in respect of any bilateral accord that might be reached. Nawaz Sharif, while addressing a joint session of the two houses of Parliament on 6 June 1998, added that today world attention has been diverted to Kashmir. They are realising now that without its solution peace cannot return to South

Asia and at the same time criticized the leading powers for their failure to implement the UN resolution on Kashmir for the right of self-determination of the Kashmiri people. In the same vein, Atal Bihari Vajpayee, the new Prime Minister of India, while taking part in a debate on nuclear issue in the Rajya Sabha on 8 June 1998, reiterated New Delhi's desire for earliest resumption of official talks with Pakistan on all outstanding issues including Kashmir but ruled out any third party mediation in the dialogue process. [87]

Two important events of the recent past were Atal Bihari Vajpayee's visit to Lahore in February 1999, followed by a return tour paid by General Pervez Musharraf to New Delhi in July 2001. On both the occasions though no forward movement seemed to be taken, exchange of views took place. The Lahore Declaration signed by the two Prime Ministers, issued on 21 February, resolved to intensify efforts to settle all outstanding issues, including Jammu and Kashmir. However the Declaration contained Pakistan's inability to reflect any softening of the Position on Jammu and Kashmir. At Agra, Musharraf insisted on the centrality of Kashmir to the peace process but also indicated at the famous breakfast on July 16, 2001 that the plebiscite idea was abandoned. Each side should 'negate' extreme proposals unacceptable to the other. On 18 December 2003 he also said, apropos the UN resolution, "Now we have left that aside, "but added," both sides need to talk to each other with flexibility going beyond stated positions, meeting halfway somewhere. Since he has consistently rejected the LoC, what could be the halfway point between the old demands of both sides – the plebiscite and the LoC ? The problem of Jammu and Kashmir is a challenge to the diplomatic creativity which would have to be met and find a happy medium sooner than most imagine.

References

1. Sarvepalli Gopal, Jawaharlal Nehru-A Biography, 1956-1964, Vol. III, Delhi, 1984, p. 84.
2. Dipankar Gupta, "Tricolour Over Kashmir – Territory, People and the Nation-State," The Times of India, 16 September 1999.
3. *Ibid.*

4. Jawaharlal Nehru, September 1946-May 1949, Vol. I, New Delhi, 1949, p. 176.
5. *Ibid.*, August 1949-February 1953, Vol. II, p. 112.
6. Kuldip Nayar, "Deadlock on Kashmir," The Hindustan Times, 11 April 1998.
7. Jawaharlal Nehru's Speeches, Vol. I, *op. cit.*, pp. 174-85.
8. Dr. Akhileshwar Singh, Political Leadership of Jawaharlal Nehru, New Delhi, 1986, pp. 230-31.
9. Nehru to Chief Ministers, 20 February 1948.
10. S. L. Poplai, Talbot Phillips eds., India and America, New Delhi, pp. 74-75.
11. Jawaharlal Nehru's Speeches, Vol. I, *op. cit.*, pp. 107-8.
12. Reply to debate on the President's Address in Parliament on August 11, 1951.
13. K. Subrahmanyam, "Flaws in Planning Programme, Need for Long-Range Assessment", The Times of India, 26 February 1990.
14. Jawaharlal Nehru's Speeches, Vol. II, p. 189.
15. N. B. Grant, "Flaws in India's Kashmir Policy," The Hindustan Times, 12 September 1998.
16. *Ibid.*
17. B. L. Sharma, Kashmir Awakes, Delhi, 1971, p. 178.
18. Yunas Samad, A Nation in Turmoil – Nationalism and Ethnicity in Pakistan, 1937-1958, New Delhi, 1995, pp. 126-127.
19. G. W. Choudhury, Pakistan's Relations with India-Story of Irreconciliable Hostility Between two Asian Neighbours, Meerut, 1971, p. 86.
20. B. N. Mullik, Kashmir, Bombay, 1971, p. 49.
21. G. W. Choudhury, *op. cit.*, p. 87.
22. Deva Narayan Mallik, Post-war International Politics-A Quadripartite Survey, Muzaffarpur, 1973, p. 480.
23. B. N. Mallik, *op. cit.*, p. 50.
24. The Hindu, 11 December 1955.
25. D. N. Mallik, *op. cit.*, p. 482.
26. As quoted in A. G. Noorani, "Words, Words, Words," The Hindustan Times, 10 June 2003.

27. Notes of Ministry of External Affairs to Foreign Ministry of Pakistan, 12 October 1956.
28. As quoted in A. G. Noorani, "First, an Agenda," The Hindustan Times, 28 June 2001.
29. *Ibid.*
30. The Times of India, 25 September 1960.
31. Pakistan Times, 4 May 1962.
32. Dawn (editorial), 27 October 1962.
33. D. C. Jha, Indo-Pakistan Relations, 1960-1965, Patna, 1972, pp. 80-90.
34. National Herald, 3 December 1962.
35. For the text of the Joint statement, see Foreign Policy of India : Text of Documents 1947-64, New Delhi, 1966, p. 368.
36. Nehru's Television interview in London on 13 December 1962.
37. Pakistan Times, 28 December 1962.
38. See the text of the Communiqué in Foreign Affairs Record, Vol. 8, 1962, p. 331.
39. Washington Post, 26 December 1962.
40. G. S. Bhargava, Pakistan in Crisis, Delhi, 1969, pp. 121-22.
41. Shelton Kodikara, Strategic Factors in Inter-State Relations in South Asia, No. 19, New Delhi, 1983, p. 40.
42. Benazir Bhutto, Foreign Policy in Perspective, pp. 32.33.
43. The Hindu, 12 January 1963.
44. The Times, 8 February 1963.
45. D. C. Jha, *op. cit.,* pp. 100-101.
46. For Bhutto's speech, see National Assembly of Pakistan Debates, Vol. 2, 17 July 1963, p. 1567.
47. Nehru's statement in the Rajya Sabha, 13 August 1963.
48. The Times of India, editorial, 27 February 1963.
49. Pakistan Times, 10 April 1963.
50. Nehru to Kennedy, 21 April, 1963.
51. As quoted in Salmaan Taseer, Bhutto, a Political Biography, New Delhi, 1980, pp. 58-59.
52. Sarvepalli Gopal, *op. cit.,* pp. 260-61.

53. The Times, 8 September 1965.
54. As quoted in A. G. Noorani, "War Hysteria Won't Work," The Hindustan Times, 26 December 2001.
55. *Ibid.*
56. Ibid., "Blinkers That Obstruct," 13 November 2002.
57. D. N. Mallik, *op. cit.*, p. 221.
58. Shelton Kodikara, *op. cit.*, pp. 39-40.
59. Salmaan Taseer, *op. cit.*, p. 65.
60. See author's book, 'Indo-Pak Nuclear Tension, 1974-1998, New Delhi, 2001, p. 98.
61. *Ibid.*, p. 99.
62. As quoted in Salmaan Taseer, *op. cit.*, pp. 66-67.
63. The Dawn, 15 January 1966.
64. The Times of India, 17 January 1966.
65. Salmaan Taseer, *op. cit.*, p. 67.
66. *Ibid.*, pp. 73-74.
67. Shelton Kodikara, *op. cit.*, p. 7.
68. D. N. Mallik, *op. cit.*, p. 389.
69. K. R. Narayanan, "New Perspectives in Indian Foreign Policy-India's Growth as a Regional Power," Foreign Policy of India, K. P. Misra, ed., New Delhi, 1977, p. 174.
70. A. N. Dar, "Solving the Kashmir Problem," The Hindustan Times, 23 March 1998.
71. Salmaan Taseer, *op., cit.*, pp. 140-45.
72. For the text of the Simla Agreement, see, H. O. Agarwal, Kashmir Problem-Its Legal Aspects, Allahabad, 1979, pp. 180-82.
73. *Ibid.*
74. *Ibid.*, p. 182.
75. Vasant Sathe, "Unwrapping Kashmir", The Hindustan Times, 7 July 2001.
76. As quoted in T. V. Rajeshwar, "LoC as the Border," *Ibid.*, 18 July 1998.
77. The Statesman, 7 September 2001.
78. Benazir Bhutto, *op. cit.*, pp. 40-43.

79. L. P. Singh, "The Line of Feud," The Hindustan Times, 14 November 1998.
80. See author's book, India's Foreign Policy–The First Study in Continuity and Change, New Delhi, 2001, p. 129.
81. Shelton Kodikara, *op. cit.,* p. 10.
82. As quoted in S. K. Singh, "Focus on Kashmir," The Hindustan Times, 18 July 1999.
83. J. N. Dixit, "Clarity on Kashmir," *Ibid.,* 23 July 1998.
84. A. G. Noorani, "Find a Happy Medium", *Ibid.* 20 April, 2004.
85. See author's book, India-South Asia Minus Congress Regimes, Patna, 2000, p. 68.
86. Kuldip Nayar, "Deadlock on Kashmir," The Hindustan Times, 11 April, 1998.
87. The Times of India, 9 June 1998.

5

Wars on Kashmir

Attack on Kashmir 1947-48

Conflict and rivalry between India and Pakistan has remained the core problem of inter-state relations in South Asia since the partition of the subcontinent in 1947. While the departure of the British removed country's colonial presence, it had, on the other, deprived her of the necessary military strength that England had represented for so many years – a strength that was clearly indispensable for the implementation of a viable defence system, or for the hitherto skilfully practised British forward policy of establishing a wide network of controlled buffer states in the north and naval protection in the South. With the disappearance of this factor the regional security environment had also changed considerably. It had become hostile and unstable. On the Western flank, the new India had now to face an unfriendly and suspicious Pakistan with whom difficulties had surged over Kashmir-difficulties that had finally exploded into military conflict. On her northern frontier – soon after the termination of the Chinese civil war – India had to reckon with the Chinese occupation of Tibet.[1] Thus, a frontier, kept quiet by the British had become alive and active.

The Kashmir war of 1947 broke out before either side could reconstitute and reorganise their respective armies; that war determined the military strategies of both India and Pakistan. India organised its Army almost exclusively as a plains army deployed for the contingency of war with Pakistan; Pakistan's plans were based on war with India. However their preparations were megre before the 3,150 km long Indo-Pak border that can broadly be divided into four sectors. The 950 km northern sector is largely mountainous and unsuitable for mechanised warfare. This sector contains several vulnerable areas such as Baramula – Poonch and Kargil. To its south is a 750 km sector along Jammu, Punjab and northern Rajasthan that is heavily defended from fortified positions supported by water bodies such as rivers and canals. The terrain is suited for mechanised, air-land warfare. The most vulnerable area here is the Chicken's Neck-Shakargarh bulge. The possibility of the Pathankot – Jammu – Srinagar artery being severed continues to be India's biggest territorial fear against Pakistan. This sector is vital for Pakistan too. Indian gains in this sector, which can be achieved with good equipment and planning, can have a devastating effect on that country. Further south is a desert sector of about 950 km where too air – land warfare is possible, and where it is far easier to make territorial gains. Still further south, the remaining border of about 500 km, up to Sircreek, is a marsh-cum-desert sector where major offensives are difficult.[2] Fluctuations in border position confirmed that Pakistan can pose a threat at several levels.

As a prelude to the outbreak of war between India and Pakistan on Kashmir, in the spring of 1947 an uprising against the then Maharaja of the state started in Poonch. It was an area in northwestern Jammu sandwiched between the Kashmir valley to the east and Rawalpindi division of northwestern Punjab to the west. Poonch had been an autonomous principality until second world war when the local ruler was deposed by the Dogra kinship. Explosive situation was created when the administration of Maharaja levied punitive taxes on local Muslim peasantry and the regime's Sikh and Dogra troops reacted with severe reprisals against the population. It was considered as a grave error on the part of Maharaja because Poonch, along with neighbouring west Punjab and NWFP districts was a prime recruiting ground for soldier's in British days. Indeed, a total of 71,667 men from Jammu and Kashmir who had served the British forces during the second World War 60,402 were Poonch Muslims. This large number of demobilized soldiers responded to government's taxation by evacuating their families to west Punjab areas beyond the boundaries of the princely state. As they came hostile to the ruler of the State of Jammu and Kashmir, in the aftermath of partition in August 1947, acquired a pro-Pakistan character. They returned to the area to confront regime's forces in which the former had gained success in Poonch district, except the town of Poonch. The success in Poonch fighting encouraged the pro-Pakistan chieftains of Western Jammu districts – Muzaffarabad, Poonch, Mirpur to proclaim the formation of a provisional "Azad" Jammu and Kashmir government in Rawalpindi, Pakistan, on 3 October 1947.

The developments in Poonch had far-reaching effects and it made the situation worse. Punjab and the NWFP were convulsed with violence in August-September 1947, communal massacres were taking place amid a collapse of civil order. Apart from this the incidents had invalidated the provisions of the Standstill Agreement signed between the State of Jammu and Kashmir and the Pakistan Government. In response to an offer made by the Prime Minister of Jammu and Kashmir in a telegram on 12 August 1947 which was accepted by the Government of Pakistan on August 16, the latter had taken responsibilities in regard to State's communication, supplies, post office and telegraphic arrangements. The Pakistan Government put pressure on the government in Kashmir, through an economic blockade and by fomenting communal troubles. In early September armed groups from Pakistan began infiltrating Jammu and Kashmir from west Punjab especially the Rawalpindi zone, looting and attacking Hindu and Sikh minorities as Nehru said in his broadcast to the nation on 2 November 1947, "We had received the reports of infiltration of raiding bands into the State territory of Jammu province and also of concentration of armed forces near the border of Kashmir, with the North-West Frontier Province. We were naturally concerned about this not only because of our close ties with Kashmir and her people but also because Kashmir is a frontier territory adjoining great nations and therefore we were bound to take an interest in the developments there".[3] But in the speech he denied to interfere and taking any step even though a part of the Jammu province was overrun by these raiders.

However, the Government of Jammu and Kashmir was unhappy with the incidents taking place in the State. By early October the Government of Jammu and Kashmir complained to Pakistan's foreign ministry that cross-border attacks were being conducted across several hundred kilometers of the Jammu border, from Rawalpindi in the north to Sialkot in the South. In reply, the Pakistani government drew attention to terror and atrocities perpetrated by Jammu and Kashmir against the Muslim population of Poonch. Later the Government of Jammu and Kashmir made a complain to the Governor-General of Pakistan for the violation of the Standstill Agreement and the border raids. Considering that still the overall protector of the Indian states, Mehar Chand, the then Prime Minister of Jammu and Kashmir complained to the British Prime Minister. He asked the British Premier to advise Pakistan to adopt a course of conduct consistent with the good name and prestige of the Commonwealth of which the latter claimed to be a member. Cross-border attacks, economic blockade and Pakistan's negative approach to Kashmir regimes' request, ultimately paved the way for a breakdown of relations between the two.

The action of Pakistan was condemned but on its part, perhaps, it was a calculated move for grabing the State of Jammu and Kashmir. As a follow up of its well-thought plan made by an over-confident Jinnah in September 1947, it decided to disperse the State forces of Jammu and Kashmir by manipulating skirmishes at several points along the border and then to launch a full-scale offensive through the tribesmen and Pakistani regulars under the overall command of Akbar Khan, a senior officer of the Pakistani army, who was given the code name of 'General Tariq'.[4] But, the Government of India, on the other, maintained strictly to the adherence of its policy of non-interference and even when the first aggression was made by Pakistan, there were no Indian Forces at all in Kashmr as acknowledged later by the Foreign Minister of Pakistan in the Security Council. A large part of that State had been under Pakistan's occupation for many years, India never intended to recapture this by force.[5] As situations warranted Pakistan's diplomatic strategy in Kashmir had backfired by mid-October.

The third and fourth week of October was crucial for all – the Government of Jammu and Kashmir, India and Pakistan. The crumbling position of the forces of Jammu and Kashmir as well as India's no otherwise signal had encouraged Pakistan to move forward. On 21 October the secrets of Kashmir drama began to unfold. On that day several thousand Pashtun tribesmen, known then and now for their impressive if unruly warrior tradition, began an offensive into Jammu and Kashmir from the sprawling Hazara district of the NWFP, located north and northwest of the princely state. This full scale invasion of the State of Jammu and Kashmir was, no doubt, a product of Pakistan's planning and design. Although invasion was carried out mainly by ex-soldiers and officers from Poonch area, it was led and conducted from outside the State of Jammu and Kashmir. The so-called raiders were well-armed and even possessed small artillery. They had competent leadership and probably officers of the Pakistan army, who helped in organising them. The actual tribesmen among the raiders were probably limited in number, the rest were ex-servicemen. Part of the Muslim element in the Kashmir forces had also gone over to them. Their equipment was good and they had a large number of lorries.[6] Pakistani hand in organising the attack was evident from the letter of Sir George Cunningham, the Governor– General of North-West Frontier Province, to General Lockhart, the British Commander-in-Chief of India. The letter contained a warning of tribal infiltrators and stated that the Government of the province was actively helping them. Pakistan's assistance to the operation was also clear from the meeting of the two Governor-Generals in which Jinnah, the Governor-General of Pakistan promised to call the whole thing off; if Lord Mountbatten, the Governor-General of India, would agree to his terms.[7] Thus, Pakistan was master-minding and commanding the whole affairs regarding the first attack on the State of Jammu and Kashmir.

The tribesmen and other Pakistani Nationals entered the state from two directions in motor vehicles to march towards the capital of the State. According to a reliable source a Pakistan Army brigade was kept ready at the frontier near Kohala and another brigade was kept at Sialkot near the Jammu frontier. The idea was that as soon as the raiders captured Srinagar, they would announce state's accession to Pakistan and then the regular Pakistan Army would march in and take possession. The invasion was a peculiar in the sense because it reminded of Nazi Germany, which was the fierce, blatant and false propaganda that had been carried on by their radio and press.[8] Although many of the raiders were motivated by the prospect of loot and rape, they were 'led by experienced military leaders familiar with the terrain and equipped with modern arms, they poured down in numbers estimated at 5,000–strong initially, with a fleet of transport vehicles numbering about 300 trucks.[9] At least 95 villages in Jammu Province had been destroyed by the raiders from Pakistan. Bhimbar, a considerable town, had also been sacked and destroyed. Other towns were besieged and a considerable part of Poonch and Mirpur areas was in the possession of the raiders. After taking the town of Muzaffarabad on the Pakistan–Jammu and Kashmir border, the raiders headed straight for the heart of the Kashmir Valley. Meeting almost no resistance from the Maharaja's crumbling forces as they advanced into the northern part of the valley, they rapidly captured the town of Baramulla, just twenty miles northwest of Srinagar.[10]

The example of Kashmir showed how feeble the administrative apparatus was in the state and how rapidly it may collapse in a real emergency. In a moment of crisis the Maharaja suddenly left Srinagar with his ministers, followed by the disappearance of other officers and there was no constituted authority worth in name. The army itself which was supposed to be strong, somehow faded away. About a quarter of it went over to the raiders or deserted. The rest was caught in small pockets and generally did not put up any good show at all. However, even in this situation it was a definite policy of the Government of India that war is a dangerous thing and must be avoided. From the military point of view there was little doubt that if there was war between India and Pakistan, Pakistan as a state would perish. But, undoubtedly, India would suffer very great injury and all our schemes of progress would have to be pushed aside for many many years. We can not be driven into extreme courses simply because thoughtless people sought and become bellicose. We must all, in our own way, try to make people understand the situation and to reduce the tension so that normal relations might be maintained with Pakistan.[11] The initial success of the raiders signalled that the Srinagar was in peril and it was not only for Kashmir but for the whole of India. On 24 October Baramulla fell into the hands of the invaders.

In the circumstances the Maharaja's administration sent an urgent request to New Delhi on 24 October for military assistance to repulse the raiders. Having assessed the alarming situation in the State of Jammu and Kashmir, the top Indian leaders were more than willing to oblige. But they were advised by Lord Mountbatten, the then Governor-General of India, not to send the troops without first securing the accession of Jammu and Kashmir to India, because prior to accession it would be an Indian invasion on a neutral territory. After completing legal formalities the State of Jammu and Kashmir was acceded to the Indian Union on 27 October 1947.

The request for accession and military assistance was made on behalf of both the Maharaja and Sheikh Abdullah. Jawaharlal Nehru, while defending the accession narrated the deteriorating situation in Jammu and Kashmir. "These raiders had crossed Pakistan territory and they were equipped with Bren guns, machine guns, mortars and flame-throwers and had at their disposal large number of transport vehicles. We gave earnest consideration to this situation in our Defence Committee on the 25th and 26th October. The position on the morning of the 26th was that the raiders were marching towards Srinagar and there was no military detachment capable of stopping them. If we had delayed the decision even by 24 hours, Srinagar would have fallen and would have suffered the tragic fate that befell Muzzaffarabad, Baramulla and other places."[12] On the day of accession Sheikh Abdullah resisted the tribal invasion because it represented an attempt to coercively absorb Kashmir into Pakistan. An another political commentator was of the view that many Kashmiris were "out raged" by the Pakistani attempt to first secure accession by wooing the hated Maharaja, and after that failed, "to decide the issue by force".[13] The news of Indian military intervention proliferated like a wild-fire and Jinnah was said to have asked the British general commanding the Pakistan army to deploy regular Pakistani troops in Kashmir but he was advised not to do so because the territory was now legally and constitutionally a part of India and such a deployment would amount to a declaration of war with India.

As the Srinagar was in peril, the Government of India decided in the afternoon of 26th October to send its troops to the State of

Jammu and Kashmir. The Indian forces landed in Srinagar on 27 October and fought a defensive war, holding operation to prevent Srinagar from being overrun in the first week of operation. Then came a series of heroic feats which had done India proud. A massive air lift of troops was arranged in an unbelievably short time. "It was", to use the words of Patrick French, "a stunning operation. Mountbatten too, was surprised and told Alan Campbell Johnson that "as a military operation, the speed of the fly-in on 27 October left our SEAC efforts standing".[14] Initially the Indian forces were small in numbers to begin with but immediately on arrival they rushed into action to stop the invaders. A number of valuable lives were laid down. Lt. Colonel Ranjit Rai, whose plane was the first to touch down at the Srinagar airport, boldly dashed to pattan and died fighting against heavy odds. Major Som Nath was another soldier who, though outnumbered seven to one, engaged the raiders at Badgam and kept them away from the airport. But when conditions looked bleak, Sardar Patel, accompanied by Defence Minister Baldev Singh, flew to the State capital, assessed the situation and on return to Delhi ordered stoppage of all airline services and diversion of all planes for flying troops to Srinagar. The timely arrival of reinforcements enabled Brigadier Sen to lure the raiders into the net of Indian forces, near Shaltang, and attack them on November 5 from three sides. The raiders were routed and Kashmir Valley was saved.

The way the Indian armed forces improvised the initial airlift using both air force and civil aircraft, as well as the speed with which the army halted the enemy and then counterattacked, were impressive. However, this initial success was for two reasons. First, some of the raiders had engaged in looting, rape and murder against the overwhelmingly Muslim population during their advance, spoiling any possibility of goodwill and support from the co-religionists they had ostensibly come to liberate. Second, the existence and cooperation of a well-honed National Conference organisation throughout the valley was invaluable to the Indians. With the signing of the accession Maharaja had appointed Sheikh Abdullah as the head of interim administration. In Srinagar the NC soon emerged as the *de facto* government and thousands of volunteers enrolled in National

Conference's "National Militia" quickly organised by the Sheikh's top aides like Bakshi Ghulam Mohammed and G. M. Sadiq, which included a women's unit. A plus point for India was the momentum of World War II, which had concluded only two years earlier.

In quick succession the Indian forces first pushed the raiders out of the vicinity of Srinagar, elimating a threat to the city's airfield. They then retook Baramulla on 8 November and Uri on 14, from which on road takes off to Domel on the Abbottabad frontier and another to Poonch where a Kashmir detachment had been beleaguered for quite some time. However, the position in Jammu was not very good at the time because communications were difficult and the area was very close to West Punjab from where supplies could reach raiders easily.[15] A large number of tribal people and ex-servicemen from Pakistan are crossing the Kashmir border into the Poonch areas. There was authentic evidence that increasing pressure was being put on our troops from fresh hordes of armed people coming through Pakistan. Thousands of Pathans had already come down to Jhelum and Gujrat districts and to some extent into Sialkot and there they were grouped, trained and kept in formation with the obvious connivance of Pakistan officials.[16] By late November the Indian counter-attack had lost momentum owing to the approach of winter and the difficult nature of the terrain.

In the meantime, Liaquat Ali Khan, the Prime Minister of Pakistan, through a telegram on 16 December 1947, expressed the desire for a peaceful and honourable settlement of the issue. He stated that the problem of Kashmir "can only be solved by an act of statesmanship......and not by legal disputations as to how Pakistan is party to the dispute or how UNO can be brought in". Nevertheless, the activities of the Pakistan authorities in regard to Kashmir belied this approach, in response, the Government of India made a formal request in writing on 22 December to the Prime Minister of Pakistan. The letter stated briefly the acts of aggression of Pakistan and the forms of aid given by Pakistan to the invaders. It also asked the Government of Pakistan to call upon Pakistani nationals to cease participating in the attack on the Jammu and Kashmir and to deny the invaders : (i) all access to and use of Pakistan territory for operation against the Kashmir state ; (ii) all military and other supplies; (iii) all other kinds of aid that might tend to prolong the present struggle.[17] Through this letter the Government of India expressed its earnest desire to live on terms of friendship with Pakistan and hoped that the request would be acceded to promptly and without reserve. Failing to get any reply from Pakistani authorities, on December 30, a formal reference was made to the Security Council of the UNO, a copy of which was sent by telegram to the Pakistan Government, the very next day. By late December Pakistan had opened a new front to the South in the Jammu – Naoshera belt, and it was one of the reasons why India approached the UN Security Council on new year's day, requesting it to intervene and stop the Pakistani aggression.

The second phase of an all-out offensive resumed by the early spring of 1948. The Indian troops had been built up to the strength of two divisions, and by the summer to three divisions. In April-May 1948 the Indian army made further gains, retaking the strategic town of Rajouri on 11 April 1948 on the Jammu front and expanding India- controlled territory farther north in the valley. This threatened the security of Pakistan and it also led to a large exodus of Kashmir Muslim refugees to Pakistan. At this point the regular Pakistani army entered the fray and the fighting stalemated. But the Indian forces had definite advance towards the border of Pakistan; the headwork's of the Jhelum canals, which is situated in Kashmir and on which the irrigation of Pakistan relied so much, was also threatened. The special correspondent of *The Times* at Srinagar reported, 'The Indian army has worked extremely hard during the winter months and its position has been improved......the force has been considerably strengthened and it should be soon ready for a limited offensive. Already some units have advanced from Rajouri in Jammu and from Uri.....'[18] In accordance with the recommendations of its Commander-in-Chief, the Government of Pakistan in early May 1948 sent its troops to Kashmir to hold certain defensive positions and to prevent the Indian army from advancing to the borders of Pakistan.

Thus began the last phase of the first Indo-Pak war on Kashmir that continued for the rest of 1948. It occurred when Pakistani forces launched a thrust towards the valley from the mountainous areas of Gilgit and Skardu to the north. The drive was repulsed by Indian light tanks at the Zojila Pass, which marks the boundary between the valley and the huge, sparsely populated region of Ladakh. The region too, witnessed remarkable feats of heroism. Air Commander Mehar Singh flew his plane on May 24, 1948, at 23,000 feet without oxygen on a hitherto unchartered course and landed at the rough strip of Leh airport located at the height of 11,555 feet. This enabled the Indian forces to be airlifted to Leh. Another unique feet was of Major General Thimayya who took his tanks to the snow-covered Zojila pass at the height of 11,578 feet on November 1, 1948. General Thimayya's feat has been compared to Hannibal crossing the Alps with his elephants. The Indian army strengthened their position by capturing the Ladakh towns of Dras and Kargil in November. The victory of the region ensured the completion of strategic road link between Srinagar and Leh, the centre of Buddhist-dominated eastern Ladakh.

However, it appeared difficult to capture the mountainous territories beyond the valley, with winter setting in. There was also a fear of general war, with two Indian armoured brigades concentrated against Lahore and two Pakistani brigades poised opposite Jammu threatening the vital Indian supply line into Kashmir. Apart from this the Indian policy-makers had, from the beginning, some kind of propensity to leave the area of so-called Azad kashmir beyond Uri with Pakistan as they knew that Gilgit and other points of strategic importance were covetted so much by the Anglo-American strategists that if India would make the recovery of that part of Kashmir a high priority objective it would bring the West to a point of war in favour of Pakistan against India or, at least, would make a hell of India's relations with the West. Such developments the Indian policy makers could not afford to risk with their country's great limitations and rational aspirations.[19] The war between the two ended after a UN-sponsored ceasefire agreement came to be effective from one minute before midnight on January 1,1949, and after protracted discussions, an agreement on demarcation of the ceasefire line was also reached on July 27, 1949. The truce of January 1949 came into effect only because each side was exhausted and convinced that it could no longer make significant territorial gains against the other.

The political decision to refer the Kashmir issue to the United Nations Security Council, to commit a plebiscite to ratify the accession, and to agree to a ceasefire have been criticised widely. The first question being raised among knowledgeable circle is why the Indian army asked to stop fighting at the ceasefire line. In 1948, we could have solved the Kashmir problem if the military had been allowed to go on with the war.[20] Just a week's further action by the Indian Army would have enabled it to vacate the Pakistani aggression from the whole of Jammu and Kashmir. General K.V. Krishna Rao says in his book '*Prepare or Perish*' : Infact, if at the end of 1948, operations were continued, perhaps the enemy could have been evicted even from the remainder of the territory under their occupation, with of course, additional forces.[21] On the issue, whether India could have cleared the Pakistani from the mountainous areas to the north and west of the valley if the ceasefire had been delayed, there are differing perceptions. However, most of the senior officers of the time had felt that substantial areas to the north could have been recaptured if the ceasefire had been delayed.

As a result of the ceasefire India had under her physical control the best and major part of the state. It left the Indians with the bulk of Jammu and Kashmir's territory 139,000 of 223,000 square kilometers, approximately 63 per cent and population. The Indians had gained the prize piece of real estate, the Kashmir valley, and they also controlled most of the Jammu and Ladakh regions. These areas became Indian Jammu and Kashmir. The Pakistanis were left with a long strip of land running on a north-south axis in western Jammu and Kashmir, mostly Jammu districts bordering Pakistani Punjab and the NWFP a slice of Ladakh (Skardu), and the remote mountain zones of Gilgit and Baltistan. With this ceasefire line and division of the State between India and Pakistan the Kashmir dispute had been born. But on the other, the ceasefire was hailed as a great achievement for the UN in its attempt to settle the Kashmir dispute, at least, stop fighting between the two nations going on for more than a year.

The War of 1965

The year 1965 witnessed two wars between India and Pakistan – one over the Rann of Kutch in April, followed by a full– fledged war in the State of Jammu and Kashmir with the use of regular armies from both the sides in August-September. Armed border clashes between Indian and Pakistani troops were a constant theme in relations between the two countries, but increased greatly in number and intensity in the early part of 1965. It was a one more in the long series of hostile clashes between India and Pakistan but the confrontation in the dismal waterland was the biggest armed clash between the two armies since the Kashmir war of 1948. The Kutch war of 1965, though fought with tanks and armoured vehicles by India and Pakistan, was a 'mini-battle' and was sparked off by a relatively minor border dispute in an area separating West Pakistan (Sind Province) from the State of Gujarat in India. Pakistan's claim to the Rann of Kutch was based on the ground that it was either a landlocked sea or a boundary lake, to which the principles of international law applied, and that therefore the boundary between the two States ran through the middle of the Rann. In the Indian view, there was no dispute regarding the Kutch boundary, since the former princely states of Kutch had always been in possession of the Rann in its entirety and since in any case it was not an inland sea or lake, to which the principles of international law applied as contended by Pakistan.

The controversy between India and Pakistan over this area dated back to 1948. In 1956 it led to border skirmishes. The matter was further discussed in the conferences of October 1959 and January 1960 between Swaran Singh and K. M. Shaikh but no solution was found. From January 1965 this area became a scene of trouble and created a very alarming situation in April 1965. The incidents which led to the armed clash between India and Pakistan started with what India called the "intrusion" of the Pakistani Rangers into the Kanjarkot area in the Rann of Kutch and with the setting up of a post by them at Kanjarkot.[22] The Indians considered the Pakistani intrusion in the Kanjarkot area, extending to more than a mile and a half inside Indian territory. The Government of India in its notes of 12 and 18 February

1965 protested against these activities, asked for the immediate withdrawal of Pakistani "intruders" from the area and for the immediate restoration of the *status quo ante*, and suggested an early demarcation of the Kutch – Sind boundary. Pakistan, on the other hand, claimed that the Kanjarkot fort was well within the area of the Rann of Kutch which had been in the *de facto* possession of Pakistan since August 1947.

A little war flared up between India and Pakistan on 9 April 1965. According to Indian sources regular armed forces of 51st Infantry Brigade of Pakistan supported by heavy mortar, MMG, and artillery fire from twenty-five pounder guns, attacked the Indian posts at Sardar. There were heavy losses on both sides in these attacks and the Government of India, on 11 April protested against these attacks to the Pakistani Government and demanded adequate compensation for the loss of life and property. However, Pakistani side alleged that India attempted to dislodge Pakistani forces from their territory at Ding on 9 April and said that India had attacked the Pakistani post at Kanjarkot on 12 April.[23] It specifically suggested on 13 April a three–point formula that envisaged; (i) ceasefire (ii) restoration of the *status quo* and (iii) negotiations to settle the Rann of Kutch dispute. But India remained adamant on Kanjarkot as Indian Prime Minister made it clear that unless Kanjarkot was vacated by the Pakistanis, India would not agree for talks.[24] Failure of peace proposals led to the further massive attack by Pakistan in the Rann of Kutch.

As reported by the Indian side a large-scale fighting took place between the two with Pakistan launching military attack on four Indian posts at Point 84, Sardar, Vigokot and Chhad Bet, six to eight miles inside the Indian claim line. It was for the first time that Pakistan had used armour in course of fighting in the Rann, which, India described as an almost undeclared war. About respective losses that lasted for a week 24-29 April 1965, each side claimed a heavy toll of life on the other side and comparatively negligible losses for itself. In the meantime, on 26 April the British Prime Minister, Harold Wilson, authorised the British High Commissioners to express the "profound concern of the British Government to President Ayub and

Prime Minister Lal Bahadur Shastri and Britain's readiness to help in any way we could". This message was also communicated to both personally by the British Prime Minister, in which the two had ultimately agreed. The fighting between the two was stopped through a ceasefire on July 1, a day after signing the Kutch Agreement. It contained three Articles and provided for a ceasefire, the restoration of the *status quo ante* as on 1 January 1965 and ministerial level talk for the determination and demarcation of the Kutch-Sind boundary. Because an alternative was made in the Agreement, the dispute was later settled by international arbitration, 32,00 square miles of the disputed territory being awarded to India, and 350 square miles to Pakistan.

The April war of 1965, was, however, only a dress rehearsal for the larger Indo-Pak conflict which followed in August-September. Establishment of a very close relationship between Pakistan and China, and the anti-Indian character of it, created a sense of injury in India because it felt that Pakistan was taking undue advantage of India's hostile relations with China. The latter's support to Pakistan encouraged it to press India for concessions, and even to use force to change the *status quo* in its favour.[25] The relations between the two countries took a serious and dramatic turn when about 3000 Pakistani armed infiltrators moved into Kashmir valley across the ceasefire line on August 5, 1965. It took several selected sectors like Chaknot, Keran and Tithwal up in the north and Uri, Poonch, Mendhar, Rajouri and Naushehra in the Western sector. They also crossed into the Chhamb and Samba sectors of the international border of the State of Jammu and Kashmir.

The large-scale infiltration that took place in August 1965 was the result of an earlier preparation made by the Government of Pakistan in consultation with the army headquarters. Around the summer of 1965, a smaller inner circle of Ayub Khan, of which Z. A. Bhutto, the then Foreign Minister of Pakistan, was one of the most influential members, made the decision to invoke an armed uprising in Kashmir. Though the inner circle included the Information Secretary Altaf Gauhar, Foreign Secretary Aziz Ahmed, Defence Secretary Nazir Ahmed and representing the army General Akhtar

Malik, it was Bhutto who convinced the President to act with his strong and forceful arguments. His persuasion was crucial and he was of the view that we wanted to pursue a policy of confrontation with India but time was running out. We had to act now or it would be too late. The idea of sending infiltrators was exclusively of Bhutto's who was trying to build up his image as a tough anti-Indian leader.[26] He prepared a working Paper – which came to be known as the Bhutto Plan to argue that if India was to be tackled at all, now was the time.

The overall code name of the Plan was "Gibraltar Operation". Broadly, the plan envisaged, on a short term basis, sabotage of military targets, disruption of communications and as a long-term measure, distribution of arms to the people of occupied Kashmir and initiation of a guerilla movement there with a view to starting an uprising in the valley eventually. The Gibraltar force consisted of approximately 7000 Mujahideen from Azad Kashmir. Most of them was given some guerilla training within the short time available before it was launched. It was armed with light machine guns and mortars, besides personal weapons and was equipped with wireless sets.[27] However, the main aim for which the hazardous missions were entrusted to them were not accomplished. They were targeted to enter the city of Srinagar, coinciding with an expected demonstration by some political parties on August 9, hoping that they could so disorganise the affair as to create a situation of an armed rebellion. Their suppression would involve Indian troops, which in turn, would cause reverberations around the world, particularly among Indian Muslims, a chain of protests and adverse reaction from world opinion. This, it was hoped, would force India to reconsider its position on Kashmir and perhaps bring about a situation where fruitful talks could be held on a plebiscite in the troubled valley.[28]

The immediate purpose of the Government of Pakistan belied as the plan was certainly audacious and perhaps foolhardy. In afterwards the causes of its failure discussed at length, at various levels of command and found that the reason was lack of necessary preparations in the valley for the extremely difficult tasks before they were undertaken. They felt, in the first place, that the adequate preparations to start guerilla was needed to consult the public leaders across the ceasefire line about our aims and intentions. The leaders had to have a proper underground organisation in the valley which should have jointly planned the operation with us and should have remained in touch with us after it was started. Because of the haste with which the operation was launched, even Azad Kashmir leaders were not taken into confidence by the advocates of guerilla raids.[29] Even those who were willing to help were unable to cooperate first, because they were not mentally prepared for it and second, due to the presence of nearly five Indian infantry divisions. The Indian Army of occupation was nearly five times stronger than Pakistan had in Azad Kashmir. They were also vigilant due to the agitation in the valley, and reacted strongly.[30] History has proved that the success of guerilla warfare greatly depends on the cooperation of the people of the area where it is carried out.

But what gave Pakistan an exaggerated picture of its military might was first, the humiliating defeat of the Indian army at the hands of China in NEFA in 1962 and second, the partial success of the Pakistani Army in its clash with its Indian counterpart in the Rann of Kutch in April 1965. Since then the Pakistanis went wild and nourished high hopes regarding their war with India. Mizanur Rahman Chowdhury said in the National Assembly of Pakistan on 10 July 1965 that optimism was generally expressed in West Pakistan that in the event of a war with India, Pakistani troops would occupy Delhi and its Red Fort and hoist the Pakistani flag on it.[31] However, in Pakistani provocation no less important role was played by Sheikh Abdullah, the controversial leader of the State of Jammu and Kashmir who made an extensive tour of Islamabad, followed by his visit to China. Before his departure for Pakistan, the Government of India had left Abdullah in no doubt about its position on Kashmir that no compromise could be made on the State's accession to India and any proposal aimed at ending the accession or the secular values of the Indian State was ruled out of court.[32] Abdullah's new posture convinced Pakistan that it would get the support of the people of Jammu and Kashmir. Further the

Government of India was alarmed by Abdullah's tough stance on self-rule and by his insistence on the need for Pakistan's involvement in finding a serious, durable resolution to the Kashmir question.

Pakistani attempts to seize Kashmir by sending a few thousand armed infiltrators had miserably failed. The Indian army had not only sent infiltrators back across the ceasefire line but occupied a number of Pakistani posts between 15 and 30 August. The Indian aggressive moves in Azad Kashmir left Pakistan with no option but to take a decisive battle in Kashmir at that time. In the circumstances Pakistan had to do something if it wanted its plan to succeed and to save its face against Indian success in the area. On 1 September, Pakistan committed its regular army and attacked Akhnur in the Chhamb Jurian sector where India's critical Jammu-Srinagar highway could be threatened. The place chosen for the attack by Pakistan was suitable to it because in the Chhamb sector Pakistan had direct and short lines of supply and a ground to manoeuvre its tanks. If the Pakistani forces had besieged Jurian, the bridges across the Chenab at Akhnur would have been placed in imminent jeopardy. The capture of the strategic town of Akhnur would pave the way for easily cut off Jammu from Poonch, by destroying the Jammu-Poonch road, one of the two main roads linking Kashmir with the rest of India.[33]

The measures taken by Pakistan had been pre-planned in consultations with Akhtar Malik and Yahya Khan. It mounted a major attack with the infantry of a brigade strength into Chhamba backed with seventy tanks and preceded by heavy shelling of the Indian positions by the Pakistani artillery. The division, being the infantry component of the main strike force in Pakistan was not committed to ground and was the only formation available at that time for employment in the Chhamb-Akhnur sector. One of its infantry brigade already formed part of the counter-offensive force from the time it was launched. The Pakistani troops fought their way forward and finding it difficult to check the advance, India sent its Air Force into action on 1 September. However, the Pakistani advance continued unabated and by 5 September their total advance in Chhamb sector into Indian territory was said to have seventeen miles.[34] Encouraged by the advance of the Army General Mohammad

Musa, the Commander-in-Chief of Pakistan, was able to send message to his soldiers "you have got your teeth into him. Bite deeper and deeper until he is destroyed". But it was not easy to capture Akhnur quickly because the Indian troops had reinforced it substantially by then. By 5 September, a hopeless situation had developed for India in Chhamb sector.

Five days later of the Pakistani attack in Chhamb sector, India responded on 6 September 1965. Like Pakistan, India selected Punjab, a region where it was in advantageous position as the former had in Chhamb. It made a three-pronged attack across the West Pakistani border from Firozepur, Gurdaspur and Wagh-Amritsar areas. With the Indian attack, a full-fledged undeclared war between India and Pakistan broke out. The occasion reminded the prophetic words of Nehru, who warned the country in his new year's message in 1952, "If Pakistan by mistake invades Kashmir, we will not only meet them in Kashmir, but it will be a full-scale war between India and Pakistan."[35] Important foreign daily newspapers including *The Newyork Times* and *The Times*, admitted editorially that they were at war. The Indian Army was reported moving forwards Lahore, Sialkot and Kasur. It justified the moving of its army because the action was necessitated in order to forestall the opening of a new front by Pakistan across the international border in the Indian Punjab. Further on 8 September Indian forces made a diversionary attack across the Rajasthan-Sind border at Gadra Road in order to hold down the Pakistani Division located in the Karachi-Hyderabad region and prevent it from either moving north to the main battle area or from attacking in Kutch again.[36] Even some noted observers were of the view that a strong reason for attacking India was to relieve the pressure on the Indian forces in the Chhamb area of Kashmir.

The Indian attack of 6 September clearly took the policy-makers in Islamabad by surprise, who till then, retained an exaggerated opinion of the Pakistan army's strength. "We thought our armoured divisions would cut through like a knife through butter. But they messed everything up dividing the armoured division......and then of course Khem Karan was a disaster.[37] From then onwards, Pakistan's security took precedence over other missions in Kashmir.

The country, in view of its limited resources and because the threat to Azad Kashmir had receded, it withdrew from Chhamb the additional artillery allocated to the counter-offensive force and an infantry brigade for deployment on the Sialkot front.[38] The 1965 war revealed the basic weakness of Pakistan's defence system : it was geared to the security of West Pakistan, and largely to operations in the Kashmir sector.

Z. A. Bhutto was not afraid of the retreating position of Pakistan because he did not feel that the outbreak of war meant abandoning confrontation. It was an extension of the same thing. A military action would be even more effective in mobilising world opinion against Indian control of the valley. But President Ayub Khan could not bear the high tension of continuing a war. He pleaded with the Ambassador of United States for American intervention to stop the conflict and appeared ready to grab at any straw which would bring about peace. Suddenly on 23 September 1965 he accepted a ceasefire based upon a United Nations resolution. Thus, the 22-day war between India and Pakistan came to an end. President Ayub had admitted later that the decision to embark on confrontation with India in 1965 was his 'weakest and fatal point.[39] From India's point of view, particularly in military terms, the 1965 war was not much more than an honourable draw. It helped greatly to restore the morale of the nation, and that of the armed forces, both badly shaken by the 1962 debacle. After the USSR mediated Tashkent Agreement in January 1966, captured territories and prisoners of war were exchanged.

The War of 1971

The Indo-Pak war of 1971 was different from the previous wars in several respects. It was not of India's making. Pakistan brought it on itself by its rejection of democracy. It was the first instance when East Pakistan was the source of the dispute and it was the first time East Pakistan was the main theatre of operations. Pakistan got trapped into it through poor internal political management and hubris, not unlike the way India had gone stumbling into the 1962 war through weak external political management and misplaced confidence.[40] The failure of the Pakistan state to allow adequate political and economic space for its eastern wing and to accommodate the latter's distinctiveness had led to inter-wing conflict. Within a year of the 1965 war, Mujib-ur-Rahman had made his six-points autonomy demand. The over-confidence of the Pakistan army and West Pakistan politicians permitted matters to go downhill, leading eventually to the military crackdown of 25 March 1971. Events apart, there was a framework of social philosophy shared by both the Indian ruling party and the Awami League – the leading nationalist force in Bangladesh that seemed to have place India in a privileged position in the Bangladesh nationalist discourse. The Awami League's political projects as broadly articulated in its Six-Point Programme, had a very close affinity to Nehru's social philosophy of the Indian Congress.[41] The mixture of a rather populist version of socialism with a reformist vision of state capitalism, and an ideological adherence to the principle of secular and democratic state brought India under the Congress and Bangladesh under the Awami League within the same general framework of state ideology. Thus, India's involvement in the liberation movement became a national policy-issue instead of being only emotional.

Things in East Pakistan went from bad to worse. The civil war of 1971 brought India decisively to the position of supporting the nationalist forces against the Pakistani state while the nationalists themselves and the East Pakistani people in very large numbers had sought refuge in India. A massive exodus of the people of Bangladesh into India commenced on the night of March 25, 1971. This was an exodus unprecedented in known history across an international frontier. For India, already overburdened with million of rural unemployed, who are increasing daily, the permanent absorption of 10 million destitutes would have been economically crippling. The refugee migration was a serious matter for India, for if the refugees were allowed to stay long, they were likely to settle permanently. It created a intolerable demographic pressures on the mostly densely populated neighbouring states and territories of India. The economic implications of the number of refugees, which stood then at ten million, and generated economic pressure on India was discernible from the fact that the Indian Finance Minister had made two additional provisions of nearly 330 crores of rupees or approximately 500 million in India's annual budget for the year 1971-72 which ended on March 31, 1972.[42] In view of the fast deteriorating conditions in the eastern wing of Pakistan and the intransigence of its military rulers Mrs. Gandhi thought it wise to take some precautionary steps. The first such measure was the signing of the Indo-Soviet Treaty of Peace Co-operation and Friendship on 9 August 1971.

Towards the end of October 1971, Mrs. Gandhi set out on a tour of Western Europe and the United States to inform the policy-makers of the countries in her itinerary that zero hour was approaching in the sub-continent and they should do something about it. The visit was aimed to build up world opinion in favour of the Bangladesh freedom struggle and on convincing even the most sceptical about the unbearable burden the unending stream of refugees was putting on India. New Delhi's arguments were: (i) there could be no military solution to the Bangladesh problem and all military action there must stop forthwith, (ii) the flow of refugees into India must stop; (iii) conditions must be created in Bangladesh to enable the refugees to return their homes in peace and security; (iv) a political solution acceptable to the people of Bangladesh was the only way to ensure normalcy; and (v) the situation was fraught with serious dangers for the peace and security of the region.[43] However, the scenario in South Asia began to change in important respects when the new forces took concrete shape, starting with the Indo-China war of 1962. In the subcontinent change also flowed from the hardening of international alignments of India and Pakistan: India with the Soviet Union, Pakistan with the US and China.

But still the international community had hoped that by counselling moderation to Pakistan and India it had done its duty towards forestalling disaster in the subcontinent. The world, in fact, was hesitating in coming to grips with the basic issue which was not the traditional India-Pakistan friction or even the refugees but the confrontation between the Pakistan Government and the people of Bangladesh following the military rulers, refusal to accept the verdict of the electorate. After great public pressure within America,

Washington came round to say that a political solution of the East Bengal issue was necessary for speedy solution of the problem. It was only in the third week of November that India was informed by America regarding its request to Yahya to open a dialogue with top Bangladesh leaders with an initial assurance that should a political settlement be found feasible, Mujib's views would be ascertained. By then, the activities of the Mukti Bahini who were assisted by India and the local population, had assumed serious proportions. Even responsible opinion in India was that a war would be cheaper than the cost of maintaining the ten million refugees. The war could also offer the solution to the refugee problem.

Though the Government of India had adopted the policy of non-interference in East Bengal crisis and wanted only that the Government of Pakistan should go for peaceful and amicable negotiation with East Bengal leaders of the Awami League, the President Yahya Khan, in his address to the country on October 12, 1971, blamed India for encouraging the 'secessionist movement in East Bengal".[44] He also viewed, in his earlier statements that any success of Mukti Bahini, the freedom fighters of East Bengal would be considered by him as an act of aggression which would justify his having "total and open war against India. It was unfortunate that from March 25 to November 15, 1971, there were over 600 military intrusions or border incidents committed by Pakistani forces on the Indo-East Bengal border,[45] the speech of Yahya was followed, within few days, by a massive build up of the Pakistani army against India's Western frontiers, including the areas adjacent to the ceasefire line in Jammu and Kashmir. Probably India was laying a trap for Yahya and he was walking into it. Without his taking the initiative to wage war, New Delhi would not have thought of going beyond a few miles into East Bengal, definitely not upto Dacca anyway. However, when situation went out of control Yahya and his generals began to feel that they had been driven into a corner. All his actions showed that he was desperately anxious to avoid launching his country on a full-scale war that might doom his forces in East Pakistan and would have unforeseeable consequences in the West Wing. Militarily, an offensive in the West would mean throwing his outnumbered and less well-equipped army against strongly entrenched Indian defensive positions.[46] India's security management was commendable during the eight months between the Pak crackdown on 25 March and the beginning of war in December.

By November 1971 the liberation struggle of East Bengal had reached a critical stage. For the military rulers of Pakistan the situation had become very desperate. Naturally, border clashes between Indian and Pakistani forces had increased and casualties were mounting every day. Yahya's threat warned India which dispensed its aircraft and took steps to protect its coast, harbour, and ships against surprise attack. In the meantime Pakistan's military rulers got an assurance of support from the United States and Peking. Their actions made it clear that they would go on helping Pakistan both economically and militarily for an indefinite period. Although Pakistan was facing an economic disaster, there was no immediate prospect of complete economic ruin which alone, it appeared, would compel her to stop the inhuman adventure in Bangladesh.

In the circumstances, first massive attack by the West Pakistani army was mounted against Indian border posts in the Indo-East Bengal border in the Bogra area on November 21, 1971. It was a full-scale attack with the armour and artillery, and where Indian resistance was firm, Pakistan brought its airforce into action. The Pakistani attacks were successfully resisted by the local commanders of the Indian Army, and Pakistan also suffered losses of its planes while attacking Indian territory over its territory. The mounting number of border incidents and the increasing ferocity of the attacks and counter-attacks clearly proved that there was a state of undeclared war. Mrs. Gandhi described the military actions between November 21 and 22, 1971, as "purely local action", thereby clearly indicating India's intention of doing all that was possible to de-escalate the situation.[47] Further on November 24, 1971, in a statement in the Indian Parliament she reminded the rulers of Pakistan that "the path of peace, of peaceful negotiation and conciliation is more rewarding than that of war and the suppression of liberty and democracy." But a day before the statement, on November 23, 1971, President Yahya Khan declared the state of emergency in Pakistan and on the same day, in a press interview he stated that he expected to be "off on a war within days."[48] The Government of Pakistan escalated the situation further and the shelling of villages and armed intrusions on the Indian border continued.

In East Pakistan the initial clashes, over several weeks, were with Indian-armed, Indian-trained and Indian-assisted Mukti Bahini guerillas, at several points along the 1400-mile long border. India had about ten divisions round the border and by repeated attacks they were encouraging the Pakistan army to use up their immunition while at the same time depriving them of further supplies. By an ever tightening blockade, they were also drawing more troops to the border in order to enable the Mukti Bahini greater freedom to operate in interior. The overall war-like situation warranted Pakistan to strike in Kashmir and on the Western front at any moment which would give rise to an all-out and bitter war on all fronts. Consequently, Indian troops deployed along the Kashmir ceasefire line had been ordered by the Indian Government to hold their ground at all costs and then make a deep thrust into Pakistan territory if a massive attack was launched by Yahya's army, in desperation, on the Western front.

Exactly the same, as expected by India the Pakistan Air Force struck at 5.47 p.m. on 3 December 1971. It carried out an extensive and unprovoked air strike against Indian cities and major air bases in northern India namely Amritsar, Pathankot, Srinagar, Avantipur, Uttarlai, Jodhpur, Ambala and Agra. Following this India had declared a state of national emergency and the Indian Parliament passed the Defence of India Act giving emergency powers to the Government. India did not declare war probably to be in a position to induce Pakistani forces in the east to surrender on terms which are not available to the forces of a country against which there is a regular state of war. On the morning of 4 December, the Indian Prime Minister stated that Pakistan's war with Bangladesh had become a war with India and that had imposed awesome responsibility. She declared that the Pakistani act of aggression would be decisively repulsed.[49] The same day Indian Armed Forces were in action not only in Bangladesh but also in the Western Sector. On 5-6 December the Indian troops moved into the Shakargarh bulge from two sides, from the north between the Basantar and Bein rivers and from the east across the Ravi from the Thakurpur Ferry area. Pakistan was in an advantageous position here because its cantonments were located quite closer to the border. Naturally, the Indian troops could only make slow progress. In a further step the Government of India offered diplomatic recognition to the People's Republic of Bangladesh on December 6, 1971. A joint Command of the Indian Armed Forces and the Mukti Bahini of Bangladesh was set up on December 10, 1971.

The fighting on both sectors, eastern and western continued for a few days. In the eastern sector, following the recognition of Bangladesh the Indian attack was intensified. Lieutenant General Jagjit Singh Aurora, General Officer Commanding, Eastern Command, observed that India's military objective in Bangladesh was to force the Pakistan army's surrender as quickly as possible. The political objective behind the Indian move was to enable Bangladesh to have a Government of its own choice. It was the first time that the Indian strategy worked out jointly by the Army, the Navy and the Air Force so effectively. The Indian Army encircled Dacca from all directions of their operation in Bangladesh. The Indian Air Force, by its highly skilful and effective raids, had already demoralized the officers and men in Eastern Command. The Indian Navy successfully operated both in the Arabian Sea and the Bay of Bengal and prevented the Pakistani ships from bringing military help to the Pak Army in Bangladesh.[50] India's preponderance of military strength was quickly demonstrated. The Army commanders continually sent messages to the Pakistani soldiers urging them to surrender, pointing out the hopelessness of their position and promising full protection under the Geneva Convention.

In the Western sector, the objective behind Indian action was to stop a recurrence of Pakistani aggression. It had certainly no plan to capture Lahore, Sialkot, or any other key town in 1971. It was disclosed by General Chaudhri, the then Chief of the Army Staff, and Lieutenant–General Harbaksh Singh, then Chief of the Western Command that their purpose was only to destroy "the enemy war machine", not to get involved in cities and towns. In Kashmir, India captured 36 of the 88 Pakistani posts in Kargil to eliminate the threat to its road from Srinagar to Leh. From the posts occupied, New Delhi could have posed a threat to Skardu and then to Chitral because there was a road along the Kargil river which was good enough for one-tonners for the first seven miles and three tonners from then onwards. India also captured Dharusian in the Poonch sector and this helped it seal one line of communication between hajira and Kotli leading to the Haji Pir bulge. In the Rajasthan sector Indian troops captured approximately 210 square miles, and it is said that had Lieutenant-General G. G. Bewoor, the then Commanding officer in the area, been given more troops a much bigger area could have been captured.

On the other hand Pakistan's strategy in the war of 1971 was the same as before : multi-directional attack, with wave after wave of troops coming in, unmindful of loss in terms of manpower. For an attacking force this perhaps was a weak strategy. Because of this there was no major tank battle in 1971 like the one fought in Khem Karan and the Sialkot area in 1965. In this war Pakistan wanted to pin down Indian forces in the East and gain as much territory it could in the West so as to be able to use it as a lever at the negotiating table after the cessation of hostilities. In West it made target, like the war of 1965, to capture the 6-mile area of Chhamb towards the Pakistan side of the Munawar Tawi, a rivulet. The area was important, as India could pose a threat to Pakistan's Marala headworks, only eight miles away. Pakistan's strategy might have been to draw the Indians deep inside Pakistan territory, straining their supply lines, before counter-attacking, but the restoration of the railway line eased the attackers' logistic problems.[51] By the time hostilities ceased in the west, India had captured 479.96 square miles in Azad Kashmir, 373.93 square miles in Punjab, and 4,765.71 square miles in Kutch and Sind. As against this, Pakistan occupied 52.57 square miles in Chhamb sector, 68.70 square miles in Punjab, and 0.5 square miles in Rajasthan.[52] Thus, Pakistan's plans to acquire real estate in the West for further bargaining over territories lost in the East had clearly failed.

Taking note of the deteriorating situation in Bangladesh Pakistan looked to the US and China for help. The dispatch of an aircraft carrier group to the Bay of Bengal by the United States showed diplomatic rather than military intent. During the 14 days war China made belligerent noises, but less threateningly than in 1965. Within a week of the start of the exhaustive war, major cities and towns around the borders of Bangladesh had been liberated and on the tenth day Indian troops in concert with the Mukti Bahini began their march towards Dacca. The Pakistani forces were reported to be fleeing to river ports in the hope of being able to escape to West Pakistan by sea. But due to a close air and sea blockade by the Indian troops and expectation of a 'big change' in the situation compelled them to stay in Bangladesh. General Niazi, army commander in the East had also declared that the Pakistani forces in Dacca would fight 'to the last man' and Dacca would 'fall on his dead body'. On the night of 14 December the Indian MIGs destroyed the official residence of the civilian Governor of East Pakistan which followed his resignation along with entire cabinet. A day after the incident came Niazi's surprise request for a ceasefire, perhaps, on instructions of President Yahya Khan.

At last, on December 16, 1971, the Pakistani Forces under the command of General Niazi surrendered to the Joint Command of the Indian Armed Forces and the Mukti Bahini which was led by General Aurora. With the surrender of Pakistani forces in the East, New Delhi offered a unilateral ceasefire in the West. It was a victor's prerogative, as it was China's in November 1962. In response to India's ceasefire offer, Yahya, at first, said that "temporary retreat on one front in such a big war" did not mean the end of the war. But wiser counsels prevailed and he accepted the ceasefire that came into effect from 20.00 hour.......IST., on December 17, 1971. The developments held so far were communicated to the United Nations Security Council in which the Prime Minister of India, through a message, stated, "We have repeatedly declared that India has no territorial ambitions. Now, as the Pakistani armed forces have surrendered in Bangladesh and Bangladesh is free, it is pointless in our view to continue the present conflict. Therefore, in order to stop further bloodshed and unnecessary loss of life, we have ordered our armed forces to ceasefire everywhere".[53] Although it was the triumphant manoeuvre war in the east that caught public attention, it was the dogged static war in the West that was tougher, and where India incurred the bulk of its casualties and material losses.

Kashmir via Kargil

The State of Jammu and Kashmir contains three different regions – the Kashmir valley, Jammu and Ladakh. The region of Ladakh is itself made up of two districts – Kargil and Leh. Like Jammu, Ladakh is a heterogeneous region and does not have a unitary regional personality. For several decades, Buddhists, concentrated in the Leh district made up a very slight majority of the sparsely populated high altitude region's mixed Buddhist – Muslim population. The census results of 2001 reveals that the demographic balance has shifted slightly but significantly and 250,000 population of Ladakh has now a thin Muslim majority of 52 per cent. Ladakh's Kargil district has almost 85 per cent Muslim, principally adherents of the Shiv version of the faith. The Leh district is over 80 per cent Buddhist, the main minority being a Muslim community called Arghuns, descendants of Sunni Muslims who migrated to Leh from the Kashmir valley in the seventeenth century and intermarried with local ethnic Tibetans.[54]

From the start the region of Kargil has been considered as difficult one. In order to get the area troops have to pass over the Zojila Pass which leads to Ladakh. In 1947-48, when the first Indo-Pak war broke out for the State of Jammu and Kashmir the regular Pakistani forces entered the fray and launched a thrust towards the valley from the mountainous areas of Gilgit and Skardu to the north, the Indians consolidated their position by capturing the Ladakh towns of Dras and Kargil. Indian forces captured Kargil in November 1948 and hoped to move forward. At the Juncture Brigadier Bagga Atal Commanding the 77th Para Brigade drove the Pakistanis from Zojila with tanks. Three weeks later he signalled 'Have taken Kargil' and requested permission to advance to Gilgit. Halted at Kargil because we went to the UN. The youngest Brigadier in the Army, Bagga was a mountain warfare expert who won the Military Cross in Eritria in World War II, and climbed two mountains of 15,000 ft.and

17,000 ft. everyday to meet his pickets.[55] We Indians have a peculiar trait of not consolidating our gains after a victory. Lapses on our part occurred under Prime Ministers known for their pragmatic national security approach. Further the territorial gains of 1965 and 1971 were bartered away at Tashkent and Simla for empty promises and imaginary peace. India repeated the same old story in 1999 when it gave a humiliating defeat to Pakistan in Kargil sector.

The letter and spirit of the Lahore Declaration signed between the Prime Ministers of India and Pakistan in February 1999 evaporated months later on the barren peaks and ranges of Kargil. In the summer of 1999 Pakistani regular units supported by Jehadi volunteers infiltrated the Indian side of the LoC and the Indian military launched a massive land and air campaign to evict the infiltrators. Originally, the plan for intrusion in Kargil, as revealed by Altaf Gauhar, a powerful Information Secretary to the President Ayub Khan, was made in 1987 and General Zia-ul-Haq authorised the then Foreign Minister Sahibzada Yaqub Khan who opposed the idea on the plea that as a former general, he knew that the posts that Pakistani soldiers would occupy were totally covered with snow almost throughout the year and it would be extremely difficult to have communication with them and meet their day-to-day needs. Secondly, he said, as Foreign Minister, he would find it extremely difficult to justify Pakistan's military action.[56] When Nawaz Sharif became the Prime Minister of Pakistan, relations between the two became tense, particularly after the nuclear explosions by both in May-June 1998. The Pakistani Prime Minister permitted the execution of that old plan and intrusion in Kargil started.

In fact, the incursion into Kargil started in September 1997, when Pakistan brought new long-range guns into Baltistan and began to sell it in Kargil town and the surrounding villages. In 1998, its gunners continued their selling, progressively improving their accuracy till they were able to target three stretches of the road at will. Pakistan's maximal goal in Kargil was to change the Line of Control by brute force, its long-term objective was to draw a large part of the Indian army away from the valley to facilitate the entry of militants.[57] The Kargil adventure was simply a continuation of its decade-old policy with added means. The brilliant gambit of seizing the heights would balance Siachen, expose the Leh road, revive the flagging militancy and, of course, internationalise Kashmir.

The causes for opting Kargil were many. It was partly due to the Indian success in handling insurgency in Jammu and Kashmir. With the downsize of the effects of insurgency in Srinagar valley, economic activity and tourism had started picking up. It blocked all other ingress routes for intrusion and only Kargil was open. The other attraction is the strategic domination of the Srinagar–Leh highway from heights overlooking it. Thus, it was the safest place for making infiltrator's hideouts. Pakistan sneaked through across the LoC into the unoccupied areas and established posts four to six kilometres deep over a hundred kilometre band width. The strategic importance of the Srinagar – Leh road has been evident since the first war between India and Pakistan in Kashmir. It is the only supply route to troops manning our defences against Chinese moves in Ladakh as well.

Surprisingly, the development of Pakistani forces was revealed by a journalist in course of the visit of Strobe Talbott in July 1998 when he reported that the Leh road was closed by Pakistani artillery firing. Although a large section of people had welcomed Vajpayee's visit to Lahore in February 1999 but some of us expressed reservations even at the time and cautioned the government in Parliament. His intentions were praise worthy, not his political judgement. Barely a month after the Prime Minister crossed the Wagah border, in response to question no 3468 someone had asked in Lok Sabha an answer, based on military intelligence report, was read out in the House by George Fernandes, the Defence Minister on March 18, 1999, "Pakistan's ISI agents in Kargil are suspected to be behind the accuracy of Pakistani firing in the Uri-Kargil sector recently". However, the picture became clear and the government belatedly accepted the intrusion as early as the first week of May. Casualties had started mounting and May 18 report quoting defence sources, declared that 75 soldiers had been killed.

On 18 May 1999, a close door meeting of India's Defence Minister with Vajpayee and Jaswant Singh was held as the 48-hour deadline for flushing out Pakistani intruders had already expired. In other words, the Indian diplomacy had failed to persuade Islamabad to see the reason and agree to pull back from the brink. It had left with no option but to use the force. India's task was not merely to undo the Pakistani encroachment in Ladakh's Kargil sector–an objective which, if pursued alone, would cost New Delhi dearly because it meant fighting at a dictated place on enemy's term, but to implement a larger strategic plan that would make Pakistan pay a price sufficient to deter it from committing such glaring aggression again or continue its unconventional warfare against this country. New Delhi had to devise a geopolitical strategy to maul the Talibanised Pakistan-Afghanistan pair, the main world exporter of extremism and terrorism. Situation demanded a robust firm yet coolheaded unharried approach.

Keeping in view the gravity of the situation New Delhi first ordered air strikes and the Indian Air Force had been pressed into service to support the army operation in the Kargil sector. With it, India has escalated the conflict in Kargil sector of Kashmir where 500 to 700 militants had crossed over from Pakistan and taken up positions deep in India–held territory. The Indian point of view clearly was that all steps have to be taken to repulse the outsiders, particularly they have secured strategic positions, possibly with the objective of altering the alignments of the Line of Control and disrupting the lines of communication between the Indian security forces. Apart from air strikes, India launched "Operation Vijay" that put relentless pressure on the intruders. Within day it saw a significant gains for India and evicted Pakistani infiltrators across the Line of Control. On several crucial positions in Kargil, Drass and Batalik security personnel acted swiftly on a tip-off and get cleared of the intruders and retaken up positions there.

As a result of New Delhi's perfect planning and war management, at the close of May 1999, Islamabad was on the verge of defeat diplomatically and militarily, although it was beyond doubt that Pakistan had prepared a well-planned thrust across the Line of

Control in the Drass-Batalik sector and executed it. The Pakistani army, the ISI, the Mujahideen and the Taliban were involved in it and an operation of this scale involving anything up to 3,000 men, would not have been possible without clearance at the highest political level. It also linked the crossing of the Line of Control in the Kargil and Drass sectors with the question of Kashmir and felt that such invasions and intrusions would continue to occur till the problem of Kashmir is resolved to Pakistan's satisfaction.

A desperate Pakistan in early June attempted to capture a ring line in the southern Siachen glacier. It was tried to do through Turtuk sector, but was detected in time and foiled. The Siachen glacier has more than passing interest for the Kargil-aiming Pakistan army. It was possible that the entire exercise in the Kargil sector was in pursuance of plans to take Siachen. Unfortunately, the Siachen glacier was neither included in the ceasefire line drawn according to the Karachi Agreement of 1949, nor in the Line of Control as drawn at the Simla Agreement of 1972. In both instances the line ended at a point known as NJ 9842. A summary verbal reference in the 1949 agreement said only that beyond this point the line went "north to the glacier". At last India launched a final assault on Tiger hills to capture this Drass sub-sector and the Indian Air Force jets intensified bombardment of well-known targets" of intruders in several parts of Kargil sector. It followed a meeting of cabinet ministers and defence forces chiefs to discuss the overall situation which was headed by Nawaz Sharif, the Prime Minister of Pakistan. In addition, with the outbreak of Kargil crisis Islamabad was under intense diplomatic pressure, led mainly by the US to withdraw forces from the Kargil-Drass sectors, where India had maintained ground and air offensive for about two months against what it called Pakistan–backed infiltrators and some Pakistani regulars.

In the circumstances, Nawaz Sharif, to save his face as well as of his country met American President Bill Clinton on 4 July 1999, where the former had surrendered all its options and was desperately willing to get rid of the mess of its own making, on any terms that Washington chose to set down. As a follow up of Clinton-Sharif Communiqué in which Pakistan had committed to take concrete steps to restore the sanctity of the Line of Control in Kashmir it decided to appeal to Mujahideen fighting the Indian Army while praising them for their courageous action leading to focussing of international attention to the Kashmir issue, to help resolve the Kargil situation. The Pakistani Cabinet at its meeting held on 3 August 1999, chaired by Nawaz Sharif discussed Kargil issue at length and decided to send 'instant message' to Mujahideen to 'cool down' in the larger interest of the country. The Communiqué of July 4, stated that they agreed that it was vital for the peace of South Asia that the Line of Control in Kashmir be respected by both countries in accordance with their 1972 Simla Agreement. It was also agreed between the President and the Prime Minister that concrete steps would be taken for the restoration of the Line of Control in accordance with Simla Accord.

After Kargil India emerged from the war with enhanced capacity for negotiation and compromise while Pakistan stood with this capacity almost destroyed. However, the Indian Army had lost hundreds of its men besides wounded and missing in action. Its action against the Pakistani soldiers who had taken up positions in Kargil sectors began on May 8 and the Indian Air Force joined the operation on May 16, 1999. According to the Indian Army about 800 Pakistani soldiers, mainly from the Northern Light Infantry had been killed in operation Vijay. Besides, about 200 militants had also been killed. During the 49-day air operation which began on May 26, Air Marshal V. Pandey said about 550 strike missions, 150 reconnaissance missions and over 500 escort flights were carried out.

But the end of Kargil war did not mean the end of continuing Pakistani hostility to India. In fact, Kashmir has always been a symbol, not the root cause of Indo-Pak conflict. As admitted recently by General Pervez Musharraf, who succeeded Nawaz Sharif in a military coup on October 12, 1999, that even a settlement of the Kashmir issue would not usher peace in the region and the root of Pakistan's hostility are in history, religion, civilization and the politics of revenge. The gulf between the two is too wide to be bridged in the foreseeable future without major geo-strategic or radical policy changes in the region.

References

1. Harish Kapur, India's Foreign Policy 1947-92 Shadow and Substance, New Delhi, 1994, p. 20-21.
2. Verghese Koithara, Society, State and Security, The Indian Experience, New Delhi, 1999, pp. 253-54.
3. Jawaharlal Nehru's Speeches, September 1946-May 1949, Vol. I, Delhi, 1947, pp. 156-57.
4. As quoted in Jagmohan "50 years of Kashmir's Accession to India", The Hindustan Times, 27 October 1997.
5. Mrs. Indira Gandhi, "India and the World," K. P. Misra, ed., Foreign Policy of India–A Book of Reading, New Delhi, 1977, p. 165.
6. Jawaharlal Nehru, Letters to Chief Ministers, 1947-1964, Vol. I, Delhi, 1985, p.7.
7. H. O. Agarwal, Kashmir Problem Its Legal Aspects, Allahabad, 1979, pp 45-46.
8. Jawaharlal Nehru, *op. cit.,* p. 7.
9. Sumantra Bose, Kashmir Roots of Conflict Paths to Peace, New Delhi, 2003, p. 35.
10. *Ibid.*
11. Nehru to Chief Ministers, 2 November 1947.
12. Jawaharlal Nehru's Speeches, *op. cit.,* pp. 163-66.
13. Sumantra Bose, *op. cit.,* pp. 36-37.
14. As quoted in Jagmohan *op. cit.*
15. Nehru to Chief Ministers on 15 November 1947.
16. *Ibid.,* pp. 39-40.
17. Nehru's Statement at a Press Conference, New Delhi, 2 January 1948.
18. The Times, 13 April 1948.
19. D. N. Mallik, Postwar International Politics –A Quadripartite Survey, Muzaffarpur, 1973, p. 471.
20. General U. N. Sharma, "National Security Can't be Left to Bureaucrats", The Hindustan Times, 17 January 2000.
21. Satish Kumar, "Mistakes in Kashmir", Ibid., 24 September 1998.
22. As quoted in The Sunday Times, 2 May 1965.

23. Pakistan Times, 10, 11 and 13 April 1965.
24. Lok Sabha Debates, Vol. 41, 12 April, 1965, col. 9106.
25. See author's book, India's Foreign Policy, The First Study in Continuity and Change, New Delhi, 2001, p. 125.
26. Kuldip Nayar, Distant Neighbours- A Tale of the Sub-Continent, New Delhi, 1972, pp. 88-89.
27. General Mohammad Musa, H. J., My Version-India-Pakistan War 1965, New Delhi, 1980, pp. 35-36.
28. Salmaan Taseer, Bhutto-A Political Biography, New Delhi, 1980, pp. 60-61.
29. General Mohammad Musa, *op. cit.,* pp. 36-37.
30. *Ibid.,* p. 38.
31. Pakistan Times, 11 July 1965.
32. B. L. Sharma, Kashmir Awakes, Delhi, 1971, pp. 140-41.
33. D. C. Jha, Indo-Pakistan Relations 1960-65, Patna, 1972, pp. 339-42.
34. The Newyork Times 7 September 1965.
35. Kuldip Nayar, *op. cit.,* p. 93.
36. G. S. Bhargava, Pakistan in Crisis, New Delhi, 1969, p. 146.
37. As quoted in Salmaan Taseer, *op. cit.,* pp. 61-62.
38. General Mohammad Musa, *op. cit.,* p. 42.
39. Shelton Kodikara, Strategic Factors in Interstate Relations in South Asia, New Delhi, 1983, p. 5.
40. Verghese Koithara, *op. cit.,* pp. 86-87.
41. Jayadeva Uyangoda, "Indo-Bangladesh Relations in the 1970s: Bangladeshi Perspective", Shelton U Kodikara, ed., South Asian Strategic Issues, New Delhi, 1990, pp. 72-73.
42. G. P. Ojha, India's Foreign Policy, Meerut, 1986, pp. 35-36.
43. Kuldip Nayar, *op. cit.,* p. 127.
44. The Times of India, 13 October 1971.
45. As quoted in G. P. Ojha, *op. cit.,* p. 39.
46. Md. Abdul Wadud Bhuiyan, Emergence of Bangladesh and Role of Awami League, New Delhi, 1982, p. 254.
47. The Times of India, 25 November 1971
48. *Ibid.,* 24 November 1971.

49. Md. Abdul Wadud Bhuiyan, *op. cit.,* pp. 256-57.
50. S. K. Chakrabarti, The Evolution of Politics in Bangladesh 1947-1978, New Delhi, 1978, pp. 214-15.
51. Kuldip Nayar, *op. cit.,* pp. 135-40.
52. *Ibid.*
53. Bangladesh Document, Vol. II, New Delhi, 1971, p. 545.
54. Sumantra Bose, *op. cit.,* pp. 191-92.
55. Aditya Nehru, "Failure at the Top". The Hindustan Times, 3 September 1999.
56. The Times of India, 13 September 1999.
57. Prem Shankar Jha, "Subversion in Kashmir," The Hindustan Times, 17 July 1999.

6

Cross-Border Terrorism in Jammu and Kashmir

Differing Perceptions

In past the border areas had served as a heaven for terrorists, who after obtaining training and arms in Pakistan, crossed over into India and fanned out all over the country. There has been a steady one-way traffic of illegal immigrants from Pakistan to the border areas. The importance of the problem lies in the fact that not only human traffic but arms and narcotics find easy access into India. Reports from various parts of the country confirm that they smuggle arms and narcotics in large quantities. Unfortunately, there are many godfathers, agents, touts, etc. on the Indian side who not only provide shelter and food to the illegal migrants but all help needed to remain unnoticed. The defence forces with the help of local people and the police must break up these gangs, round up the agents and touts and send the godfathers to prison. What is needed is not a fence along the border but a highly efficient intelligence machinery capable enough to identify the illegal migrants and stop the trans-border commerce in humans, drugs and arms.[1] In August 1986 the Indian Parliament adopted a resolution in pursuance of Article 249 of the constitution whereby the Centre assumed special powers to create a security belt to deal directly and swiftly against large scale infiltration, illegal traffic in arms, drugs and secessionist and terrorist activities on international borders. Not only the entire border of Pakistan from Kashmir to Kutch but our borders with Bangladesh and China also need to be protected. It is time India told its people the real and full story about Pakistan's role in the unrecognised war in Jammu and Kashmir which the latter has been waging since its first invasion in October 1947.

Terrorism, it is said, has become endemic to modern society. It continues to be generated by recurrent social crises, arising from the increasing marginalisation of some sections of society caused by the indescriminate spread of capitalism and the free market economy, through the much vaunted process of globalisation. At its root the terrorist movement is born out of frustration and despair. Despair caused by social marginalisation, economic decline and political defeat. Someone once said that "young hope betrayed, transforms itself into bombs". Perceived injustice if allowed to continue unresolved, would transform into despair and then violence. According to Leon Trotsky the two emotions central to terrorism, are despair and vengeance.[2] The causes of these issues and the form they take, whether it be terrorism or otherwise, must be studied and understood in a scientific and objective manner.

With the start of cross-border terrorism by Pakistan the Kashmir dispute assumed alarming proportions. Pakistan's historical record of its commitment to honour its agreements and treaty obligations, which it freely entered into, not only with India, but also with other countries has been extremely poor. The 1947 Standstill Agreement with Jammu and Kashmir, the 1948 UN Resolution, 1949 Karachi Agreement, 1954 SEATO and CENTO Agreements, 1966 Tashkent Declaration, 1972 Simla Agreement, 1988 Geneva Accords with Afghanistan, 1999 Lahore Declaration, and so on stand out. When the Kashmir agitation picked up steam the Berlin Wall was being pulled down, the mighty Red Army had been forced out of Afghanistan by rag-tag bands of Islamic guerillas a year earlier and geographical boundaries were being redrawn across Eastern Europe and Central Asia.[3] Thus it was no surprise then that the votaries of azadi thought that India too would close shop in Kashmir. But this did not happen.

However, Pakistan's waging a covert war through trans-national terrorism has a strong religious base. It was during the regime of General Zia-ul-Haq that Islamabad began to use terror as a weapon to fight war. The strategy had found a sound footing from a book '*Quranic Concept of War*' written by Brigadier S. K. Malik (Lahore, 1979). In it, the Holy Quran was interpreted as requiring the believers to use terror as weapon of war. Unfortunately, the military dictator at that time, strongly recommended the book and its conclusions by stating that it brings out the "Quranic philosophy on the application of military force, within the context of the totality that is "JEHAD". The volume concluded that "jehad", the Quranic concept of total strategy, demands the preparation and application of total manpower and military instrument is one of its elements. It went on to say further that "The holy Quran lays the highest emphasis on the preparation of war. The test of utmost preparation lies in our capability to instil terror into the hearts of the enemies". The merging of the concept of jehad, war and terrorism has also been pursued by Pakistan in the trans-national terrorism it imposes in Jammu and Kashmir. Incidentally, a combination of jehad terrorism war has also been pursued by Pakistan in Afghanistan for nearly three decades.

There can be no doubt that India is the victim of sustained low-level aggression by secessionist forces encouraged and abetted by Pakistan. The present thinking on terrorism can be divided into two schools of thought. One school of thought places the terrorist beyond the pale of civilized society and considers him anathema to civilization and stigmatises him as a plain murderer who needs to be eliminated. But the second school of thought encourages an in-depth study of, and a systematic approach to understand and eradicate, the reasons that bring about such upheavals. The rational political, social and economic aspirations of peoples which when frustrated continuously give rise to full blown terrorism of the modern day, must be sifted out of the process of terroristic actions and looked at separately. Those political aspirations must be addressed honestly and seriously. The solutions that are employed must be made effective–legally and constitutionally, politically, economically and socially. The overall gained impression from the cross-border terrorism is that it relates to the second school of thought. Peace is more than the simple absence of war. It entails active engagement in the battle for identifying and rectifying the root causes of conflict.

The problem of cross-border terrorism took an alarming shape during 1988-89 for which solid ground had been prepared by the parties concerned. First, on the part of New Delhi it was a time to face realities on the ground and examine carefully the causes for the sense of alienation that the Kashmiris feel. The government is well advised to go into the history of the Kashmir issue in order to understand and appreciate how and when things went wrong and how the impass of this particular type came about. It is an open fact that the Government of India has, from the beginning, been ignoring the political, social, economical as well as cultural needs of the people of Jammu and Kashmir. The successive governments of the National Conference well alternated by the direct rule of New-Delhi proved a disaster in real sense of the term. Farooq Abdullah's behaviour during his curtailed first term in 1983-84, has been described as that of "a little boy with a toy", and during the second as "a virtual abdication of governance."[4] He acquired the *sobriquet* "disco chief minister" because he was frequently sighted in discotheques in Indian cities, and he spent much of the rest of his time playing golf or vacationing abroad. His colleagues in government earned a reputation for corrupt practices. In nutshell, the Kashmiris feel that Delhi's behaviour has been atrocious in that it has chosen to ignore them completely.

The wars of 1965 and 1971 had succeeded in freezing the problem of Kashmir, however, the post-war agreements with Pakistan failed to keep the promises inherent in those documents. The Simla Agreement of 1972 in particular provided that the two would respect the ceasefire line of December 17, 1971, and that neither side would seek to alter it unilaterally irrespective of mutual differences and legal interpretations. They also agreed to refrain from a threat or a use of force as the agreement itself was based on the principles of bilateral diplomacy and durable peace. Notwithstanding the benevolent spirit of Simla Pakistan continued to raise the issue of Kashmir at various international fora. A little latter of the signing of the agreement, Zulfikar Ali Bhutto, the then Prime Minister of Pakistan, had clearly stated that there would be no compromise on the principle of self-determination in Kashmir. General Zia-ul-Haq followed the same militant line on the matter and succeeded in keeping the issue alive at both, bilateral and international levels. However, the issue had become critical and closely related to it was

Pakistan's perception regarding its role in the State of Jammu and Kashmir.

Domestic as well as international are the two important determinants that govern Pakistani action in the State. The period that was responsible for initiation and growth of cross-border terrorism largely witnessed the power rivalry between the democratically elected ruling elite and the military. Prime Minister Benazir Bhutto inherited a mixed economy. Tied to these were two experiments of democratic rule, one of which was carried out by her father; and populist Islamisation process that was used by all as a tool for legitimacy. Her task was not just to undo autocracy but build an economy and industry that had for long been propped up by external aid. Her success at keeping the army at bay had also been uncertain. Therefore, militant posture for her became a need of the hour and in such a situation Kashmir remained the most readymade tool.[5] In addition, it was just a chance that both India and Pakistan were embroiled in grim problems outside Kashmir–India in Punjab and Assam and Pakistan in the volatile steamy city of Karachi where armoured personnel carriers were now common sight in the streets. There were host of problems for Pakistan in other states as well apart from the continuing and running battle between the federal and Punjab government.[6] The then government of Pakistan was beholden to the army and to the President to remain in office.

At that time India too was ruled by a minority and weak government headed by V. P. Singh, supported by Bharatiya Janata Party and Hindu fundamentalism. The situation in India convinced Pakistan that this was the time to liberate Kashmir. Among the military stalwarts, General Chisti, Arif and Gul were of the view that when the government in India is weak it is vulnerable to military and political pressures in the valley along with direct and indirect international wish to settle the issue of Kashmir. Hence they calculated that the situation would either lead to the decapitation of India by the loss of Kashmir and parts of Punjab as a result of developments on the ground or to an Indo-Pak deal by a softened and chastened India, and a tough and principled Pakistan. Finally they concluded that in either way, militarily or diplomatically, India would lose in Pakistani thinking and 1971 would be revenged and with Pakistani getting its parity with India.[7]

So far as the international determinants of the Pakistani action in Kashmir was concerned, it was tied to Islamabad's perception about India's position regarding the State of Jammu and Kashmir. In the first place, Pakistan must have reason to believe that India would be reluctant to mobilise itself into a war over the issue. Reason for such a reluctance would lie both in civilian and military thinking in India. Democratic systems are rarely tuned to instantaneous response in the face of crisis because it is linked to the decision-making process of the political system. In India, while the military would be consulted, the decision about the war would be basically political. Islamabad's second perception was related to the situation in Kashmir itself. As the Government of India had implemented democracy in Jammu and Kashmir half-heartedly and on the other Pakistan perceived the accession of Kashmir to India as one attained by force, the Kashmiri population would welcome intervention by Pakistan to liberate it from India.

But finally was the consideration of international support that Pakistan hoped, particularly from the US and China. Pakistan has reason to believe that both United States and China along with others would extend international sympathy. Given the religious dimension of the issue Pakistan also counted on the continued support of the West Asian countries. At that time the Soviet Union, India's only ally was in a state of internal influx and Gorbachov himself had been supporting freedom movements in Eastern Europe. The Soviet system was also trying to cope with demands for change from its own ethnic minorities and nationalities. In Pakistan's perception India would find it difficult to get international support over its position in Kashmir. However, Pakistan's initial efforts to project Kashmir on the world stage failed because the major Powers had other preoccupations and were loath to add a hoary contentious issue to their agenda.[8] The Simla agreement came in handy for the world to put away the issue of Kashmir as the world knows that there can not be a radical solution short of war.

Diplomatic Channels Reactivated

In case of cross-border terrorism Pakistan is pursuing its own brand of 'two track' policy. While it wants a dialogue with India, it has kept up the level of violence. In its latter part of the strategy, Afghanistan's utility is the greatest. To wage proxy war against India, Afghan heroin pays for the weapons and salaries of Kashmiri militants. To escape the "terrorist state "label Pakistan places its jehadi camps across the Durand Line. As said by the official of the Foreign Ministry a good chunk of the militants are Afghans and "Afghanistan is the fountainhead of militancy".[9] In fact the movement of Kashmiri people was hijacked by the Afghan– based elements. And from the start the real thrust of Pakistani terrorism in Jammu and Kashmir is not to give a chance to the people of the state to vote for their future but to channel the overflow of arms and mercenaries from the war-ravaged areas of Afghanistan, which would flood Pakistan if not sent elsewhere. It is true that the idea has caught the imagination of the Pakistani people and become a sort of precondition to any "settlement" of India-Pakistan question. Even today this precondition exists in Pakistani establishment. In June 2001, on the eve of his arrival in Agra, Musharraf told the Karachi monthly, *The Herald* that violence would decline as talks on Kashmir made progress. After the collapse of the Agra summit, a noted Indian writer on military affairs realistically noted, "The only real bargaining leverage that Pakistan wields in Jammu and Kashmir is through its proxies, the jehadi groups operating in the state. For Pakistan, therefore, cross-border terrorism has to be retained as a lever until the end of the peace process.[10] While India depended entirely on the hope that a resumption of negotiations would end the problem.

In the meantime change of guards took place in Islamabad and New Delhi respectively. While a democratic government was sworn in under the premiership of Benazir Bhutto in Pakistan, it followed the taking over of the second non-Congress government of National Front headed by Vishwanath Pratap Singh in India. Though both the countries had been obsessed with an inexorable state of "new cold war" on the subcontinent in the light of Pakistan's covert or overt support to secessionists in Punjab and Jammu and Kashmir, the new Indian government adopted the policy of friendliness and mutual understanding with neighbouring countries, particularly with Pakistan. A foreign office spokesman said, "It is our hope that Pakistan will exercise similar restraint and desist from giving encouragement to terrorism directed against India. Such action violates bilateral, regional and international obligations including the terms of the Simla Agreement and is not conducive to peace in the region".[10] The provocative statements of Pakistan and terrorist support by it were considered by India as "unfortunate" and despite threatening posture the new dispensation did not abandon normalisation process entirely. In three respects the National Front Government's record had been creditable. First, inspite of developments in the Kashmir valley and a certain amount of militancy[11] in Islamabad's attitude, V. P. Singh's Government considered it appropriate to keep the dialogue open. Secondly, when Benazir's Government was dismissed, New Delhi avoided making any comments except for wishing well for a strong and stable Pakistan.[12] Third, India's active diplomacy in the Arab countries and western world it was instrumental, to a large extent, in containing Pakistani efforts to internationalise the Kashmir issue.[13]

Since January 1990 political atmosphere between the two countries was vitiated due to statements of Pakistani leaders, particularly the Prime Minister who maintained that no compromise would be done with India on the question of the right of self-determination for the people of Jammu and Kashmir. She also announced through a state-run television that a joint session of Parliament would be convened in the first week of February 1990 to discuss the 'deteriorating situation in Kashmir. It added fuel to the fire and compelled India's ruling as well as opposition circles to react sharply. They all condemned the statement of Pakistan's Prime Minister and conveyed its resentments in a message communicated to Sahib Zada Yakub Khan, country's Foreign Minister. India's concern involved terrorist activities directed against India in Jammu and Kashmir. It reiterated that Jammu and Kashmir is an integral part of India and any interference in our internal affairs would be unacceptable.[14] In this tense situation a balanced statements of Pakistani President Ghulam Ishaq Khan appeared that Pakistan can not afford war and added that there was no immediate threat from India. Inder Kumar Gujral, India's Minister for External Affairs, stressed the need to resolve their differences through dialogue and Confidence Building Measures to promote peace and cooperation in South Asia.

Earlier, at the close of the 1980s in order to avoid war and normalise ties New Delhi and Islamabad agreed to take some concrete CBMs. The turning point came following the holding of the military exercises by India called "Brasstacks" along the borders of Pakistan during the winter of 1986-87. Taking cognizance of the situation, both governments belatedly called for a reduction in their military presence and talks were held in New Delhi on 30 January 1987 between senior foreign ministry officials of the two countries. On 4 February 1987 a memorandum of understanding was signed that provided for the withdrawal of forces from both sides to a "peace time position over the next fifteen days.[15] The CBMs between the two countries strengthened further in December 1988 when on the occasion of the fourth SAARC summit held in Islamabad, Rajiv Gandhi, the then Prime Minister of India, as a gesture of goodwill, announced the cancellation of routine exercises by the Indian military along the Pakistani borders. Pakistan also responded to invite international observers, including those from India to see military exercises in December 1989 called "Zarb-i-Momin".[16] Such steps taken by India and Pakistan proved to be useful for building mutual trust and confidence and the de–escalation of tension. Now it became possible for New Delhi and Islamabad to communicate directly at the times of crisis along the border.

Concrete steps and bold decisions taken by the two countries relating to CBMs had reduced the risk of an accidental war. Given the success of military CMBs agreed to between New Delhi and Islamabad India and Pakistan could embark on adopting non–military CBMs. However, both sides undermined the necessity to simultaneously adopt military and non-military CBMs. India had its own reasons to emphasise the adoption of non-military CBMs before settling the Kashmir dispute, and Pakistanis feel it is meaningless to go for these CBMs without settling the dispute with India. In other words, Indo-Pakistan difference in perceptions concerning CBMs is two fold : First, New Delhi wants Pakistan to agree on applying CBMs related to political, economic and cultural fields and argues that outstanding disputes should either be frozen or left aside for future discussions. In this regard, India cites the Simla Agreement as a model for its normalisation of relations with Pakistan. But Pakistan feels that the entire process of CBMs can not render positive results unless some measures are not taken to settle the bilateral issues.[17] Apart from this Pakistan also needs a nuclear parity with India to cope effectively with the Indian threat and to use the capability as a deterrent to any future Indian designs against Pakistan's territorial sovereignty.

When in the summer of 1990, the Kashmir dispute threatened a new outbreak of hostilities in the subcontinent, the two had decided to launch bilateral talks at the foreign secretary level for de-escalation of tension and normalisation of relations. The readiness on the part of India and Pakistan to start foreign secretaries' talks despite escalation of Kashmir and other disputes could be termed as an "exercise in confidence building. As scheduled Muchkund Dubey, India's foreign secretary, met Tanvir Ahmed Khan, his Pakistani counterpart in Islamabad 18-20 July 1990 for talks to defuse the year long tension between the two countries over Kashmir. Benazir Bhutto was happy with the development and described Indian response as "Positive".[18] But in the talks India and Pakistan failed to make much headway to defuse tensions between them with the two sides sticking to their different perceptions on the situation in Kashmir.[19] The meeting ended without agreeing on any confidence building measure but it was decided to continue the dialogue in Delhi in the second week of August 1990.

Several rounds of talks at both levels had been held since, and almost half a dozen CBMs have been adopted by the two countries. Amid the dismissal of Benazir Bhutto's Government and Organisation of Islamic Conference (OIC) not endorsing Pakistan's call on Kashmir, India, in August 1990 proposed five non–military CBMs which were directly related to the cross-border terrorism. They were :

- ➢ Statements [should be] made by political and military leaders in Pakistan disassociating themselves from [acts of] terrorism and subversion in the [Indian states of] Punjab, Jammu and Kashmir.
- ➢ The handing over of [ten] fugitives who have been operating from Pakistan. India also asked Pakistan to handover Jammu and Kashmir Liberation Front leader Amanullah Khan. Such request was promptly turned down by Pakistan.
- ➢ Seizure [by Pakistan] of arms and ammunition [that are] being smuggled into India and the arrest of infiltrators [who have been] crossing into India.
- ➢ Cessation of official statements and pronouncements from Pakistan inciting violence and striking communal passion in India.
- ➢ Closure of officially sponsored funds that have been put in Pakistan in connection with recent developments in Jammu and Kashmir.[20]

In 1991 when militancy was at its peak, on 16 April, two accords on CBMs of military significance were signed. In this connection two conclusions could be made from the Indo-Pak normalisation talks. First, these talks were held at the official level and agreements signed were merely restricted to military security matters. Second, because of Political reasons, progress achieved in these talks were not durable. For example, after the sixth round of talks held in August 1992 and the subsequent defence secretaries' talks held in November of the same year, political relations between the two countries deteriorated to an alarming extent. Therefore, gains achieved in Indo-Pakistan talks are lost when something goes wrong, quickly the two countries are back to square one.

In between the change of guards Pakistan formally proposed "negotiations on the settlement of Jammu and Kashmir in terms of Article 6 of the Simla Agreement", India responded with two stipulations : Pakistan must be "in a position to adopt an effective and practical approach and next, it must end "support for secessionist elements" in Kashmir. At a later date Narasimha Rao rebuffed Nawaz Sharif, but waived the stipulations when Benazir came to power. On 19 October 1993, he himself proposed "a comprehensive dialogue for discussing all matters of mutual concern, including issues related to Jammu and Kashmir. Unfortunately, Bhutto adopted this time a hard line that wrecked the talks in January 1994.

In 1997 Nawaz Sharif returned to Power second time and the dialogue was resumed. A joint statement was issued in Islamabad on June 23, 1997, announcing a decision "to set up a mechanism, including working groups to address eight issues. Militancy was not absent when Vajpayee went to Lahore in February 1999. Kargil derailed the process. On 13 June 1999, Vajpayee said, "India is for the continuation of Lahore process.......but for that process it is absolutely necessary for the *status quo ante* to be restored on the LoC." He added, "You withdraw your troops from Kargil and then we are prepared for talks". Of late when Abdul Majid Dar, the sacked commander of the Hizbul Mujahideen was asked, "You talk about a peace process, but you do not call for an end to militancy, why ?" Dar replied : "We want a political process, but unless we see a positive attitude from the Government of India we can not put the gun down. According to press reports the unsigned Arga Declaration of July 16, 2001, also set up a similar mechanism to discuss precisely those eight issues. 'Jammu and Kashmir' and terrorism and drug-peddling were listed separately for talks on different levels.

Thus, implementation of military and non–military CBMs along with results of the peace talks have always been marred by the preconditions by either side. For Pakistan, the problem of Kashmir has become the "core issue" without which there can never be any settlement between Islamabad and New Delhi. Likewise the Indian leaders have stressed, on times without number, that any fruitful peace talks must be preceded by the end of cross-border terrorism in Jammu and Kashmir. It seemed that the whole exercise of CBMs and peace talks were directed in scoring competitive points rather than anything else. In fact, India and Pakistan have not moved systematically towards the goal of tension free relations. There is lack of political will on the part of the regimes in power–past and present to institutionalise the normalisation process by giving serious consideration to non-military CBMs to which the problem of cross-border terrorism is closely related. The need to act against terrorist camps, their support bases and the Pakistani army posts near the LoC which assist the cross-border infiltration will form one dimension of Indian strategy.[21] However, the larger and lasting dimension of Indian strategy must remain with the people of Jammu and Kashmir. They will isolate the militants and the terrorists and leave them exposed to military action, if their aspirations are met through good governance.

Men

General Zia-ul-Haq, who became martial law administrator in July 1977 had not only exploited religion to the maximum for legitimisation of his rule but delayed the return of democratic government for eleven long years. When the US-Pakistan Mujahideen nexus was formed, he sold thousands of brainwashed to fight against the erstwhile USSR. He exploited this jehad to strengthen religious parties with state's backing to marginalise the influence of political parties, particularly, the Pakistan's Peoples Party. The regime of Zia faced the Afghans inflow both as refugees and Mujahideen as well. The latter was provided all possible assistance on humanitarian grounds and in the spirit of Islamic brotherhood. Zia identified himself with the cause of the Mujahideen, stating that their sacrifices would be written in 'golden letters' in the annals of history, for 'the safety and security of Afghanistan and of Pakistan depended on them.[22] With the increasing post-cold war surge in Islamic fundamentalism on India's western flank, the situation has become even more serious. Afghanistan, a long time friend of India since its independence had increasingly embraced Islamic fundamentalism and many violent movements in the Indian state of Jammu and Kashmir has apparently developed a 'dangerous nexus with the Afghan Mujahideen.[23] They based on for their material and moral support to the emergence of what may be described as a militant Pan-Islamic jehad. Moving across the state borders in clandestine manner, equipped with lethal armaments and owing allegiance to no flag except the paymasters of the moment, these groups have the ability to cause mayhem and disappear into the murky mist of subnationalism and religious zealotry. For India the stakes are high since what is threatened by this proxy war is not mere territoriality but a concerted attempt to hack at the roots of the often taken-for-granted Indian independence and nationhood, based on democratic principles and abiding secularism.

Originally, rumblings of discontent appeared in Jammu and Kashmir were perceived as the normal expression of legitimate demands from a rapidly changing India.[24] But a little later disaffected Kashmiri youths formed the bulk of the cannon fodder. They were members of the Jammu and Kashmir Liberation Front (JKLF). The dream of Azad, independent Kashmir seemed but not a short struggle away. However, the unravelling of the independence struggle started with the inter-faction killings. Pakistani agencies involved in formulating and running Pakistan's Kashmir strategy worked hard not just to build up the Hizbul Mujahideen and other client groups but to actively undermine and weaken the JKLF. The former had also an important advantage over JKLF within Kashmir. It is politically connected to the Jama'at-i-Islami, which has a well-organised, well-funded Party apparatus in Jammu and Kashmir. Thus, the Hizbul Mujahideen could rely on the Jama'at's infrastructure in Kashmir, while nothing comparable was available to the JKLF. Nonetheless, the HM never succeeded in winning the kind of spontaneous mass support the JKLF enjoyed in its prime.[25]

The authorised and controlled use of violence which was earlier kept within the purview of state machinery barring stray criminal acts has undergone a radical transformation since World War II. The deliberate targetting of civilian populations by the principal interlocutors in that war had opened the door to extending the scope of 'war' and over the decades, the explosive cocktail of military technology and misplaced fundamentalism of different hues has abetted the myriad subterranean forces that have been unleashed in the aftermath of the cold war. The ability to inflict mass destruction is no longer the sole purview of the state and the non-state actor and fringe group zealot has emerged as a new challenge to state security and stability. A heady infusion of religious fervour and the proliferation of lethal small arms, the prefix being a complete contrast to the massive destruction possible have enhanced the profile of the practitioners of this proxy war. The terrorist / militant / proxy war waging group in the state of Jammu and Kashmir now too possess fire power capability including artillery pieces and anti-aircraft missiles that would normally be associated with a regular army brigade.

Other causes that had speeded up the momentum of proxy war included three events of 1980s that accelerated the process of fundamentalist terrorism in the Muslim world. First was the 1978-79 revolution in Iran. It has ripple effect which spread Shiite militancy throughout the Middle East. Second, there was the war in Lebanon, where terrorists, particularly of the Hizbullah group, achieved signal success against the Western and Israeli forces. And, third, the war in Afghanistan, where the Russian army was defeated by the Mujahideen, the Islamic warriors drawn from all over the Muslim world committed to fighting Western civilization. In due course, the Mujahideen spread to different parts of the world wherever Islam was considered to be in danger.[26] For decades, India is facing a multi-pronged attack from the fundamentalist forces through Afghanistan and Pakistan into Jammu and Kashmir. Islamic warriors from Afghanistan, Sudan, Alegeria, Tajikistan, Saudi Arabia, Chechnya, Bosnia and several other countries have been spearheading the separatist movement in the valley. The fact was evident from The Pattern of Global Terrorism, 1996 of the US State Department that noted, "Afghanistan remained a training ground for Islamic militants and terrorists" and that individuals trained in its camps were involved in insurgencies in several countries including Kashmir.

The greater challenge for India is that such acts are receiving purposeful state support from across the border and thereby straining state resources and societal tolerance. Certain sections of the Pakistani establishment have vowed that the liberation of Kashmir is a "sacred mission" and the steady attempt at bleeding Indian secularism by a "thousand cuts" as the ISI describes the mission to its mercenaries represents an entirely new challenge to state and society.[27] One of the reasons why Islamabad is reluctant to talk to India on the issue is that now Pakistan is in the grip of elements who not only lacks legitimacy but who seem to be driven by the medieval concept of jehad or holy war against infields. The open manner in which various jehadi groups operate in Pakistan uttering dire threats against India, and the close involvement of these militants with official Pakistani agencies like the ISI in organising acts of terrorism in Kashmir and elsewhere in India, leave little scope for any purposeful dialogue with Islamabad.

The whole episode took a new turn when hundreds of graduates from Pakistan's terror camps came to India, a battle for supremacy between the pro-Pakistan Hizbul Mujahideen and pro-independence JKLF began. After 1993 on account of Hazratbal crisis Kashmiri militants weakened that made Pakistan worried who soon shifted the focus with ISI. It gave the "Afghan alumni," the rag-tag mercenary remnants of that country's war against the Soviet's, a new cause. India believes that infiltration and other foreign groups are solely responsible for militancy in Jammu and Kashmir. In the post-Hazratbal phase, the Harkat-ul-Ansar with its Afghan alumni began to push into the state. They shifted their routes south of the Pir Panjal range, through Jammu's Poonch and Rajouri districts. These areas are mountainous too, but they receive less snowfall.

The way to peace is never easy and a straight one. Not at least in the troubled state of Jammu and Kashmir. The Indian establishment is aware that the biggest task in Kashmir today is of engaging and eliminating "fidayeens" and foreign mercenaries, which it is doing with incremental success. In fact militancy in Kashmir is profitable. Brigadier Mohan Bhandari, terms it as a "blue-chip" industry. He reveals that apart from the millions of dollars that the ISI gets from the narcotics trade to fund militancy, many Islamic countries also give it liberal donations for jehad. Militancy actually makes for a good career. Most local militants are paid between Rs. 2,500 to Rs. 5000 per month. Foreign mercenaries are paid about Rs. 5000 to Rs. 8000 per month. A deceased militant's kin get a pension of Rs 1,500 to 3,000 per month. There are good rates for each strata in the militant's hierarchy. Apart from this foreign militants get Rs. 2 lakhs while entering India and another Rs. 5 lakhs at the end of the two–year contract period. The reward for killing an Indian is around Rs. 150. If it is a soldier upto the rank of major the reward is around Rs. 7,000. While Lieutenant Colonel carry a price of Rs. 50,000 the Brigadiers command over Rs. 1 lakh.[28] Perhaps no one would like to give up such a lucrative career easily.

Since 1989 in Jammu and Kashmir the conflict between assorted militant organisations and the security forces has been one of the most important internal security issues in India. While the armed forces are equipped with a number of extraordinary legislations, insurgency has shown no signs of declining in the affected states. There are some of the more active terrorist groups, apart from JKLF, who fought for the unification and independence of India-Pakistan held Kashmir.

Hizb-ul-Mujahideen (HM), originated in November 1989, stands for the integration of Jammu and Kashmir with Pakistan, but will not oppose independence of Kashmir. It was patronised by the Inter-Services Intelligence of Pakistan who use and guide it to counter the influence of the Jammu and Kashmir Liberation Front. Before its birth the ISI had been supporting the JKLF but the former had a golden opportunity in 1988 when Kashmiri youths agreed to take up arms against Indian rule. Unlike the activists of the HM, the JKLF, the agent and the vehicle of the uprising, was dogmatically committed to the ideology of an independent, reunited Jammu and Kashmir state, separate from both India and Pakistan – an ideology elaborated as early as 1970 by the movement's veteran ideologue Amanullah Khan. From 1991 the ISI cut off aid to the JKLF and adopted a twin-track strategy to mould the valley uprising to Pakistan's conception and interests. It was done to divide and weaken the JKLF.

As a part of its second strategy or to weaken the JKLF, a pro-Pakistan guerilla organisation the HM was not only formed but nourished with outside help and support. As the armed revolt rapidly acquired a popular character owing to the severe and indiscriminate nature of Indian repression during 1990, thousands of valley youths started to cross the Line of Control in search of weapons and training. Hizbul Mujahideen is militarily the strongest force among the guerilla groups presently operating in Indian-administered Jammu and Kashmir. More than 50 per cent of the militants operating in the valley are from this outfit. The number of foreign mercenaries in this group is estimated to be around 30 per cent. It comprises mainly of local militants but most of foreign militant outfit operating in the valley are dependent on it for logistics and internal support.

Since the early 1990s the leader of Hizbul Mujahideen has been Yusuf Shah of Muzaffarabad in Pakistani controlled "Azad" Jammu and Kashmir, who now goes by his *nom de guerre*, Syed Salahuddin. Salahuddin was a legendary Muslim warrior who fought against the Christian Crusaders. At the sametime Syed Salahuddin, the commander in chief of Hizbul Mujahideen was critical of Indian rule in the state and said an interviewer in 1992 that he had chosen to fight for the cause of Pakistan in Kashmir because experience had convinced him that "slaves have no vote in the so-called democratic set-up of India.[29] The Mujahideen's halo of heroism was gradually giving way to a painful realisation among the public that because of the phenomenal expansion of the armed struggle the ranks of freedom fighters contained politically. Though in 1993-94 HM emerged as the leading guerilla organisation in the field, its ideology that Kashmir will become Pakistan remained a minority orientation. Its sacrifices in the cause of azadi were widely admired, but its political affiliate Jamma'at-i-Islami's brand of orthodox Islam, preached in a network of religious schools run by the Party, is regarded with distaste by most Muslims in the valley and other Kashmir-speaking areas.

However, the Hizbul Mujahideen has a significant presence, especially in the Pir Panjal mountains, a range that traverses a massive east-west arc across the northern Kashmiri-speaking part of Poonch district, the southern part of the valley, the mountainous Gujjar and Kashmiri-Muslim dominated upper reaches of Jammu's Udhampur district, and finally Doda district. The HM's fighting units in the area are called the Hizb-ul-Mujahidden Pir Panjal Regiment and, as in the valley and Doda, are mostly recruited from the local population. It has no effect either of the threat of Indian war, American pressure or General Musharraf's curtailment of activities in Azad Jammu and Kashmir as HM sources pointed out, "We have many mobile training camps in the hills and forests of Indian Kashmir where youths are trained ...... and we have munitions stockpiled over the years."[30]

The HM is an alien guerilla organisation having a strong social base in the Indian Jammu and Kashmir. A prepared ground was provided to it by the Jama'at-e-Islami of Kashmir which also has branches in Pakistan and Bangladesh. The jama'at-e-Islami of Kashmir is not affiliated to the Indian jamaat and is known for anti-secular and anti-national character. It is doing the greatest damage in the state by preaching sentiments that go against the basic secular traditions of the Kashmiri. Its followers are trying to poison the minds of Kashmiris in cities, towns and villages. If one listens the sermons they preach in village mosques, attends their study circle and just go through some of their literature which they circulate so widely, one would be convinced that they are sowing the seeds of discord and hatred.[31] Initially its stronghold area in the valley was Soporc, but slowly, the organisation spread to Anantnag and Kulgam followed by Srinagar city where it has much larger support. They are also not scarved of fund and their money comes from Pakistan and Gulf countries, particularly Saudi Arabia. Today the jamaat has a network of about 200 fairly efficiently run schools in the valley and study circles and mosques are used to propagate anti-secular and anti-national ideas.[32] Apart from the guerilla warfare alignments with jamaat-e-Islami, Hizb-ul Mujahideen owes a close link with other jehadi groups dominated by Pakistan, such as, Lashkar-e-Taiba (LeT), Jaish-e-Mohammad (JeM), Al-Badar, Tehreek-ul-Mujahideen, Harkat-ul-Mujahideen and Harkat-ul-jehad-e-Islami which are active in the area.

Lashkar-e-Taiba (LeT), is an insurgent group active in Indian Jammu and Kashmir since the mid-1990s, spawned by a Pakistan-based movement professing an ultra-orthodox variant of Sunni Islam. Like JeM, it is predominantly composed of Pakistani religious radicals, and its leader is Hafiz Muhammad Sayeed, a Pakistani academic-turned fundamentalist activist. Its peak period along with JeM is known as Fidayeen (suicidal) phase. Between mid 1999 and the end of 2002, at least 55 Fidayeen attacks were made usually executed by two-man teams and were targeted against police, paramilitary and army camps, and government installations in Indian Jammu and Kashmir, mostly in the valley. Though the LeT denies that its raids are suicide mission-preferring to call them "daredevil" actions – since the group follows an ultra-orthodox version of Sunni Islam that strictly prohibits suicide. However its attackers almost never return from these penetrate and kill missions – their aim is not to save their own lives but to maximize the frightening psychological impact on the enemy by inflicting death and destruction on their targets.[33] It is also evident from LeT's mouthpiece jehadi *Times* published from Islamabad until 2001, which has always discussed the suicidal warfare in Kashmir.

Keeping in view the continuing acts of violence, engaged in by the Lashkar-e-Taiba, the United States Government had issued stern warning to Pakistan in January 2001. Further the LeT's squad managed to enter the compound of India's Parliament building in New Delhi and then attempted to enter the building itself, on 13 December 2001 where hundreds of Parliamentarians and government ministers were present at the time. The attackers were killed by the security officers after a forty-five minute battle with guns and grenades. Its cadres have been responsible for the majority of fidayeen attacks in Indian Jammu and Kashmir since 1999, and are the prime suspects in a number of massacres of non-Muslim civilians.[34] At the root of India's terrorism it is not the LeT, JeM or another group but their common father – the Pakistani military. The latter's alliance with narco-terrorism has criminalised even its top echelons, blurring the line between civilian and military terrorists cloaked as jehadi. Without reform of the Pakistani military, there can be no regional peace, or an end to transnational terrorism, or nation-building in Pakistan.[35]

India and the US share the goal to moderate the Pakistani state, where fundamentalism and militarism feed on each other. It might be far more effective if Pakistan is squarely held responsible for patronising and instigating the extremist outfits operating from its territory. These groups operate openly, protected by the military regime's umbrella. They train, arm and indoctrinate young men and turn them into dogmatic jehadis in well-established camps in Pakistan. Primarily in response to US pressure, in January 2002 General Musharraf announced a crackdown on jehadi groups operating across the LoC from Pakistani territory. It followed a formal banning of LeT and JeM along with several other violent sectarian groups active within Pakistan.

Jaish-e-Mohammad (JeM), formed in early 2000 by Maulana Masood Azhar, a Pakistani cleric, is another zealot group led by Islamabad. It has a predominantly Pakistan membership and is direct descendant of Harkat-ul-Ansar which was active in Indian Jammu and Kashmir in the mid-1990s. Like a number of other militant groups, Pakistan's Inter-Services Intelligence (ISI) facilitated formation and promotion of Harkat-ul-Ansar. With material aid and indoctrinated cadre drawn largely from the madarsas in Pakistan and Afghanistan, this pro-Pakistan militant group has been instrumental in killing a number of armed personnel and civilians in the valley. After the US declared Harkat-ul-Ansar a terrorist organisation in 1995 after the kidnapping of five Westerners in Pahalgam, the group changed its name to Harkat-ul-Mujahideen.

Earlier Maulana Masood Azhar, the leader of JeM was captured by Indian forces in the Kashmir valley in 1994 but released in December 1999. He was one of three jailed militants released by the Indian government in exchange for the freedom of 160 hostages after a group of Pakistani religious radicals hijacked an Indian Airlines plane flying from Kathmandu to Delhi to Kandahar. JeM's mouthpiece fortnightly Urdu journal also published from Pakistan but unlike LeT it refers to self sacrificing martyr's unit.[36] It was involved in suicidal raid on India's Parliament on 13 December 2001. Apart from this its members are also implicated in sectarian Sunni violence against minority Shia Muslims and Christians in Pakistan. Along with LeT, JeM was formally banned in Pakistan in January 2002.

Both the insurgent groups LeT and JeM and their suicidal attacks are known as the Fidayeen phase in Kashmir. However, three points can be made about their aim and strategy.[37] First, the use of suicidal tactics as a weapon of war is neither novel nor the monopoly of militant Muslims. In recent past among the contemporary political movements, Palestinian militants – especially but not exclusively their Islamic wing – have resorted to the tactic with increasing frequency and decreasing discrimination. But the most effective and most deadly practitioners of suicidal warfare in the South Asian subcontinent – and possibly in the world have been the Tamil Tigers of Sri Lanka. Second, it is true that the main ideologues and practitioners of suicidal warfare in the Kashmir war are radical Islamist groups of Pakistani provenance, particularly in case of Kashmir it is not exclusively a "cross border" phenomenon, but rather it is the product of the incendiary infusion of the ideology and tactics of trans-national Islamist militancy into a brutalized, desperate local environment – that is, of a conjunction of internal and external factors. The third point to be noted is that its most spectacular and most publicized attacks have been directed against such high profile targets as the Indian army's cantonment and operational headquarters in Srinagar, the headquarters of the SOG in Srinagar, Srinagar's airport, and the legislature's premises in Srinagar. But the crucial theaters of war in this phase lie away from urban centres, in the rural areas of Rajouri and Poonch districts, Jammu and in the Kupwara region of Kashmir valley.

Inter-Services Intelligence (ISI), is Pakistan's military's premier intelligence agency which has coordinated the US backed war against the Soviet Union and its allies in Afghanistan. The ISI runs Pakistan's 'Kashmir Programme' and is deeply involved in supporting and controlling the insurgency in Indian Jammu and Kashmir. It got prominence during the 1980s military regime of General Zia-ul-Haq, acquired vast resources and autonomy as the nodal agency. By 1989 when the Soviet forces were on their way out of Afghanistan it was in a position to focus on the new war in Kashmir, Pakistan's sacred national cause since 1947. The passing time witnessed an unexpected windfall for the ISI as sizeable number of youths from Indian Kashmir were, for the first time since 1947, ready to take arms against their country. On the other hand, formerly Pakistan did assist the JKLF in launching the uprising but it soon demanded a price for continued support. When JKLF by and large refused to change its pro-independence line, Pakistani agencies, the ISI in particular, promptly terminated all aid to it. Further it set about engineering defections from the JKLF ranks, and began building the same with Hizb-ul-Mujahideen.

Thus, the ISI has opened a new horizon of proxy war in Kashmir from across the border. In a well-thought calculated move it divided and weakened the JKLF by encouraging its pliable elements to break away and form pro-Pakistan guerilla groups. By 1991 at least two such factions had emerged – Al-Umar Mujahideen and Ikhwan-ul-Muslimeen. Al-Umar was led by Mushtaq Ahmed Zargar, alias Latram, a Srinagar JKLF militant who had become notorious for executing suspected collaborators by exploding grenades tied to their bodies.[38] It promoted Hizb-ul-Mujahideen, a pro-Pakistan guerilla organisation to replace the JKLF from its centre place. However, it appears that Pakistan has been reluctant to place all its eggs even in the HM's basket. Since 1993 Pakistan has floated several new armed groups in Indian-administered Jammu and Kashmir. The ISI had further diversified its Kashmir portfolio by encouraging zealot Islamic groups in Pakistan, such as Harkat-ul-Ansar to enter the Kashmir war. India is affected by terrorism sponsored both by the Pakistani State agencies as well as by the fundamentalist Islamic organisations operating from Pakistani soil.

Mission

Pakistan's foreign policy has always revolved round the idea of annexing Kashmir. If anything, Islamabad's intentions have acquired greater urgency since the Bangladesh war for it to do to India what it believes India did in 1971. This is why Pakistanis do not hesitate to tell their Indian interlocutors that they feel insecured and incomplete without Jammu and Kashmir. Several US congressional studies, think tank reports, task-force-on-terrorism findings and CIA revalations have named Pakistan for aiding and abetting the proxy war. Yet, not a day passes without Pakistan passing strictures on India's management of Jammu and Kashmir. The proxy war waged by Pakistan has also falsified the latter's claim that it is interested in the plight of Kashmiri Muslims. Its true interests are geostrategic and economic. Although it is more than the truth that the proxy war is unwinable by either side, Pakistan's aim is to make the cost for India holding Jammu and Kashmir high, diplomatically, politically and militarily.

Traditionally, terrorism is a highly organised enterprise that fits into a clear political strategy. It has been filling the news for most of our lives, and will doubtless go on demanding the attention of our children and grand-children as well. Even in the past terrorism was almost a part of the strategy of an armed national liberation movement, and in the colonial context it usually worked in the end. The reason why it worked so well in anti-colonial struggles was that it did not have to defeat the imperial power's superior military forces in order to win. They were a long way from the home, and there was a limit to how many lives and how much money the imperial government would spend to hang into its possessions. But the early, easy successes of terror tactics in the anti-imperial context left everybody with a great inflated notion of what the technique could achieve against an established national government with local roots.[39] Governments and armies that cannot "go home" – because they are already at home – simply do not give in to terrorism. After several years and more than 80,000 deaths, the Islamic fundamentalists, terrorist war against Algeria's crypto-military regime is no closer to success. They are capable of doing much harm but they are not politically serious people.

While India has traditionally been on the defensive, Pakistan made Jammu and Kashmir the core issue and the root cause of India-Pakistan dispute. Pakistanis and the world are fed on a routine diet of propaganda on television, radio and print media about Indian Army atrocities and human rights violations in Jammu and Kashmir.[40] Pakistan's initial strategy in Kashmir has settled down to three-pronged mutually supportive thrust line;

- Work for negotiations with India in an agenda which would discuss the Kashmir issue on the basis of not only the Simla Agreement but also the UN Resolutions, thus bringing the issue of plebiscite/self-determination into bilateral/multi-lateral talks. So far Pakistan's own obligations under the UN Resolutions (the basic reason why the resolution could not be implemented) are not even alluded to;

- Strategy of overt support and covert action for a low - intensity proxy war fought by non-regular forces constructed on the ideology of religion-based subnational separatism;

- Prepare for, and if necessary escalate to a regular war preferably in a manner that creates perceptions of India being the initiator of such war.[41]

The above strategy was aimed to seek the Pakistan's objectives of destablising India and its developmental plans, undermine its secular policy and feudal structure, push the Indian states towards increasing dependence on force and damage India's standing in the international community particularly at a time when it is receiving added recognition and respect. Pakistan would actually be pursuing a low-cost high-benefit strategy where the real price would be paid by the Kashmiri and other Indians. The proxy war could bc sustained by Pakistan for a long time as long as some Kashmiris are willing to keep the conflict alive. Pakistan would try to avoid war as long as it sees the basic objectives being met by the other elements of its strategy without paying a direct price which is bound to be heavy.[42] We can hardly hope to win the low-intensity proxy war being waged against us if we do not have the undoubted capacity to win a possible regular war, whether it is of short or long duration. Winning the proxy war was itself requires a cool assessment of the evolving situation and elements of the Pakistani strategy so as to evolve appropriate responses, political as well as military.

It is said that the situation in the valley could not have taken such a serious turn since 1989 had the government handled militancy more effectively in its earlier stages. The policy makers of India were knowing Pakistan's plan. The details of the Pakistani plan were given in "Operation Topaz", published in one of the issues of the *India Defence Review* in 1988. Later on the plan was put into operation in stages. At each stage it tested government's will and preparedness to fight it. First, a number of explosions, without causing much damage, took place in Srinagar. This was followed by attacks on police stations and selected killings to terrorise the people. The three main objectives before the militants were : (i) to demoralise the state police by targeting those officers who dared to take action against them; (ii) to drive out the Kashmiri Pandits from the valley; and (iii) to create a communal divide between Hindus and Muslims.[43] The key to the Kashmir problem lies in controlling its internal situation.

India has been for years at the receiving end of cross-border terrorism in Kashmir and surrounding areas. Scores of innocent civilians are mercilessly gunned down at all to frequent intervals, and bomb explosions kill and maim hapless victims in buses and trains as well as in the market place. At this stage our own strategy will have to rest on five concurrent elements :

- Keep the avenues for peaceful solution of the conflict with Pakistan open;
- Political and administrative measures to restore normality in Kashmir with the use of force where incapable;
- Sustained politico-diplomatic efforts to mobilise international support in countering Pakistan's proxy war for sub-national separatism;
- Active use of force against infiltration and terrorist activities which are an important component of the proxy war;
- Adequate preparedness to deter imposition of a direct war.

Management

Pakistan has been using terrorism as an instrument of State policy, waging a low-intensity covertly planned conflict against India for over the last 25 years. This policy is predicated on the Pakistani calculation that as long as the levels of intrusive terrorist violence remains short of a threshold, Pakistan could inflict damage upon India without attracting any punitive action against itself. There is also the Pakistani assessment that important powers would be willing to tolerate the situation in Jammu and Kashmir as long as this terrorist violence does not expand into a general conflict between India and Pakistan. As a result the latter's collusion with jehadi groups operating in Kashmir has weakened Islamabad's ability to influence any future political dispensation in the Valley. Pakistan's chosen Kashmir policy has also exacerbated domestic problems in multiple ways that do not require retelling. This debilitating condition can only be changed if the Pakistani leaders come to accept the proposition that a principled position on the Kashmir dispute can not be successfully advanced through unprincipled means.[44] The real thrust of Pakistani terrorism in Jammu and Kashmir is not to give a chance to the people of the state to vote for their future but to channel the overflow of arms and mercenaries from the war-ravaged areas of Afghanistan. The involvement of foreign mercenaries and international religious extremist organisations has become a challenge for the Indian agencies. Unfortunately these covert mercenaries are supported not only by Pakistan but by some other Islamic countries as well. Extraneous vested interests have developed in terms of Pan-Islamic agendas, narco-terrorism, arms sales and so on, which negatively affects the prospects of a reasonable dialogue focused on specific issues related to Kashmir.

Sporadic cross-border incidents along the Indo-Pak border were so surprise for New Delhi because it did not pose a threat to the either side. However, it got an alarming rate at the close of the Eighties and especially with the Soviet's withdrawal from Afghanistan. The Pakistani military's Inter-Services Intelligence (ISI) had, during the 1980s military regime of General Zia acquired resources and autonomy as well in co-ordination with the Central Intelligence Agency (CIA), who sponsored war against the Soviet take-over of Afghanistan. In the post-withdrawal phase the ISI was in a position to focus on the new war in Kashmir. It began to recruit Kashmiri youths for training and arming in Pak-controlled camps. It got, for the first time since 1947, a large number of Kashmiris' prepared to join the terrorist organisations managed and maintained by the ISI.[45] It was revealed in the recent book, *The Lost Rebellion*, written by Manoj Joshi, that once General Zia and Pakistan's ISI concocted the scheme of recruiting local disaffected Kashmiris, and arming and training them to become insurgents. Till 1987, Pakistan received only a trickle of recruits, but that turned into a flood after Rajiv Gandhi forced the National Conference into a shot-gun marriage with the Congress in 1987 and Farooq Abdullah allegedly rigged elections in the Valley to ensure his return to power. What followed then was a genuine insurgency.

The whole story began in late 1986 when Farooq Abdullah concluded a rapprochement with the Congress regime at the centre. Under its terms, he was reinstalled as chief minister pending fresh Assembly elections in March 1987, which he undertook to contest in alliance with the Congress Party. This alliance was deadly opposed by the Muslim United Front (MUF) coalition. It was mainly represented by a new generation of young men who born in the 1960s. The organisation was formed as an independent, pro-people entity to fight NC's opportunistic alliance with the detested Congress at the polls. The process and its outcome irrevocably tainted Farooq Abdullah and his supporters in the eyes of their former voters as just another clique, serving as tools of the Indian state in return for the spoils of political office.[46] This was the moment when the valley and some of its contiguous areas lost all residual confidence in India's political system. With this, the Kashmir conflict witnessed a changed mood of the younger generation in the Valley.

Apart from this internal factor, there were international elements too that gave a helping hand to Pakistan and the ISI in spreading their network in the state of Jammu and Kashmir. International events, particularly that took place in late 1989 and early 1990, played an important role. The first Palestinian intifada against Israeli occupation was a significant reference point, as was the collapse of repressive one-Party regimes in central and eastern Europe after mass demonstrations in the autumn of 1989. It was noted by a Srinagar scholar, "We felt that if the Berlin wall could be dismantled, so could be the Line of Control".[47] The young Kashmiri guerillas, for their part, were inspired by the 1989 Soviet withdrawal from Afghanistan in the face of Afghan Mujahideen resistance and success of Tamil Tiger guerillas in Sri Lanka against the vastly superior

Indian force. It also became clear soon that these foreign expeditions were fundamentally misguided and increasingly costly in terms of resources and combat casualities.

From here onwards, the ISI has successfully financed, cultivated and armed a powerful section of the Kashmiri people. By 1990 there were over 30 militant groups in Kashmir and 29 of these had been receiving assistance and shelter in Pakistan. A US task force on terrorism and unconventional warfare, set up by a House Republican Research Committee, covered, in its report, various aspects of Islamic terrorism, its origin and spread to Afghanistan, Sudan and Iraq. The report held ISI responsible along with Pakistan for abetting and sponsoring terrorism in Kashmir as part of its over all effort to promote Islamic international terrorism. It noted that in 1986 Pakistan expanded its operations to sponsor and promote separation, primarily in Kashmir, as a strategic long-term programme.[48] Among the most crucial activities of ISI were to propagate religious fundamentalism in small but lethal doses and train and indoctrinate selected leaders from Kashmir to create militant cadres. The report said that several youth from Kashmir valley and Poonch district in Jammu region were given extensive training in the use of automatic weapons, sabotage and attacks on security forces.[49] The US State Department and the various reports published by several agencies confirmed that the extent of the growing state support for terrorism and insurgence in Kashmir is clearly reflected in the evolution of the organisations operating there.

The relation between the two had undergone a sea change when they exploded nuclear devices in May-June 1998. After the explosion, Tariq Altaf, a Pakistani Foreign Office spokesman, reiterated Nawaz Sharif's assertion saying that Pakistan was ready to have a non-aggression pact with India but 'after just settlement of Kashmir dispute. He urged India to take up the Kashmir issue on "priority basis" as it was root cause of tension between the two neighbours. Despite the fact that Vajpayee had cautioned Pakistan not to internationalise the Kashmir issue, the militants–mostly from Afghanistan and Pakistan find it easier to shoot and kill the people in the mountainous parts of Jammu and Kashmir region. Further

Pakistan's ISI wanted to involve the Jammu region in violence to show the international community that the entire Jammu and Kashmir was disturbed – to strengthen its points of plebiscite in the state.[50] In nutshell, the militants were doing what they had been assigned to do while Pakistan was claiming that it was not involved in any manner in the armed militancy in Jammu and Kashmir.

The net result of cross-border terrorism was the full-fledged war between the two at Kargil sector. It broke out in May-June 1999 which ended in a humiliating defeat of Pakistan at India's hand. Formerly Islamabad had fully expected the big powers to intervene because of the potential nuclear peril, thereby effectively internationalising the Kashmir dispute. When nothing of the short occurred, and the entire exercise became dangerously counter-productive, Islamabad decided to pull back the intruders from Kargil.[51] But the end of Kargil war did not mean the end of continuing hostility to India. The so-called withdrawal of Pakistani forces from Kargil the border had not regained normalcy and guns continue to boom. Added to this was the calculated revival by Pakistan of cross-border-terrorism, and resort to provocative anti-Indian action along various points across the LoC.

As an after-effect of Kargil the Government of Nawaz Sharif was overthrown in a military coup on 12 October 1999. General Pervez Musharraf, Chief of Army Staff, took over the Administration and again a new chapter of military rule was opened in Pakistan. The new ruler, in a televised announcement on 17 October 1999, as a gesture of goodwill towards India, declared unilateral military de-escalation along the border. His address also included an offer to resume "result-oriented" talks with India on "all issues" but said, "Pakistan would continue its support to the Kashmiri people for their right to self determination" and added that India must honour all UN resolutions on Kashmir. At a later stage in July 2000 when Bharat Bhushan, a correspondent of *The Hindustan Times*, asked General Musharraf about different aspects of terrorism, the latter had replied that as far as the hardware and the weapons of terror were concerned, "We certainly want to curb the uncontrolled display and holding of weapons and we are taking action in this direction. But this is easier said than done. To disarm and de-weaponise a region completely is next to impossible".[52] On the ideological front he presented his own definition of jehad and distinguished it from terrorism. He refused to equate these two perhaps in reference to Kashmir and said, "jehad means struggle in the path of God, opposing victimisation against Muslims wherever it exists. But the world at large did not share Musharraf's perception of jehad.

In this context, on times without number Islamabad has been told by countries of the world and its leaders as well to stop cross-border terrorism and reminded the assurance that the former had given to world organisations. Recently in the year 2002, the two most powerful associations of nations–the Group of Eight and the European Union through their adopted statements agreed that "Pakistan must put a permanent stop to terrorist activity organising from territory under its control. It called on Pakistan to take further concrete action in accordance with the assurances it has already given and with its international obligations, including UN Security Council Resolution 1373 (2001), to stop infiltration across the Line of Control and to prevent terrorist groups from operating from territory under its control, also through closing of training camps".[53] What seems to be clear, and all agree, is that the General has not done enough to curb militants. As military head and President Musharraf would have no problem in ordering terror camps in PoK to be closed. Of the powerful nations, Washington and London even doubted the power the General has over the jehadi groups. They believe that Musharraf's influence is limited, that large numbers of ISI officers operate independent of him. They refer to the December 13, 2001, attacks on Indian Parliament and the Karachi suicide attack on French nationals as evidence that Musharraf is not the puppet master of all jehadis.

But despite many stresses and strains on the Pakistan military over the last few years, the present day regime's chain of command remains intact. The logistical and communication linkages between the ISI and the Pakistani army units on the one hand and terrorist cadres on the other continue. The pattern and number of infiltrations from Pakistan into India across the LoC have been more or less at the same level. The terrorist training and launching camps which were closed briefly after January 12, 2002, in which Musharraf promised a crackdown on terror, have been reopened and relocated in other parts of Pakistan and PoK, the northern areas, the Punjab and the North-West Frontier Province. There are an estimated 70 to 75 such camps which continue to be active. India also has information that the Harkat-ul-Mujahideen and Lashkar-e-Taiba cadres are now located in PoK. There are at least 12 launching camps being used for funnelling terrorists across the LoC into India in Jammu and Kashmir. The estimate of the Indian security forces is that there are about 3,000 to 3,500 militants under training in Pakistan.

India and the US both are uncertain about the future course of action that Musharraf would like to take. But they need to keep the working closely on the goals they share in relation to Pakistan. Not only for the present but also in recent past India's threat of war and US diplomacy have worked well in conjunction, with each reinforcing the other's message to Pakistan. Recent revalations of Pakistan's help to Iran, North Korea and Libya in their nuclear weapons programmes have further fuelled American distrust and the latter had expressed its unhappiness. Equally on the other the Western world, including the Chinese should also pause and reflect on the consequences of supplying sophisticated arms and technology to Pakistan. Transferring the M-11 missiles to Islamabad, even in unassembled form, is to give into the hands of potential forces of destruction, the wherewithal to strike at civil society in the name of jehad.

One possible way to minimize Indo-US pressure on Islamabad to end the cross-border terrorism is to start a dialogue between the two and thereby improve relations. Difficulties are more with Pakistan than with India. Today there is a rare consensus on this in Pakistani civil society, born of very diverse reasons. The religious parties favour this on the ground that it would increase Pakistan's capacity to resist pressure by the US to get more deeply involved in the 'war against terror', Pakistan's liberals, both in politics and business, want it in order to further consolidate the economy. With its much smaller economy, it cannot indefinitely continue to try and match India. While nuclear weapons now provide it security against any alleged Indian hegemonism, nuclear sabre-rattling of the Kargil war period will not work. Equally, it is no longer possible for Islamabad to back proxy forces, even in the name of religion. This is more so because such forces are now turning against their Pakistani army mentors.[54] The demands for public funds for education, public health and so are no less compelling.

Kashmir is the speed-breaker on the road connecting India and Pakistan. Kashmiri Muslims are unhappy with our presence, but they are also doubtful about having close relations with Pakistan. With its best chance ever to end the scourge of cross-border terrorism, India needs to closely monitor the ground situation, continue to breathe down Pakistan's neck, and speak up whenever the circumstances demand. India's insistence on deeds, not just words reflects not only the emergent maturity in its foreign policy but also signals that war as an Indian policy option remains primed for exercise if Musharraf refuse to understand the matter in proper perspective.

References

1. S.K. Ghosh, Muslim Politics in India, New Delhi, 1987, pp. 113-17.
2. As quoted in Chandrika Bandaranaike Kumaratunga, "Original Sins," The Hindustan Times, 29 April, 2002.
3. Bharat Bhushan, "Match Fixing Won't Help in Kashmir", *Ibid.*, 21 April 2000.
4. R.K. Jain, ed., Soviet-South Asian Relations, Vol. 1, 1947-1978, Atlantic Highlands, 1979, pp. 3-4.
5. Shrikant Paranjpe, "Dangers of Indo-Pak Confrontation on Kashmir", The Times of India, 21 February 1990.
6. The Tribune, 17 April 1990.
7. The Indian Express, 26 July 1990.
8. Pramit Pal Chaudhuri, "The Return of the Great Game," The Hindustan Times, 14 October 2001.
9. A.G. Noorani, "The Blackwill Thesis," *Ibid.*, 12 November 2002.
10. The Hindu, 15 January 1990.
11. Manorama Kohli, "Foreign Policy Initiatives of the National Front Government in India," Ramakant, ed., South Asian Studies, Vol. 25, no. 1 and 2 January-December 1990, Jaipur, 1990, p. 141.

12. The Times of India, 9 August 1990.
13. Dileep Padgaonkar, "Pak Crisis and India's Choices," *Ibid.,* 6 August 1990.
14. Foreign Affairs Record, Vol. XXXVI, no. 1, January 1990, pp. 18-19.
15. Rikhye Ravi, The War that Never Was : The Story of India's Strategic Failures, New Delhi, 1988, p. 2.
16. Moonis Ahmar, "The Role of CBMs in the Post Cold War Era," ACDIS, Occasional Papers October 1993, Pakistan, 1993, pp. 9-10.
17. *Ibid.,* p. 15.
18. The National Herald, 30 June 1990.
19. The Hindustan Times, 19 July 1990.
20. The Indian Express, 12 August 1990.
21. V.R. Raghavan, "The Right Kind of War," The Hindustan Times, 22 March 2002.
22. As quoted in Pakistan Times Overseas Weekly, 4 November 1984.
23. India Today, 15 July 1992.
24. Harish Kapur, India's Foreign Policy, 1947-92, Shadow and Substance, New Delhi, 1994, p. 29.
25. Sumantra Bose, The Challenge in Kashmir, Democracy, Self-Determination and a Just Peace, New Delhi, 1997, p. 194.
26. Prakash Singh, "Militancy from Kashmir to Coimbatore" The Hindustan Times, 23 February 1998.
27. C. Uday Bhaskar, "Strategic Implications of the Proxy War," Ibid., 18 August 1998.
28. As quoted in Anita Kanungo, "Peace Pangs" *Ibid.,* 7 August 2000.
29. The Illustrated Weekly of India, 10-16 October 1992, p. 4.
30. Sumantra Bose, Kashmir, Roots of Conflict Paths to Peace, New Delhi, 2003, p. 163.
31. Udayan Sharma, "Kashmir's Anti-National Jamaat-e-Islami, Sunday, 2 December 1979.
32. *Ibid.*
33. Sumantra Bose, *op. cit.,* p. 142.
34. *Ibid.,* p. 295.

35. Brahma Chellaney, "An Act of War," The Hindustan Times, 18 December 2001.
36. Kashmir Times, 23 December 2001.
37. Sumantra Bose, *op. cit.,* pp. 145-47.
38. *Ibid.,* p. 126.
39. Gwynne Dyer, "The Slow Decline of Terror," The Hindustan Times, 24 August 1998.
40. Ashok K. Mehta, "The Truth About the Proxy War," *Ibid.,* 11 August 1998.
41. The Hindu, 15 May 1990.
42. *Ibid.*
43. Ved Marwah, "Hostage to Misrule," The Hindustan Times, 16 July 1998.
44. Michael Krepon, "Forbearance is the Key Word," *Ibid.,* 14 October 2001.
45. Sumantra Bose, *op. cit.,* pp. 125-26.
46. *Ibid.,* p. 94.
47. As quoted in Victoria Schofield, Kashmir in Conflict, London, 1996, p. 231.
48. Indian Express, 23 February 1997.
49. Indian Recorder, a weekly of events and happenings, Vol. IV, No. 15, April 9-15, 1997, New Delhi, 1997, p. 2726.
50. Author's book, Indo-Pak Nuclear Tension 1974-1998, New Delhi 2001, pp. 103-4.
51. *Ibid.,* p. 126.
52. The Hindustan Times, 3 July 2000.
53. Brahma Chellaney, "Pakistan as Problemistan," *Ibid;* 8 July 2002.
54. Manoj Joshi, "The Marathon Begins," *Ibid.,* 30 June 2004.

Index